# Performance in the Twenty-Fir Century

*Performance in the Twenty-First Century: Theatres of Engagement* addresses the reshaping of theatre and performance after postmodernism. Andy Lavender argues provocatively that after the 'classic' postmodern tropes of detachment, irony, and contingency, performance in the twenty-first century engages more overtly with meaning, politics and society. It involves a newly pronounced form of personal experience, often implicating the body and/or one's sense of self.

This volume examines a range of performance events, including work by both emergent and internationally significant companies and artists such as Rimini Protokoll, Blast Theory, dreamthinkspeak, Zecora Ura, Punchdrunk, Ontroerend Goed, Kris Verdonck, Dries Verhoeven, Rabih Mroué, Derren Brown and David Blaine. It also considers a wider range of cultural phenomena such as online social networking, sports events, installations, games-based work and theme parks, where principles of performance are in play.

*Performance in the Twenty-First Century* is a compelling and provocative resource for anybody interested in discovering how performance theory can be applied to cutting-edge culture, and indeed the world around them.

**Andy Lavender** is Professor of Theatre and Performance and Head of the School of Arts at the University of Surrey.

**Cover image**: 'Feast of Dawn', *Hotel Medea*, presented by Zecora Ura Theatre Network. Persis-Jade Maravala (Medea) and Thelma Sharma (the Nurse) await the audience for a communal breakfast. Photo: Ludovic des Cognets.

**Author's note**: The scene that this image depicts is staged at dawn – *Hotel Medea* is durational, and runs from midnight to daybreak (the production is discussed in detail in Chapter 4). This is an invitation to eat together, for the audience has breakfast with the company at the end of the show. So the image awaits completion by its (immersed) spectators who have also been participants in the drama, and will now engage in an extra-theatrical way. The Medea story ends with the sharing of food, a different sort of ritual, from those that it customarily presents. The photo features two actors who have been playing the characters of Medea and her Nurse, although at breakfast they are (sort of) out of character, post-show. This image is from the London run of the production, by the River Thames – you can see the O2 Arena on the Greenwich peninsula in the background. The dawn breakfast, in this iteration, took place outside, further enhancing the sense of event and theatre-in-the-world. I like the image's frontality, which is not untypical of the performance discussed in the book – people looking out, directly engaging you with their gaze. The photo is more broadly appropriate as a cover image for *Performance in the Twenty-First Century*. Everything about it is liminal, both actual and pretending. It draws us in, and invites our involvement in its staging of an encounter.

# Performance in the Twenty-First Century

## Theatres of Engagement

Andy Lavender

Routledge
Taylor & Francis Group

LONDON AND NEW YORK

First published 2016
by Routledge
2 Park Square, Milton Park, Abingdon, Oxon OX14 4RN

and by Routledge
711 Third Avenue, New York, NY 10017

*Routledge is an imprint of the Taylor & Francis Group, an informa business*

*British Library Cataloguing-in-Publication Data*
A catalogue record for this book is available from the British Library

*Library of Congress Cataloguing-in-Publication Data*
Names: Lavender, Andy, author.
Title: Performance in the twenty-first century : theatres of engagement /
Andy Lavender.
Description: Milton Park, Abingdon, Oxon ; New York : Routledge, 2016. |
Includes bibliographical references and index.
Identifiers: LCCN 2015042640 | ISBN 9780415592338 (hardback) |
ISBN 9780415592352 (pbk.) | ISBN 9780203128176 (ebook)
Subjects: LCSH: Performing arts – History – 21st century.
Classification: LCC PN1584 .L38 2016 | DDC 790.209/05 – dc23
LC record available at http://lccn.loc.gov/2015042640

ISBN: 978-0-415-59233-8 (hbk)
ISBN: 978-0-415-59235-2 (pbk)
ISBN: 978-0-203-12817-6 (ebk)

Typeset in Bembo and Gill Sans
by Florence Production Ltd, Stoodleigh, Devon, UK

# Contents

# Figures

# Acknowledgements

I am grateful to the organizers of the following events and symposia, who invited me to give presentations that have subsequently found their way into this book, one way or another: *Spring Academy Symposium* on Dries Verhoeven, part of the *Spring Festival*, Stadsschouwburg Utrecht, Holland, 30 May 2015; *Media, Politics, Performance: The Role of Intermedial Theatre in the Public Sphere*, symposium as part of the *Fast Forward Festival*, Onassis Cultural Centre, Athens, 4 May 2014; *Journeys Across Media* conference *The Body and the Digital*, University of Reading, 19 April 2013; *Cultural Exchanges Festival*, De Montfort University, Leicester, 28 February 2013; and *The Scenographer in the Rehearsal Room*, Theatre and Performance Research Association (TaPRA) Scenography Working Group Interim event, Rose Bruford College, London, 17 April 2012.

A version of Chapter 3 was published as 'In the mix: intermedial theatre and hybridity', in Amine, Khalid and George F. Roberson (eds), *Theatre and Intermediality*, Amherst (Massachusetts), Denver, Tangier: Collaborative Media International, 2014, 26–42. A version of Chapter 7 was published as 'Viewing and acting (and points in between): the trouble with spectating after Rancière', *Contemporary Theatre Review*, 22:3, 2012, 307–326.

A number of my visits to events and productions discussed in this book were supported by the Research Offices of the University of Surrey and Royal Central School of Speech and Drama, University of London. My thanks to colleagues for this assistance.

I'm especially grateful to Talia Rodgers, Theatre & Performance Studies publisher at Routledge until just prior to publication of this book. I owe much to Talia's belief, patience and always sage advice, and I couldn't have had a more supportive editor. My thanks, too, to colleagues at Routledge, Taylor & Francis and Florence Production for their work on the project.

Pursuing new theatre and performance can sometimes be a lonely task. Some of the pieces that I write about (and others that I chose not to) I attended with friends and colleagues, and I'm most grateful for personable companionship along the way. Not least I am grateful to colleagues in the Intermediality in Theatre and Performance working group of the International Federation of Theatre Research for discussions around some of the ideas in this book.

My thanks to Marvin Carlson for sharing his unpublished conference paper; and to Noah, Bridget and Robin Keam for their permission to recount aspects of a trip to Dickens World. Thanks too to Annie Wharmby for showing me round Hong Kong Disneyland. I am grateful to my parents for their continuing support. This book is dedicated to three people who have suffered stoically while I worked on in the British Library or the loft room. I'm especially grateful to them for their forbearance and support, and for growing up/older with aplomb in spite of my inattention.

The publishers wish to thank the following for permission to publish work in full or extracts:

dreamthinkspeak, excerpts from programme notes by Tristan Sharps.
Jim Stephenson, images of dreamthinkspeak's *Before I Sleep*.
Derren Brown, excerpts from programme notes for *Svengali*.
BBC Sport, excerpt from Tom Fordyce's blog, 2011.
Judith Butler, transcription by A. Lavender of speech made at 'Occupy Wall Street'.
Luke Garai Taylor, still from video of Judith Butler speaking at 'Occupy Wall Street'.
Dries Verhoeven, excerpts from *No Man's Land*.
Stavros Petropolous, images of Dries Verhoeven's *No Man's Land*.
Jorg Baumann, images of Rimini Protokoll's *Situation Rooms*.
Barbara Braun, image of Rimini Protokoll's *Annual Shareholders Meeting*.
Blast Theory, image from presentation at InterCommunication Centre, Tokyo, 2005.
Brinkhoff & Mögenburg, images of Punchdrunk's *The Drowned Man*.
Robert Day, image of Ontroerend Goed's *Audience*.
Peter Combs, images of Dog & Pony's *The Twins Would Like to Say*.
*Pixelated Revolution* by Rabih Mroué, 2012, courtesy the artist.
Rabih Mroué. *Riding on a Cloud*. 2013. Performed at The Museum of Modern Art, April 21, 2015, in Projects 101: Rabih Mroué. © 2015 The Museum of Modern Art, New York. Photo by Julieta Cervantes.
Ludovic des Cognets, images of *Hotel Medea*.
Reinout Hiel, images of Kris Verdonck/A Two Dogs Company *Dancer #3 in Actor#1* and *Stills*.
Stavros Petropolous, image of Kris Verdonck/A Two Dogs Company *Stills*.
Dickens World, image of boat ride. Discontinued 2012.

# Introduction

As with some performance installations or immersive theatre productions, there is no necessary sequence to this book. You can roam as you wish. Even so – as with some performance installations or immersive theatre productions – it has units (here essays) within sections that are deliberately arranged.

*Performance in the Twenty-First Century* is about various sorts of theatre and performance after postmodernism. As a whole, its argument is that subsequent to the 'classic' postmodern tropes of detachment, irony and contingency, many theatre and performance events in the twenty-first century entail altered modes of engagement on the part of both practitioners and spectators. They connect more overtly with social process. They involve a pronounced form of personal experience, often implicating the body and sometimes even one's sense of self. And they entail certain sorts of commitment.

I tend to use 'theatre and performance' as a compound in the book, for reasons that I expand on in the opening chapter. While both terms can mean different things – and are routinely contested in theatre and performance studies – I incline to conflate them in the same spirit as Alan Read in his conception of an 'expanded field' for theatre. Read provides a tabular comparison of what might be thought norms of theatre and performance, in order to suggest that the 'order and history' of the former is 'irritated and disturbed' by the latter. Read's chart proposes that 'linearity (theatre) is infused with 'simultaneity' (performance); 'character' with 'autobiography'; 'acting' with 'authenticity'; 'invention' with 'revelation' (Read, 2013: xx). You don't have to agree with Read's specific mappings to grant a general point. Performance as a disciplinary construction now finds theatre in its field; while theatre can be thought of through the patterns of performance, and provides a paradigm for the organisation of that which is encountered.[1]

*Performance in the Twenty-First Century* explores such developments in relation to three mainstays of theatre and performance: mediation, performing, and spectating. That's to say, the mediality of the event and the way in which it is structured and conveyed; the sorts of acting and performance involved; and what this means for audiences, who often become participants in some way. The book features close analysis of a number of performance events in a range of international settings. It also examines a wider array of cultural phenomena – including installations, online video performance, sports events, games-based work and theme parks – where principles of performance are in play. In each instance, new forms of interaction are facilitated between creator, performer, spectator and event, and personal experience is often foregrounded. Most of the instances I discuss in the pages that follow are shows or events that I attended between 2003 and 2015. I don't hold that you have to see a piece of theatre in order to write about it – otherwise how could we ever say anything about Garrick's *Hamlet*, for instance? That said, the essays that follow set store by the phenomenological stuff of encounter, visceral response and contextual engagement. A procedure that situates the critic in face of the event is not inappropriate here. In part through a form of immersed analysis, I address some key developments in contemporary theatre and performance, and critical paradigms for discussing such work. This all makes for a reengagement with meaning in and around theatre and performance; a change to our understanding of registers of performing and what it is to be an 'actor'; likewise a new set of possibilities for spectatorship, increasingly drawing on participatory models of engagement, and privileging sensory experience.

Each essay has a specific focus and usually addresses one or more representative instances of performance, although the first is more synoptic and outlines a context for those that follow. Chapter 1, 'Theatres of Engagement: performance after postmodernism', discusses a timeframe for developments that have shaped contemporary cultural production: the quarter-century from 1989. It considers two key tributaries: significant historical events that have remodeled our sense of what Rancière describes as the sayable and doable; and the extension of digital culture, enabling new forms of communication and interaction (therefore, new *ways* of saying and doing). We arrive beyond postmodernism at a changed cultural paradigm, albeit one attuned to continuing postmodern tactics and techniques. I propose that the notion of 'engagement' describes the mode of this cultural scene. I discuss the intertwining of motifs of reality and performance, as a way of thinking about underlying features of a broad 'reality trend' to performance that goes hand-in-hand with a pervasive theatricality to contemporary culture.

Three sections address core features and procedures. The first, 'On mediating performance', explores changing processes through which performance is shaped, presented and engaged. Chapter 2, 'The visible voice (or, the word made flesh): political presence and performative utterance in the public sphere', examines an interest in apparent truth-telling in performance, particularly through a privileging of the 'authentic' speaking voice. I explore reasons behind the growth of testimony, witness, and first-person speaking, and their platforms including vox-pop radio, reality TV, verbatim and documentary theatre and 'reality trend' performance. I discuss the relationship of 'authentic speaking' to both personal experience and social process, and how this marks a shift in the Habermasian public sphere towards plural public spaces for diverse discourse.

By way of example, I explore Judith Butler's polemical and poetic utterance at an Occupy demonstration in Washington Square Park in New York; *No Man's Land*, a walking tour conceived and directed by Dries Verhoeven, featuring testimony drawn from immigrants; *Riding on a Cloud*, in which Yasser Mroué speaks of his life, near-death, and amateur artistic endeavours; and (by way of counterpoint) *Annual Shareholders Meeting*, whereby the actual AGM of the Daimler Corporation is framed as a theatrical event by Rimini Protokoll.

In Chapter 3, 'In the mix: intermedial theatre and hybridity', I consider hybridity as a signal feature of contemporary cultural production. Hybridity suggests both a becoming and a beyond: here, the emergence of cross-disciplinary formations. I explore this with reference to scholarship in bioscientific, aesthetic, cultural, postcolonial and performance studies; and look at hybridity in relation to intermediality, as a way of explaining developments in media form and function. I discuss dreamthinkspeak's *Before I Sleep*, a promenade production that includes models, installations, live performance and scenic design, to consider the strategies and implications of a blended aesthetic. In Chapter 4, 'Feeling the event: from *mise en scène* to *mise en sensibilité*', I argue that we observe a shift in performance-making from *mise en scène* (the arrangement of the stage) to *mise en événement* (the arrangement of the event) to *mise en sensibilité* (the arrangement of feeling). I explore critical perspectives developed by scholars including Pavis, Franko, Foucault, Fischer-Lichte and Lehmann, and literary critics writing about sensibility. The developments here are exemplified by Zecora Ura Theatre Network's *Hotel Medea*, a durational, immersive event. Based on the Medea story, the piece runs from midnight to dawn and involves its spectators in an array of scenarios of affect, as they witness the drama from within.

The next section, 'On (not) being an actor', addresses changes to acting and performance in the first decade or so of the twenty-first century. Chapter 5, 'Sincerely yours: from the actor to the persona', examines the notion of 'character' in performance. I note the apparent shift in postmodernism from characterization to the presentation of a persona, in part theorized by Auslander, Fuchs and Lehmann. I suggest that nonetheless a conception of character often underpins performances that are otherwise rooted in non-acting. I explore this as it applies to magicians (David Blaine and Derren Brown) and machines (those presented in Kris Verdonck's installations and performance pieces). In each case, a mix of apparent sincerity and evident fabrication helps to present a form of characterful personhood that provides an enjoyable kind of presence. In Chapter 6, 'Me singing and dancing: YouTube's performing bodies', I consider a more obvious kind of digital performance, by way of the rapid spread of self-curated performance online. I examine the growth of YouTube, enabling serial presentations of the self and a shared reiteration of motifs of performance. I discuss the memes of 'me dancing' and 'me singing', digitally-enabled cultural practices that re-inscribe the body at the heart of virtual performance.

The subsequent section, 'On (not) being a spectator', examines changes to spectatorship, and particularly a movement towards participation, interaction and agency. Chapter 7, 'Viewing and acting (and points in between): the trouble with spectating after Rancière', examines Jaques Rancière's celebrated notion of the 'emancipated spectator'. I trace some significant contributory currents in Rancière's work (particularly concerning 'equality', '*dissensus*' and '*sensus communis*') to unpack 'emancipation' here as a combination of critical detachment and commitment. I explore the application of this to scenarios of spectatorship by discussing four instances of events in Chicago in which the spectator is ingrained: a promenade-style studio theatre production, a civic sculpture, a museum event and a basketball game. I conclude by suggesting that, in these examples at least, we observe spectators who are pleasurably implicated within events, rather than emancipated in the more politically-oriented sense of the term. Chapter 8, 'Audiences and affects: theatres of engagement in the experience economy', starts by addressing characteristics of the 'experience economy', whereby transactions are developed precisely in order to provide certain sorts of experience. I discuss the notion of affect as a key to developments in this larger cultural ecosystem, and examine diverse studies of affect to build a framework for analysing the experience-inducing work of performances and events. I focus on four instances of audience engagement – an end-on theatre production by Ontroerend Goed; a sporting event; an immersive production by Punchdrunk; and an interactive game-based piece by Blast Theory – to explore how each facilitates the experience of its audience/participants.

In my concluding chapter, 'Performance engagements across culture', I draw threads of the book together to suggest ways in which we have moved not only beyond postmodernism and the postdramatic, but perhaps even beyond theatre itself, as performance suffuses cultural production and is itself suffused with effects of encounter, experience and actuality. I look briefly at civic installations by Kris Verdonck and Dries Verhoeven to gather several strands, including the convergence of performance, digital production and civic space; and the incorporation of the spectator in scenarios of actuality. The chapter closes with a discussion of three theme parks – Disneyland in Hong Kong, Dickens World in Chatham and Banksy's Dismaland in Weston-super-Mare, the latter two in unprepossessing towns either side of south England – that help reverberate the book's wider themes. Whatever else you make of them, theme parks depend upon our engagement in an 'eventful present'. It hardly needs saying that this applies to nearly all the performance work discussed in the book.

## Note

1   In their volume Theatricality, Davis and Postlewait are cautious of the wide embrace of performance, which they suggest is no different from the idea of *theatrum mundi* (2003: 33). Nonetheless, in their view 'theatricality' is concept, system, 'quintessentially the theatre' and 'the theatre subsumed into the whole world' (1). If theatricality is different from performance, it is no less pervasive.

# Chapter 1

# Theatres of engagement
## Performance after postmodernism

As so often, ours is a story of changing realities. Consider this, the publicity blurb for a new theatre festival, inaugurated in May 2014, for the economy-raddled city of Athens:

> Digital cameras, iPods, mobile telephones, the Internet, and live-cinema, documentary and editing techniques are all mobilized in the interactive, multimedia and site-specific spectacles the OCC [Onassis Cultural Centre] will be hosting as part of the **1st Fast Forward Festival** (FFF). Because the theatre of now is restless and hybrid, a collage of arts, techniques and media and an exciting, groundbreaking, holistic experience closely bound up with the technological advances and quickening socio-economic pulse of our times.[1]

Several themes are harnessed: the rapidity of cultural change; the defining role of digital technologies in contemporary culture; the increasingly hybrid nature of theatre form; and *experience* as a main attraction. It is perhaps not surprising to see this initiative emerge from amid Greece's economic chaos. Artistic production here is a marker of resilience and connectedness. The Fast Forward Festival (supported by the financially independent Onassis Foundation) looks out to an international circuit of festival theatre production. It looks back to a scenario – we might even call it Athenian – where festivals mark the cultural currency of a place. And it looks forward, embracing work that is new and emergent.

The Festival included productions by the Berlin-based company Rimini Protokoll, the Dutch scenographer and performance-maker Dries Verhoeven, and the Lebanese writer and director Rabih Mroué.[2] This small selection represents much of what *Performance in the Twenty-First Century: Theatres of Engagement* addresses, for these pieces variously deal with perspectives on fact and reality, adopt hybrid performance modes, and are intrinsically shaped by digital culture. Rimini Protokoll's *Situation Rooms* is a piece for 20 spectators. Each has a set of headphones connected to an iPad (Figure 1.1). The event is split into eleven segments. In each, the spectator hears the story of an individual

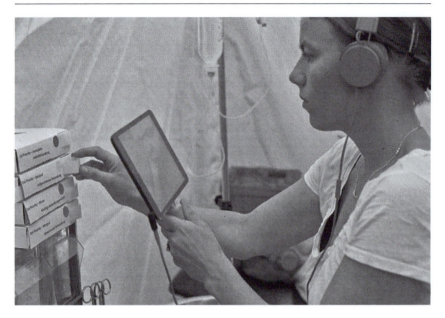

*Figure 1.1* The spectator in action: iPad immersion in Rimini Protokoll's *Situation Rooms*
Source: Baumann-fotografie.de.

in some way connected with contemporary warfare – a surgeon, a child soldier, a hacker. The iPad shows a video that mixes documentary footage with a recorded version of the performance setting in which you find yourself. This enables you to navigate the space, in which you encounter different rooms (scenically arranged within a realist aesthetic), and other spectator-participants who stand in for the additional characters that are described in the scenes that you inhabit.

Dries Verhoeven's *No Man's Land* is also for 20 spectators (indeed, auditors), whom it also asks to don headphones. These are connected to MP3 players. As distinct from *Situation Rooms*, the voiceover that you hear is the same for all spectators simultaneously, and is a merged account of the experiences and musings of a group of immigrants who contributed to the process of creating the piece. Each spectator is taken on an individual journey through the surrounding streets by an immigrant or refugee, the latter acting as a guide and, in effect, standing in as a witness for her or his community. (I discuss the piece more fully in the next chapter.)

The Lebanese theatre-maker Rabih Mroué presented two pieces. *The Pixelated Revolution* was a lecture-performance in which Mroué considered the prevalence of mobile phone recordings of demonstrations and activities in the Syrian conflict, still ongoing when I saw the piece in 2014, looking particularly at moments in which the phone's camera recorded the moment of death of its owner (Figure 1.2). In *Riding on a Cloud*, Mroué's brother Yasser presents a possibly partly fictionalized account of his biography. This much is true: he was shot in the head by a sniper in Beirut but survived, paralysed down his right hand side. He sits at a table and plays a series of cassette tapes containing his own voice track; and DVDs whose images appear on the large screen at the rear. He indicates early in the show (by way of his voiceover, accompanying an image of him with a guitar) that at one point he wanted to be a musician. The piece provides a moving finale by way of the brothers playing the guitar together, Yasser shaping chords and trills with his left hand, Rabih strumming and picking with his right.

Theatre has been exploded, and it has regathered. It is no longer what we knew, and it sustains its root in communal live encounter. Theatre has become more than itself, a compound of media. *No Man's Land* and *Situation Rooms* cannot properly be described as 'mixed media' pieces. They stage a more complex interrelation of media and modes (video, scenography, utterance), forms (drama, documentary, testimony) and structures (dramaturgical, architectural, spatial and temporal). Theatre has become something other than an encounter between actors, or between actor and audience. There is no longer a separation between the space of performance and that of spectatorship. Scenic space is

*Figure 1.2* A performance lecture: Rabih Mroué in *The Pixelated Revolution*,
            dOCUMENTA 13, Kassel, 2012

Source: Pascheit Spanned, courtesy of Gallery Sfeir-Semler

inhabited. *Riding on a Cloud*, while presented in a conventional end-on studio setting, walks a similar line between personal and public, the actual and the aesthetic. Each piece participates in the broad 'reality trend' described in the German term *Theater der Zeit*, adopted by Rimini Protokoll and applicable to a much wider range of work.[3] Theatre enters the world, and the world is presented back to us as theatre. Meanwhile all these pieces engage with both personal and political concerns.

What kind of theatre do we see here? Three particular phenomena help answer this question: the rise of forms of 'truth-turning' after the erosion of settlements of the post-Second World War era and the cultural relativism of postmodernity; the incursion of digital technologies and their relation to performance; and the ingrained nature of performance in contemporary culture. These contribute to a hybrid cultural scene that looks very different from that of the mediatized but pre-digital 1980s. We find ourselves in a cultural space that has the look and feel of one that is now definitely beyond the postmodern, even while it continues to trade in certain postmodern strategies. This scene finds pleasure, meaning and pertinence in scenarios of actuality, authenticity, encounter and experience (terms that reverberate in discussions of contemporary theatre and performance); the involvement of bodies (including ours as spectators) in events; and mixed modes of production that are, not infrequently, enabled by specific developments to or adaptations of digital communications technologies. There has been a shift in our perceptions of the real and how we might deal with it, which relates to different engagements with fiction and fabrication. Indeed, the term 'engagement' provides a useful stamp for the cultural processes and aesthetic formations that arise during the period, that typically negotiate actuality and fabrication. 1989 provides us with somewhere to start, for it presents a particularly vivid historical moment and an epicentre of new engagements (authenticities, experiences). It lies a quarter-century behind us as I write this, and somewhere within a fuzzy boundary between the postmodern and whatever cultural formation takes shape beyond it.

## Timeframe | Timeline: 1989 – 2001 – 2014

In *Riding on a Cloud*, Yasser Mroué meditates on those defining moments where we can say there is a before and an after. He mentions the fall of the Berlin Wall; the attacks of 9/11; the Arab Spring; and (reminding us that perspective depends on where you stand, for the Mroués are Lebanese) the withdrawal of Israel from Lebanon. I reflect, below, on the defining moments provided by the fall of the Berlin Wall (1989) and 9/11 (2001), with respect to their place within a trajectory of cultural production that bears upon the performance events discussed in this book.[4] More immediately, they also help us to think about a period beyond that of 'classic' postmodernism. I will address the latter in due course – but let us go beyond, in order then to look back.

The notion that 1989 provides a watershed is not uncommon. As Jeffrey A. Engel observes:

> The world changed in 1989. At the start of the year, the globe's strategic map looked much like it had since the end of World War II. . . . A year later, communism would be dead in Eastern Europe . . . The future – our twenty-first-century present – would be at hand. And no one had seen it coming.
>
> (Engel 2009: 1)

The fall of the Berlin Wall was the most visceral and immediate symbol of wider developments (particularly in Eastern Europe) that appeared to herald the arrival of a progressive populism, through which major structural political reconfigurations were performed. Partly enabled in Eastern Europe by the policy of *glasnost* and *perestroika* overseen by the Soviet Union's President Gorbachev, the drastic national reorganisations of 1989 were bookended by the elections of Lech Walesa (a shipyard trade union leader) as the Polish prime minister and Vaclav Havel (a novelist) as the President of Czechoslovakia, the first non-communist incumbent for 41 years. In October, East German troops refused to fire on crowds in open demonstration. On November 9, crowds from both East and West Berlin congregated in the area between the Brandenburg Gate and Checkpoint Charlie, following an announcement earlier that day that the East German authorities were permitting permanent emigration across all border-crossing points between East and West Germany. One of the border guards, interviewed amid the unprecedented flow of people, observed with sanguine understatement, 'The last twelve hours, travel possibilities have improved enormously' (quoted in Buckley 2004: 164). Over the next few days, people from both sides of the wall dismantled the edifice that had divided them for over 28 years. A domino effect ensued across other parts of Eastern Europe. New governments took office in Bulgaria, Czechoslovakia and (after initially violent repression) Romania before the end of the year.[5]

This was different from the ideological fixity manifested in the stark Cold-War distinctions between East and West. In his account of the 'short twentieth century' (which he dates from 1914 to 1991) Eric Hobsbawm proposes the end of the Soviet era as the effectual truncation of the century. As he suggests, 'there can be no serious doubt that in the late 1980s and early 1990s an era in world history ended and a new one began.'[6] (Hobsbawm 1994: 5) The new disruption arose from popular uprising that was nationalist or anti-governmental in its fervor, separatist in its political preference, and economically integrative by desire. This shape – individualized (even atomized), yet plurally convergent – comes to define a good deal of personal, cultural, civic and political transaction over the subsequent two decades.

Other sorts of walls were tumbling. A potent symbol of hope was celebrated globally on 11 February 1990, when Nelson Mandela, former President of the

African National Congress, was released from Victor Verster Prison in Cape Town after being incarcerated for over 27 years. Mandela had been exploring the prospect of a negotiated settlement with the government since 1985. His release came without him compromising on key positions of principle, including the release of other political prisoners and the recognition of the ANC as a legitimate political organization. President F. W. de Klerk announced the unbanning of the ANC on the opening of parliament on 2 February 1990 (see Limb 2008: 95, 100).[7] Mandela's release just over a week later was momentous. When he walked through the prison gates arm in arm with his then-wife, Winnie, and raised his fist, the triumph wasn't only that of an individual; it stood as an emblem of the rights of black people and a form of triumph over adversity and injustice. Mandela's release heralded the end of apartheid as South Africa's state system, and pre-empted the election on 9 May 1994 of Mandela as the country's first black president. This turn of events seemed all the more remarkable given the previous intransigence of the apartheid regime, not unlike that of East Germany under Erich Honecker or Romania under Nicolae Ceauşescu. Ozymandias-like, old orders, certainties and, it seemed, injustices were not just crumbling, but doing so with extraordinary rapidity.

If the world looked different in 1989 and 1990, it appeared even more altered in 2001. On 11 September, four hijacked passenger planes flew respectively into the North and South Towers (each 110 stories) of the World Trade Center in the financial district of south Manhattan in New York City; the Pentagon in Arlington County, Virginia; and farmland in Pennsylvania following the intervention of passengers. Arguably, 9/11 provides the most categorical threshold between postmodernism and that which lies beyond, at least from a western perspective. For Jeffrey Melnick

> 'Post-9/11' indexes a profound rupture in time and space. It is clear that the events of 9/11 shape not only our understanding of nearly everything in the political and cultural lives of Americans since that date, but that those events also shape our understanding of much of what came before. . . . Once we loved irony and took refuge in that distancing strategy: now we are earnest and authentic. Once we fragmented into our various political and social identities; now we stand united.
>
> (Melnick 2009: 18)

If Melnick overstates, he nonetheless describes a comprehensive shift from ironic disengagement to refigured engagement. Other commentators are more cautious, but it is broadly accepted that 9/11 propelled a reconsideration of previously uninspected assumptions, and a restatement (and in some respects retrenchment) of core positions.[8]

Historical phases and, in particular, moments of identifiable change are figurings of what Jacques Rancière calls a 'new landscape of the visible, the sayable and the doable' (2010: 149). The three iconic instances, above, provided sudden definition to shifting formations in culture and geopolitics. More than this, they helped us *think differently*. This series of falls (Berlin Wall, apartheid regime, twin towers) was relayed in still and moving images that imprint the retina because of their clarity and the astonishment that they evoke – people dancing on the Wall, Mandela's walk to freedom, the planes flying into the twin towers, the towers' collapse. Each instance provided a massive cultural and political *verfremdungseffekt*, where we saw as changeable that which we had previously taken to be fixed. Historical process also implied, at least, a shift from understanding the state (*polis*) as the organizing power, to seeing a different distribution of agency – expressed by historically impactful forms of individual intervention. Such shifts in the visible, sayable and doable feed into changing cultural formations, and these in turn shape the nexus of assumptions, desires, behaviours and practices that contribute to cultural production.

The revolutionary surges of 1989 were reported by television and radio networks – news-oriented media in a media-saturated age, enabled by satellite broadcasting technology following the consolidation of the satellite TV industry in the 1970s and 1980s. 9/11 was also experienced and discoursed in and through social media. As Melnick observes, 'Blogs became, in the aftermath of 9/11, a kind of wireless wire service, and undefined, anarchic first-responder news and opinion service' (Melnick 2009: 13). Other events, from terrorist attacks (such as those in Madrid on 11 March 2004 and London on 7 July 2005) to popular demonstrations (such as those of the Arab Spring between 2010–12), were facilitated by mobile telecommunications. Their hour-by-hour and day-to-day developments played out on social media. Helena Grehan argues that 'The condition of witnessing what one did not (and perhaps cannot) see is the condition of whatever age we are now entering' (2009: 172). Witness is adjacent to testimony, which also runs through contemporary cultural production (as I discuss in Chapter 2, below). The condition of witnessing, here, arises from communication systems that can capture and disseminate plurally in close to real-time; along with platforms and spaces for regular reiteration. This very intersection between the event and its simultaneous mediation points towards another defining feature of the quarter of a century that straddles the millennium: the rapid, pervasive and culture-changing growth of digital communications.

## Digital paradigms

Following their initial development in military and governmental settings, computers for personal use started to enter homes and offices in the late 1970s, gathering pace as desirable labour-saving devices throughout the 1980s. By 1991 http (hypertext transfer protocol) procedures were sufficiently developed to enable the transmission of information from a server to a browser, thus providing the operational backbone of the World Wide Web. In its initial phase, html (hypertext mark-up protocol) was information-based rather than interactive, depending on the transfer of pages like a form of rapid special delivery. Between 2000 and 2002 the development of Web 2.0 technology and RSS (Really Simple Syndication) provided the underpinning informational schemata for weblogs (blogs), enabling users to add content to pages and recirculate the results in an endless chain of iterations – sending as well as receiving. In 2004 RSS protocols made podcasting possible: the syndication of audio and video files as well as images and text. This enabled the ready exchange of user-generated content across platforms including MySpace (established in 2003), Facebook (2004), YouTube (2005), and Twitter (2006), along with an array of wikis and blogs, and ushered the Internet into an era of fluid information-exchange and demotic publishing.[9]

The statistics that evidence the uptake of digital culture are often virtually incomprehensible in their magnitude, although they also depict a significant divide between developed and developing countries. According to the International Telecommunication Union (ITU), the United Nations agency for information and communication technologies, 'The number of mobile-cellular subscriptions worldwide is approaching the number of people on earth. Mobile-cellular subscriptions will reach almost 7 billion by end 2014, corresponding to a penetration rate of 96 per cent.' Mobile broadband continues to grow, with 'an estimated global penetration of 32 per cent [in 2014] – four times the penetration rate recorded just five years earlier.' The number of Internet users globally, meanwhile, is around 3 billion, representing a penetration rate of 40 per cent (78 per cent in the developed countries, 32 per cent in developing countries). Around 44 per cent of the world's households have Internet access at home, up from 30 per cent in 2010 (ITU 2014: 2, 3; and ITU website[10]). Newton Lee observes that 'Facebook as a nation in 2012 would be the third largest country in the world with over 955 million citizens, after China and India.' (Lee 2103: xiii) Lee reports that in 2011 more than 100 million Americans watched online video on an average day. This doesn't denote an entirely passive audience. (Lee 2013: 23, 24) David Gauntlett conservatively estimates that 'at least 100 million new blog posts were produced each month in 2012' (2013: 81). The period we are addressing – the quarter-century or so since 1989 – is swept up in the march of digital culture, where the information-communications economy replaces the commodities economy of the 1980s.

This has had unpredictable and sometimes counter-intuitive effects. In *Convergence Culture*, Henry Jenkins discusses the case of Osama Bin Laden and Bert, a puppet from the US children's TV series *Sesame Street* (2006: 1–2). Dino Ignacio, a high school student, photoshopped the pair into the same image in a series entitled 'Bert is Evil'. The casually satirical image was recirculated in the Middle East, in different earnest, as part of a collage that appeared in signs wielded by anti-American protestors. As Jenkins notes:

From his bedroom, Ignacio sparked an international controversy. . . . Welcome to convergence culture, where old and new media collide, where grassroots and corporate media intersect, where the power of the media producer and the power of the media consumer interact in unpredictable ways.

(Jenkins 2006: 2)

Digital dissemination is varied and volatile. It has facilitated global corporatism across national and geographical boundaries; and community-based expressions of identity, protest and action. It has enabled mega-monoliths of the digital era (Facebook, Google, YouTube, Twitter) to provide platforms for individual agency and interaction. It has liberated a swathe of one-to-one, one-to-many, and group-oriented communications beyond the closely-controlled flow of information through large-scale print and broadcasting organisations. It also facilitates surveillance and 'dataveillance' (the tracking of individual activities by way of the digital footprint left by phone transactions, online bookings, credit card purchases and so on). It supports faceless bureaucracies that transact behind online paywalls, or through geographically fractured call-centres, or by way of complex corporate mechanisms across the diverse reporting and taxation regimes that facilitate global commerce. In another characteristic convergence of opposites, virtuality has gone hand-in-hand (so to say) with a sharpened enjoyment of co-presence, corporeality and embodied sensation.

Cultural production in the twenty-first century reverberates with this paradoxical mingling of capabilities and effects. Havens and Lotz characterize this within a longer trajectory of post-Fordism – whereby service-oriented transactions replace a factory-based model of production – as 'a complex web of centralizing and decentralizing tendencies' (2012: 187). Mass customization (a form of centralization) clearly applies to the glide of the computer across the globe, and the convergence of user systems, platforms and creative processes that go with it. On the other hand, there is room here for bespoke and unique creative outputs, reflecting the particular circumstances of the individual creator, or emerging through group processes that can only result from that specific combination of people. This kind of cultural production typically operates through what Thrift calls 'hybrid assemblages: concretions, settings and flows' (2008: 9).

If historical events such as 9/11 and the fall of the Berlin Wall required new ways of thinking, the technologies and devices with which we performed our thinking also changed. In so doing they remade the procedures (both cognitive and technical) by which we expressed our cultural engagement. They *restructured* our experience of and transaction with the real. By way of an instance, consider the mobile phone, a device that started rather obviously as a portable telephone, but has since become a multifunctional computer used for anything from watching videos to posting pictures to navigating from one place to another. As DeLuca, Lawson and Sun suggest:

In its introductory stage, a medium is just a tool for specific tasks within an environment created by other media and cultural practices. So, for example, that was the case for mobile phones in the early 1990s and smart-phones around 2005. If diffusion accelerates enough, however, the medium reaches saturation and a tipping point and moves from being a tool within an environment to helping create the environments within which we operate. . . . With the spread of smartphones, space and time cease to be barriers to living in a mediated world all the time.

(DeLuca, Lawson and Sun 2012: 486)

The same goes for a wider array of digital devices and interactions, allowing real-time information-sharing concerning activities that are variously public and personal, momentous and banal. In *The Practice of Everyday Life*, first published in 1984, Michel de Certeau suggests that 'The floodlights have moved away from the actors who possess proper names and social blazons, turning first toward the chorus of secondary characters, then settling on the mass of the audience' (1984, v). Little could de Certeau have known the extent to which the mass of the audience would come under a spotlight of its own everyday positioning in the age of social media. 'We witness the advent of the number', de Certeau writes. 'It comes along with democracy, the large city, admin-istrations, cybernetics' (v). The Internet and social media return the name to the number.

The ongoing mediatization of culture (at least in postindustrial parts of the world) facilitated this extension of individual engagements with the social sphere. In 2008, reviewing the position he took in his influential monograph *Liveness* (first published in 1999), Philip Auslander notes that when writing the book

it still seemed possible to insist that television was the dominant medium. By now, there is a strong case to be made that the honor belongs to the computer, although it seems more accurate to say that there is an ongoing, unresolved struggle for dominance among television, telecommunications and the Internet.

(Auslander 2008: xii)[11]

The virtual domain of Web 2.0 has refigured this scene into a mutually intersecting mediascape, not so much a struggle between monolithic media forms as a merging of platforms and protocols. Corporations and companies (indeed individuals) will of course remain in competition, but a different meta-phor from that of struggle also applies to contemporary communications. The sociologist Zygmunt Bauman proposes the notion of *liquid modernity*, in his book of the same name published in 2000 (just before the embedding of Web 2.0 technology). Bauman infers that 'fluidity' is 'the leading metaphor for the present stage of the modern era' (2000: 2). He describes processes of flow, lightness and speed, and new ways of conceiving and managing time (in part through the near-instantaneity of communication). He observes older structures being dissolved in cultural processes that privilege decentring, disaggregation and dispersal (unfixity). He notes that 'The disintegration of the social network, the falling apart of effective agencies of collective action is often . . . bewailed as the unanticipated "side effect" of the new lightness and fluidity of the increasingly mobile, slippery, shifty, evasive and fugitive power' (2000: 14). Bauman uses the term 'social network' in the sense of stable practices and spaces that circumscribe a community, and is uncomfortable at its seeming erosion. Now, however, we understand it differently. The cultural liquidity that has dissolved fixed practices and solid spaces also provides the tools for a new form of social interrelation, the 'social network' as we have come to express it as a multifarious set of interpersonal connections. Liquid modernity has enabled the reestablishment of a social scene – through some of the forms of fluid dispersion that characterize late-capitalism.

We observe a characteristic doubleness of digital culture. We lament its splintering and atomizing effects, the erosion of personal liberty in an age of electronic surveillance, and the separation between digital haves and have-nots. On the other hand, social media have facilitated popular protest as diverse as the Occupy movement and the Arab Spring; and digital culture has allowed us to present ourselves diversely – playfully, seriously, actively – in public, and share knowledge faster than ever before. It enables bespoke personal expression. It is disposed to participatory citizenship and collective action. It has extended the relativizing work of postmodernism, but also helped us to rediscover our voices and values, and our singular selves. Which suggests that postmodernism as a cultural force has shifted to become something other than itself.

## After the postmodern

A gathered view of postmodernism is that in the period after the Second World War – particularly through the 1960s and 1970s, after the austerity of the post-war years – culture in late-capitalist societies underwent a series of shifts that changed patterns of work, social habits, attitudes and modes of artistic expression. (For summative accounts of postmodernism, see Bertens 1995; Billig and Simons 1994; Docherty 1993.) As ever, there was a political context. The Cold War fed off the ideological separation behind the post-war settlements that divided Europe following the demise of Nazism, with Russia emerging as a superpower alongside the USA. Each treated the other with an untrusting scrutiny that came to a head in the Cuban missile crisis of 1962. The sense of geopolitical fragility was exacerbated by the increased sophistication of nuclear technologies. Not only were nuclear power stations now part of the reckoning for electricity generation (for a self-selecting few countries), but the bombing of Hiroshima and Nagaskai in 1945 had indicated that the superpowers could effect military will with drastic immediacy. The superpower states were meanwhile affirming their own territories and hegemony; the USSR, for example, through the invasion of Czechoslovakia on 20 August 1968, the USA through

the Vietnam War (1955–75) and in its support for the Contras and other anti-leftist movements in Latin America. In this political scenario the popular voice surfaced – as in the Civil Rights Movement in the USA, or *les événements* in France in 1968 – as counter-cultural protest, where the prospect of real and lasting change seemed distant.

While the superpowers dominated geo-politics, commercial corporations became powerful multinationals, operating across borders with increasing scope and flexibility. In manufacturing, the lithe and flexible systems of post-Fordism came to predominate over the Fordist structures of factory-based production-line economics. Postmodernism was associated with technological advance and complexity, intertwined with economic development towards post-industrial models of social and commercial transaction, segmentation and the differentiation of markets. Through all the above, it was a key feature of globalization (Henke and Middeke 2007: 2).

A similar dispersal was happening culturally. Postmodernism drew on and contributed to the growth and ubiquity of plural media. Against the grain of the dominance of major media networks, it also enabled new forms of counter-cultural expression. The era was marked by the Happenings, the growth of hippy culture, the incursion of pop, rock and then punk. In parallel, postmodern criticism offered a challenge to stable and even knowable senses of self and personal identity. This marked a set of disengagements – from politics, precedence, the very idea of coherent personhood. The postmodern age displayed 'incredulity toward metanarratives' (Lyotard 1984: xxiv) – those defining stories of progress, dominating systems, or monolithic political positions. It embraced instead the rhetoric and practices of fracture, detachment and irony. Intellectually and critically this cultural tendency was powered by the rubrics of poststructuralism in Europe and its American counterpart deconstruction, as exemplified in the writings of Derrida, Lacan, Jameson and de Man.

Bertens reasonably depicts two major trains of thought: a Foucauldian examination of social and civic structures along with histories to reveal 'the workings of power, and the constitution of the subject' (1995: 7); and a Derridean analysis of language and texts that depicts representation as untrustworthy and tenuous. Foucault's writing disputed the notion of a linear development of history in favour of seeing histories as plural, while any historical analysis was a record of discourse, power and the discriminations of cultural practices. Derrida performed in his own writing the elusive nature of poststructuralist thought, which holds that language is (de)structured by gaps and slippages, and full of fissures through which constructs of truth and stability evaporate. It traps its users in delay, deferral, *différance*. Knowledge itself became an unstable commodity. As Bertens suggests:

> If there is a common denominator to all these postmodernisms, it is that of a crisis of representation: a deeply felt loss of faith in our ability to represent the real, in the widest sense. No matter whether they are aesthetic,

epistemological, moral, or political in nature, the representations that we used to rely on can no longer be taken for granted.

(Bertens 1995: 11)

Postmodernism's playful and resistant critiques circle around an epistemological black hole. When language is untrustworthy, it becomes difficult to say something that commonly appears to matter. Bauman characterizes this as 'the celebration of the "demise of the ethical", of the substitution of aesthetics for ethics, and of the "ultimate emancipation" that follows' (1993: 2). Bauman doesn't approve of this kind of freewheeling, seemingly amoral postmodernism. He proposes instead that the postmodern allows a 'tearing off of the mask of illusions' to reveal 'sources of moral power' (1993: 3). Two years later he argued that 'some sort of coordinated and concerted action is imperative. And the name of such action is politics; the promotion of a new and badly needed ethics for the new age can only be approached as a *political* issue and task.' (Bauman 1995: 281, original emphasis. See Bauman 1997 for further development of this argument.)

By the mid-1990s, then, the tide has turned. Postmodernism had performed the healthy function of destabilizing assumed norms and notions of the real. Yet the tools that it introduced proved limited in dealing with new scenarios that changed our relationship (historically, politically, technologically) to realities and their expression. Matters of truth, transparency and commitment took on a different face with the incursion of the network (al-Qaeda) and network culture (the Internet and the spread of social media). Bauman's call to action was realized in ways that he could not have anticipated, nor, in all probability, quite meant. The real had returned, and so had the evident presence of politics and imperative questions concerning ethics. Culturally, the real could not be avoided, even where it was contested. And we developed a new taste for it.

Any significant shift in representation is usually a return to the real, as the expressive conventions of older forms are seen to be, precisely, conventions. Newer modes, technologically enabled, allow us to see and present things differently. Moreover we *experience* culture differently because we do so with our minds and expectations adjusted to the speeds and shapes, flows and frames of the expressive apparatus with which we live. How different is this from what came before? A consistent question, even during its heyday, concerns the extent to which postmodernism marked a development of, or departure from, defining features of modernism. Taking a long view, Henke and Middeke, for example, treat modernism, and postmodernism in its wake, as a break from Enlightenment rationality (2007; see also Brown 1994: 16; and Foster 1985: ix, xi–xii). Bertens sees it as a complexifying and continuance of Enlightenment-shaped concerns with the place of reason, logic and social process. In the shorter run, postmodernism can be depicted as an extension of practices that modernism had set in play; or as a break from modernist aesthetics and social processes.

A similar tension runs through the book you are reading, between a sense that the theatres of engagement that I discuss mark a break from the ironies and decentrings of postmodernism, or alternatively a continuance through different artistic strategies of its larger project of dispersal and its insistence on context. Hal Foster suggested in 1983 that 'modernism is now largely absorbed. Originally oppositional, . . . today, however, it is the official culture' (Foster 1985: ix). Likewise the precepts, techniques and assumptions of postmodernism are now largely absorbed, albeit refigured and extended in post-millennial culture.

Feminist scholarship helps exemplify the conceptual shifts over the period. Writing at the turn of the millennium, the editors of *Transformations: Thinking Through Feminism* observe that 'the late twentieth century has been a difficult time to think about transformation. . . . Somewhat ironically, recent social, political and intellectual transformations seem to have left many of us without a vocabulary or framework for discussing transformation' – this in the wake of postmodern epistemologies and evident limitations to a variety of 'new' mainstram agendas (Ahmed *et al.*, 2000: 4–5). In order to engage afresh, the authors observe in feminist projects 'the process of *re-membering* themselves in order to understand how aspects of the past may enter into the future' (6; original emphasis) – a process that implicates the body, retains advances already made, but requires the work of continual transformation of histories and practices. Writing in the same year, bell hooks (2000) likewise presents a case that is celebratory and recuperative, advocating continued change through wide cultural engagement. In the preface to the second edition of their *Manifesta*, reflecting on differences between the book's first publication in 2000 and its new edition a decade later, Baumgardner and Richards note a sustaining theme: a call to women 'to do the big thing that feminism invites us to do – to recognize our power to create social justice in our own unique ways' (2000: xiii) – in other words, a compound of individual agency and communal engagement that is characteristic of the period. This sense of reappraisal and re-engagement provides a bridge to 'fourth wave' feminism, a decade into the twenty-first century, that diversely negotiates the media systems and identity repertoires of contemporary culture (see, for instance, Nally and Smith 2015).

Postmodernism marked a scepticism about universalizing truths, grand narratives, and dogmatic statements of intent or belief. Historical process either side of the new millennium demonstrated that individual agency could be effective, overt and drastic, and that established systems were vulnerable and couldn't be taken for granted. This made for a return to some forms of universalizing (in the categorical expressions of particular faith positions or political ideologies, for example), but also entailed more individualized forms of felt experience and personal commitment. Digital culture and social media helped individuals to reinscribe their opinions and their bodies in social and cultural discourse. In so doing they were often armed with the tools, techniques and many of the assumptions of postmodernism: no truth is without its context; no exchange is innocent of its mode of mediation. Yet these tools were taken up in a new engagement with the world, and with the individual selves and bodies within it. After decentring, we found ourselves diversely centred. To address a tense present: we are amid interdisciplinary cultural formations, interested in meaning, representation, utterance and *content*, but also mindful of display, surfaces, *presentation*. We depend upon flattened hierarchies of creation, multiple modes of dissemination, and geographically wide distributions of labour, production and consumption. We remain at the behest of mega-corporations and suave political systems, but in some instances we adopt diverse means of instantaneous communication to convey our own modes of certainty and identity. After the clarion calls of modernism, and the absences and ironies of postmodernism, come the nuanced and differential negotiations, participations and interventions of an age of engagement.

## The world has become theatre (or, *Re-Enter Truth and the Real*)

Running alongside the development of postmodernism is a common conceit: the world has become theatre (or performance); performance (or theatre) provides not just a metaphor but also a *modus operandi* for our relationship to the world. Jon McKenzie provides a celebrated orientation in his book *Perform or Else* (2001). McKenzie sees the emergence of 'performance' over the last half-decade of the twentieth century as 'an onto-historical formation of power and knowledge' (2001: 18), akin to that of 'discipline' in the eighteenth and nineteenth centuries. He identifies three fields in which this is manifest. The first is 'organizational performance', to do with the business of business, the stuff of profits, prices and efficiencies, and the protocols of 'performance management' whereby objectives are achieved by calibrating the work of individuals. The second is 'cultural performance', including the major media of television, cinema and theatre, as well as communications within specific social, cultural and behavioural settings – what McKenzie describes as 'the living, embodied expression of cultural traditions and transformations' (8). The third field is 'technological performance', which concerns specifications for manufacture and end-use, 'a sense of performance used by engineers, technicians and computer scientists' (10).

'Performance' as a term is thereby particularly resonant, since it acts as a compound for an interrelated set of practices to do with presentation, efficiency, and advantage. As part of this analysis, McKenzie provides a history of the academic discipline of Performance Studies from its inception in the 1950s, moving through Erving Goffman's 'social psychology of everyday life' (2001: 33), to Victor Turner's 'social drama', to Richard Schechner's discipline-shaping account of performance in an array of social and cultural settings, to Marvin Carlson's discipline-defining *Performance: A Critical Introduction* (1996). McKenzie notes that performance in each of these approaches is often conceived as liminal, marginal, disruptive or subversive. This points to one way in which the field has developed further in the couple of decades since Carlson articulated its parameters. We tend now to see performance all around us, as a norm rather than an expression mainly of corporate drive or subversive resistance. McKenzie reflects upon Carlson's comments, as the latter concludes his study, and the citation from Carlson bears repetition here:

> [Performance] is a specific event with its liminoid nature foregrounded, almost invariably clearly separated from the rest of life, presented by performers and attended by audiences both of whom regard the experience as made up material to be interpreted, to be reflected upon, to be engaged in – emotionally, mentally, and perhaps even physically.
> (McKenzie 2001: 49–50 [Carlson 1996, 198–9])

For McKenzie, this is part of a continuum: liminality as a feature of both performance and Performance Studies. But if Carlson's statement accurately described the landscape when McKenzie turned to it in 2001, it looks a little different from the perspective of a further decade or so. As I review this in 2015, we would not necessarily say that the liminoid aspect of performance is always foregrounded – rather, that performance finds ways to imbricate the actual and virtual, presence and absence, the real and fabrication. It is not 'clearly separated from life' but of and within it. Nor is it necessarily presented by performers and attended by audiences, but comprised of performers and spectators who shift roles or may not appear at all (as performers, or spectators) in the constitutive roll-call of the performance event. Nor do we observe 'made-up material to be interpreted' – rather, presentation to be experienced, consumed, lived within. As John Corner observes, 'there is hectic innovation around combinations of the "real" with the self-declared and openly per-formative "artificial"' (2004: 292).

This is meant not to dispute Carlson's analysis, but as an observation about shifts in the trajectory of performance insofar as it is thinkable and observable from particular vantage points. Here we move from liminality to embeddedness, while performance nonetheless retains its ability to operate across boundaries. It's just that we now expect this to be the case, and – since it is the case – we observe performance operating at our centre rather than at various margins. If anything, certain margin-behaviours have moved into our common ground. This bears out McKenzie's coinage of the notion of the 'liminal-norm' (2001: 49–53, 166), although in slightly different terms. McKenzie describes a scenario 'where the valorization of liminal transgression or resistance itself becomes normative' (2001: 50). The continuing valency of performance as a mode appropriate to – vital within – twenty-first-century culture has proved yet more extensive. Performance has mainstreamed. Its liminal-norm now concerns its intermediality, its operation across 'high' and 'low' registers, its consistent merging of actual and presentational, as opposed to something more structurally subversive (although it can still operate in these terms).

Shortly before the turn of the century, Hans-Thies Lehmann expanded a critical apparatus designed for this development.[12] *Postdramatic Theatre* (published in German in 1999 and English in 2006) established fresh coordinates for performance analysis, with its focus on physical, material and sensual aspects of theatre production, and practices that depended less on the dramatic text and more on regimes of scenic, spatial and somatic organization. For all that Lehmann's work has been contested, the rubric of the postdramatic remains luminous in theatre and performance studies. As the editors of a retrospective volume suggest:

> Lehmann had deployed the term [postdramatic theatre] as an alternative to the then ubiquitous term 'postmodern theatre' in order to describe how a vast variety of contemporary forms of theatre and performance had departed not so much from the 'modern' as from drama.
>
> (Jürs-Munby *et al.* 2013: 1)

Lehmann indeed traced continuities reaching back to archaic and classical forms of theatre, across into Aristotelian and Hegelian philosophy and beyond theatre to Schechner's performance studies and interdisciplinary and multimedia work. The theatres of engagement that I discuss below share many of the attributes that Lehmann assigns to postdramatic theatre, but they mark a further extension of theatrical paradigms *beyond* theatre, into a wider performance scene that is defined not so much by its departure from drama, as its re-engagement with the real.

This returns us to the question as to whether performance in this scenario has moved beyond postmodernism. I tend to agree with Henke and Middeke's assessment:

> Virtually all aesthetic characteristics of postmodern art . . . can be found in contemporary drama: a fascination for self-reflexive, metadramatic modes which reflect upon epistemological uncertainty, ambiguity, and blanks; a mistrust of totality which results in fragmented formal structures: collages, cut-up forms, paradox, pastiche, parody – signifiers that disperse unidirectional attributions of fixed meanings, intentions, or propositions.[13]
>
> (Henke and Middeke 2007: 13)

Within this continuity, however, we must entwine a new fascination with authenticity, and the fixing of performance at the heart of contemporary experience. A way of considering this is to return to 9/11. What could be more actual than the attacks of 9/11, in their categorical violence on bodies, their political consequences and their effects on attitudes and perceptions? And what could be more theatrical, in their spectacular imagery, the shock they provided and their extraordinary staging of protest?[14] In an essay written not long after the event, Slavoj Žižek argues that following the twentieth century's fascination with getting closer to the Real, 9/11 brought a 'Third World' style of authentic horror to the USA. He articulates an interlocking compound, actual | theatrical:

> The Real which returns has the status of a(nother) semblance: precisely because it is real, that is, on account of its traumatic/excessive character, we are unable to integrate it into (what we experience as) our reality, and are therefore compelled to experience it as a nightmarish apparition. This is what the compelling image of the collapse of the WTC [World Trade Center] was: an image, a semblance, an 'effect', which, at the same time, delivered 'the thing itself'.
>
> (Žižek 2002: 19, original emphasis)

The real is unassimilable except as a sort of grisly fiction – it is nevertheless real. This is one aspect of the irruption of the real as theatre onto the world stage. Another, however, is provided by the polar opposite of the eventual, spectacular 9/11, and it is found in the tissue of quotidian, banal, everyday figurings that suffuse the contemporary media landscape by way of their appearance on social media sites such as Instagram, Facebook and Twitter, and in curated media outlets such as reality TV programmes, radio phone-ins, stand-up comedy acts and art installations that stage our ordinariness. We can invert Žižek's statement to outline an also-applicable feature of contemporary actuality: the Real has the status of a semblance precisely because it is *mediated as quotidian*, expressed in and through performance as the theatricalized image of our everyday selves.[15]

Reality incurs not as reality but as it is *performed* (presented) and *perceived*. Performance *expresses* insofar as it can be matrixed against a reality. This figuring of the real as both assimilable through its *appearance* and available because *presented* provides a perspective on theatre and performance of the period. In her introduction to *Dramaturgy of the Real on the World Stage*, addressing theatre in the first decade of the twenty-first century, Carol Martin observes 'an emerging theatre of the real that directly addresses the global condition of troubled epistemologies about truth, authenticity and reality' (2010: 1; see also Forsyth and Megson 2009: 2, 3). She relates this more broadly to 'a great expansion of ideas about "reality". Restored villages, Civil War enactments, network television, blogs, YouTube and other internet innovations, cellphones, photography, plasma boards, surveillance cameras, and mainstream film in all its modes' (2010: 2). Taken together, this swathe of mediation–machines leads her to a question that also weaves through *Performance in the Twenty-First Century*: 'are reality and representation so inextricable that they have become indiscernible?' (2010: 2; see also Reinelt 2010: 28).

*Dramaturgy of the Real on the World Stage* addresses documentary, testimony and verbatim theatre, but its scope is much wider, as its globally embracing title suggests. It focuses on discourse and practices that circulate around notions of truth and actuality. Let's call this 'truth-turning', in order to avoid simply ascribing Truth in any one place. For (after postmodernism) 'truth' is always contextual and often subject to shift, while the 'real', as Rancière has it, 'is always a matter of construction, a matter of "fiction" ' (2010: 148) – aesthetically, at least. The circumstances in play do not necessarily have to be factually correct for truth-turning to be with us. They will appear to be truthful to some people; or their apparent truthfulness matters in context; or they can be seen to involve people in action or agreement concerning matters of fact. This is not to deny that the nature and accuracy of the facts frequently matter a good deal. Rather, it is to point up the nature of a regime of (re)presentation in which facticity, actuality and truth-turning have such potency, indeed necessity, for artists and audiences. This obtains, as Reinelt suggests, in relation to the 'hypertheatricalization of contemporary culture' (2010: 39), where facticity provides a form of ballast:

> audiences know that documents, facts, and evidence are always mediated when they are received; they know there is no raw truth apart from interpretation, but still, they want to *experience the assertion of the materiality of events*, of the indisputable character of the facts . . . I see the potential for this gesture as an ethico-political revolt, as a demonstration of caring, engagement, and commitment.
>
> (Reinelt 2010: 39–40, my emphasis)

Not the least pertinent part of this account is its notion that truth-turning is *experienced* as a feature of engagement. Theatrical tropes can help to clarify and present new perspectives on realities, while anchoring audiences experientially in a specific material context (Reinelt 2010: 41). This reminds us of Bauman's call for an ethics for the new age, and Lehmann's for an *aesthetic of responsibility (or response-ability)* . . . [that can] make visible the broken thread between personal experience and perception' (2006: 185–6, original emphasis). It provides an opening for certain sorts of political agency, where it is possible to reclaim a sense of theatre and performance doing a particular kind of work in the world – and doing it in resistance to norms or uninspected assumptions, with the ability to make us see things differently and perhaps take action as a consequence.[16]

The sorts of 'caring, engagement and commitment' that Reinelt observes moves us into a notably different lexicon from that employed during the height of postmodernism. The terms that resonate now in performance studies are 'actuality', 'authenticity', 'encounter', 'engagement' – a set that would have seemed naïve or faintly ridiculous if wheeled out a generation or so ago. The difference is that theatricality itself has been riveted at the heart of these terms, as part of a combined effect of cultural production that finds urgency and excitement in the joint operation of ostensible realities and overt presentation. Musing upon a world of simulacra in which grand narratives have been discredited, Tomlin observes 'an ultimate collapse of the boundaries between the fictional and the real' (2013: 35). Another way of putting this might be to suggest that the boundaries have *become inhabited* (we are back to McKenzie's liminal-norm), where actuality and fabrication remain mutually in play, with all their respective phenomenal and ontological distinctness.

As the real returns – through transformative events like the fall of the Berlin Wall and 9/11, communications technologies that enmesh us in a sustained present, and aesthetic procedures that offer experience and encounter to their audiences – theatricality takes on a different relationship to the spaces, objects and concepts that it references. It re-presents them in their immediate presence and function. It offers a presentation structure that permits (indeed sometimes requires) representation, in an era when mediation (also) empties representation. This takes us towards Thrift's sense of performance as a cultural knowledge, whereby 'performance has become a general art which concentrates especially on the conduct of the now and which can be appropriated' (2008: 71). The appropriation is not only to do with the *presentation* of performance in the now-moment, but the *intertwining* of performance and experience, performance and witness, performance and encounter, performance and actuality. Herein lie our contemporary theatres of engagement. They arise when we observe a sharpened focus upon actualities (of situation, the body, the moment) framed within spaces and scenes of mediation that are also sites of encounter and experience. Theatres of engagement are neither, necessarily, virtuous nor vicious, popular nor coercive. But they are all around us, for they provide a shape and a means by which things are presently sayable and doable. If the world has become theatre, what of the theatre that finds itself within this particular world?

## Being engaged

The term 'engagement' describes the mode of this theatre. It conveys a sense of component parts coming together in order to *work* – as when gears engage and an engine or a machine performs its function. A theatre of engagement, in this sense, comprises diverse technical aspects that are brought together in order for the whole to perform appropriately (in McKenzie's formulation of technical performance). The term can also be taken to mean being *of* the world and *in* the world. In this sense it suggests a set of performances that are turned towards their society, deliberately invested in social process, political perspective, matters of import to gathered groups of people. This is a theatre that is socially committed, not necessarily in order to espouse a particular perspective (although it might), but to perform an age-old function: provide a seeing place (*theatron*) where matters of significance are shared communally, and a gathering ground where events are inhabited in common. 'Engagement' also suggests a mode of involvement on the part of individual spectators (who become participants in some performances in this field). Relevant markers on this particular spectrum include participation, corporeal interaction and experiential encounter. 'Engagement' in these latter instances is not just an attitude but also an act. You are engaged because this is required of you, body and mind. The term thereby also conveys a sense of commitment. It can mean both an assignation – an agreement to meet at a particular time – and, more momentously, a decision to join in marriage. In all these latter scenarios, it indicates a process of offer, decision and mutual accord, a cleaving to the mast. It is about arrival and concreteness rather than deferral and slippage. In this sense the term catches the wider disposition to affect of much contemporary theatre and performance, and the associated arsenal of feelings – allure, threat, trepidation, thrill, delight – that spectators report amid various encounters with performance.

Theatres of Engagement, then, mix it with the world. They get in amid social process. They face outwards rather than inwards, albeit that they might also involve the most intimate personal sharing or exposure. They ask commitment and sometimes sacrifice of their participants and spectators. They depend on and produce feelings and experience. They involve sometimes high-tech calibration of diverse component parts and media. In this field of intersecting attributes, 'engagement' appropriately describes performance after postmodernism.

The term has been used elsewhere. In *Theatre, Intimacy & Engagement* (2008) Alan Read infers its usefulness as a way of describing both social and intimate encounters with theatre, in an analysis that seeks to recuperate a reading of the political in and through performance. In *The Engagement Aesthetic: Experiencing New Media Art Through Critique* (2013), Francisco J. Ricardo discusses engagement from a broadly phenomenological perspective, in relation to subjective perception through the aesthetic affordances of new media art, and in virtual and actual spaces. In *Engaging Audiences: A Cognitive Approach to Spectating in the Theatre* (2008) Bruce McConachie particularly addresses audience encounters with playtexts in production. In her book *Engaging Performance: Theatre as Call and Response* (2010), Jan Cohen Cruz addresses 'the act of choosing performance to respond to social controversies' and 'the compelling expressive potential of performance that draws on a broad range of people involved in the social situation in question', doing so through lived experience and professional expertise (2010: 1). In a UK context we would think of this kind of 'engaging performance' as 'applied theatre', a field that has grown considerably over the past decade or so. While it doesn't always respond to social controversies, applied theatre engages with various communities small and large, including the young, the elderly, the imprisoned, the displaced, the traumatized and the abused, and often with people who find themselves outside social norms or tolerances. As reality-trend performance has spread, works that might previously have been encountered only in applied theatre contexts have appeared on different stages, as in Ontroerend Goed's *Once And For All We're Gonna Tell You Who We Are So Shut Up And Listen* (2008, featuring teenagers), She She Pop's *Testament* (2010, featuring three elderly fathers of members of the company) and Rimini Protokoll's *Radio Muezzin* (2008, featuring four men who give the call to prayer in Egyptian mosques). Engagement here is with particular communities of interest or expertise, but also with specific social and cultural issues that arise from their situation and experience. Engagement likewise indicates the involvement of individuals as performers who might otherwise not have so public a voice. Noting that Jean-Paul Sartre 'advocated for all art to be *"engagé"*' (*committed*), Cohen Cruz suggests that contemporary engaged art goes further than the existentialists' call for artists to act as witnesses, for it provides 'opportunities for people to speak for themselves in some phase of the process' (2010: 3, 4).

This re-expression of a political sensibility, along with a desire for more direct political engagement with and through performance, is shared by a number of authors (see, for instance, Harvie 2013, Jackson 2011, Spencer 2012, Thrift 2008, Tomlin 2013). All, nonetheless, remain mindful of the changing context in which political theatre must now be thought. Carol Martin promotes the notion of 'constructivist postmodernism', for example, as a way of recognizing the continuity of postmodern techniques and perspectives within scenarios of commitment and meaning-making (Martin 2010: 3). Tomlin proposes 'an alternative mode of poststructuralist resistance which seeks to reconfigure contemporary notions of reality, rather than merely highlighting the simulated nature of all representations of the real' (2013: 143–4). This leads her towards 'alternative models of performance which . . . seek to engage the participant (now neither performer nor spectator in any conventional sense) in a more direct and experiential relationship with their own subjectively constructed reality' (2013: 144). The models are not solely appropriate for resistance. They express, more broadly, contemporary cultural transactions with and through performance, where a consistent theme is the meeting of performance and the real.

As we have already seen, *engagement* trails a set of related terms that have been useful in discussions of this meeting-point, such as actuality, agency, authenticity, encounter and experience. Indeed this lexicon reverberates more widely across disciplines including sociology, computing, art and aesthetics, human geography and economics. Pine and Gilmore describe a society in which experiences have become a core commodity alongside goods and services (1999; see also Schulze 1992; and Boswijk *et al.* 2007). Groot Nibbelink notes the rise of the term 'theatre of experience' to describe early-millennial Dutch and Flemish theatre that focuses on the single or isolated spectator (2012: 416). In their discussion of the experiential arrangement of cultural attractions in Denmark, Baerenholdt *et al.* see experience as the outcome of a matrix of activities, that together make for 'a form of *connective authenticity*' (2008: 199, original emphasis).

The recourse to 'authenticity' has something almost plangent about it, for this was a term not much in currency in postmodernist discourse. For the philosopher-psychologist Eugene Gendlin, 'Authenticity can become the new "centre" after the decentring by postmodernism' (1999: 206). Boswijk *et al.* suggest that it marks a fundamental development in contemporary society: 'Authenticity is about rediscovering values and traditions and interpreting them in a new way within a progressive context. The individual is looking for genuineness and originality: for the core and essence of things' (2007: 46). Paradoxically, perhaps, this essence is often found through the virtualities of digital culture. The authors argue for a set of 'important watersheds in history' (2007: 39). These include (in recent times) Network, Experience, and Engagement, and while this problematically splits out the paradigm-shift of the digital era across three whole 'revolutions', the trajectory plausibly suggests that a networked cultural scene moves into more routinized provision of experience, which in turn extends into a wider facilitation of engagement.

The incursion of games and gaming, enabled by computers, provides an instance in microcosm of this kind of trajectory, by way of the sorts of intensely affective play that will be familiar to many (and the parents of many). In their most pervasive form, games offer a 'blur of the real and the fictive' (Stenros *et al.* 2009: 258), and provide encounters that may be social as well as virtual (see also Calleja 2011: 10; Douglas and Hargadon 2001: 152; and Dovey and Kennedy 2006: 8). Many games offer an extension of play-frames through online discussion fora, 'how-to' videos and conventions such as Comic-Con, further blurring the lines between performative play and quotidian activity in the world.

We can extend Bourriaud's influential notion of a changing relation between the artwork and its spectator. If 'Art is a state of encounter', it is so, Bourriaud suggests, in order to facilitate 'the transposition into experience of spaces constructed and represented by the artist, the projection of the symbolic into the real' (2002: 18, 82). An important correlate in subsequent developments of spectator engagement is the extent to which the event is *realized* or *changed* by the spectator-participant through what we can describe as an *agency function* (which is a form of both reality matrix and reality effect). In many events, one can choose how one watches, where one goes within the event, and the pace at which one does things (as in a number of immersive theatre shows or gallery-based works, for example). More directly, one can determine flows of action through decisions as a participant or gamer. Such involvement is also experiential. That's to say, when we are immersants within a Punchdrunk show, gamers in a Blast Theory piece, or interactants at a residency by Marina Abramovíc, we experience the event differently from, say, an evening spent sitting in the auditorium at the theatre, because we make a greater range of choices, find ourselves performing a larger array of actions, and have our senses pressed in a wider variety of ways. Our bodies are in play and we recognize that our own actions contribute to the figuring of the event. This self-reflexivity is part of the echo-chamber of contemporary performance encounters. We have moved from a society of the spectacle to a society of involved spectaction; in turn, we experience ourselves having experience.[17] Authenticity is, so to say, bodied forth and understood in the body, which is one means by which it performs an act of centring amid the separations of digital culture and in the wake of postmodernism.

It's not startling to suggest that experience is all around us; but the way in which experience is accorded significance marks a shift in focus in theatre and performance studies, where theatre itself expands as a domain in and through experiential performance in (for example) museums, galleries and games (Bennett 2013; Bishop 2006; Calleja 2011). Claire Bishop, for instance, observes that installation art *presents* (for us to experience) rather than *represents*. 'This introduces an emphasis on sensory immediacy, on physical participation (the viewer must walk into and around the work), and on a heightened awareness of other visitors' – making for what Bishop celebrates as an 'activated spectatorship' (2005: 11; see also Bishop 2006: 10–17, and Bishop 2004). Such work is not solely concerned with its own meanings or representational schema. It 'presupposes an *embodied* viewer' (Bishop 2005: 6, original emphasis). The very circumstance that the art critic Michael Fried notoriously lamented in 1967 – the blurring of an artwork and its context, the joining of spaces of presentation and spectatorship, the irreducible importance of the self-aware, *necessary* spectator – has become the condition of much twenty-first century art and, by extension, performance.

A good example is provided in the opening chapter to *The Audience Experience*. Radbourne et al. discuss *Haircuts by Children*, a piece developed by Toronto-based company Mammalian Diving Reflex, in which children between the ages of 10 and 12 cut the hair of adults. According to the authors, 'So thorough is audience engagement in *Haircuts by Children* that the audience and the art offering have become one' (2013: 3). The piece embodies more widespread developments, including shifts in the nature of spaces for performance (here the space is also an extra-theatrical workplace); the performance of *concept* in and through the realization of the piece; and what Alston (discussing Punchdrunk's work) sees as a characteristic conjunction, where 'acts of participation . . . become sites of reception' (2013: 130). That's to say, the older model of reception as something conveyed from elsewhere is confounded when reception is *produced by* your own active engagement.[18]

Such involvement isn't the case with all theatres of engagement, but it does characterize a larger scene. The performance that surrounds us now is often affective. It is also of the world – not solely because it is among our entertainments, but because it is suffused in our lives within culture. Performance engages with and puts us in the face of actuality. It is a means by which we can express positions and negotiate perspectives. Social space is differently inhabited. Stages extend into the world. Performance is re-theatricalized as the presentation of shifting realities, mediated in and through our own necessary presence and participation.

## Notes

1 www.sgt.gr/en/circle/53.
2 I discuss *Situation Rooms* by Rimini Protokoll and *The Pixellated Revolution* by Rabih Mroué in greater detail in Lavender 2014.
3 The term literally means 'theatre of the time', but has been rendered in English as 'reality trend theatre'.
4 Lehmann remarks that the 'motives for a certain re-entry of the political and social dimension . . . are rather obvious', including 9/11, the fall of the Wall, 'new wars, the rise of rightist populist leaders in Europe . . . [and] new social problems of different kinds' (cited in Jürs-Munby *et al.* 2013: 2). I state the obvious here to open into a wider discussion of relations between historical process, a reality aesthetic, and developments in techniques and technologies of (re)presentation.
5 For an analysis of the political context for developments in the Soviet Union, see Engel 2009: 20–6. See Engel 2009: n.1, 30–1, for a bibliography on the Cold War; and n. 2, 32 for a bibliography on 1989 in East Europe. For a narrative account of the political and social events leading up to the fall of the wall, see Buckley 2004: 137–67.
6 Hobsbawm sees the last part of the century, from the 1970s, as 'a new era of decomposition, uncertainty and crisis' after a 'Golden Age' of social and economic growth over the preceding three decades (1994: 6).
7 See Limb 2008: 99–100 for the wider political context that contributed to Mandela's release.
8 It is easy to agree with Sherman and Nardin's observation that the 'dark times' referred to by Hannah Arendt in her discussion of the Holocaust provide a 'far more appalling period of war and depression, terror and oppression' (Nardin and Sherman 2006: 4). Their caution partly concerns the sense that 9/11 was used to legitimize geo-political interventions in service of the 'war on terror' (so-called by US President George W. Bush) and broader neo-liberal agendas (see also Spencer 2012: 2; n.9, 14). For a consideration of 9/11 in light of faith-based perspectives, see Morgan 2009b (one of a series of six examining 9/11). For a consideration of responses in the arts and wider cultural outputs to 9/11, see Melnick 2009: 3, 4; and Morgan 2009a.
9 For discussion of the growth and affordances of social media and digital culture, see Benkler 2006; Bunz 2014; Castells 2012; Jenkins 2006; Palfrey and Gasser 2008; and Trend 2001 (including sections on communication and the performance of identity). For brief overviews of competing positions concerning digital culture, see Bohman 2004: 131–3; and Castells 2001: 116–33. For discussion of social media and protest, see De Luca *et al.* 2012: 501. See Teigland and Power (2013) for a collection of essays on a next-phase to Internet use that entails seeming blurrings between the virtual and the physical. See Trottier 2012 for an account of social media and surveillance. For discussion of digital culture in relation to theatre and performance; see Bay-Cheng 2014; Causey 2006; Dixon 2007; and Lavender 2010.
10 ITU, 'ICT Facts and Figures', www.itu.int/en/ITU-D/Statistics/Documents/facts/ICTFactsFigures2014-e.pdf.
11 For further discussion see Auslander 2011.
12 Lehmann's work is discussed, disputed and developed in Pavis 2014 and Jürs-Munby *et al.* 2013. Watt (1998) tackles similar ground – theatre in light of postmodernism – from a very different perspective granted his American location and interest in playtexts. For celebratory responses to *Postdramatic Theatre* see Balme 2004 (introducing a special issue of *TRI* on postdramatic theatre) and Carlson 2006; and for a notoriously scathing review, see Fuchs 2008.

13 See also Heddon and Milling's list of adjectives that apply to postmodern performance, which continue to have resonance (2006: 203).
14 Engle (2009) discusses a range of images from and about 9/11, within the rubrics of cultural production and signification. See also Spencer 2012: n. 1, 13, for references to interventions by Carlson, Sell and Stockhausen concerning the relation between 9/11 and aesthetic organization; and Kubiak 2012: 2.
15 It is worth pointing out that Žižek is caustic about the liberal interpretation of the end of postmodernism and 'The End of the Age of Irony' (2002: 34).
16 See Lehmann 2013 for discussion of the prospect of a political postdramatic theatre, in relation to the mode of tragedy.
17 We can trace a line of thought from Debord to Baudrillard to de Certeau, concerning the cultural ecology of representation within society within and beyond postmodernism; initially a separation of images from their referents (Debord's 'society of the spectacle'), to an endless circulation of simulations (Baudrillard's simulacra), to a multiform presentational system that underpins felt encounters and material practices (De Certeau's 'thrice-narratable culture', comprising the 'stories' expressed in advertising and informational media, along with their citation and re-citation [1984: 186]). Tomlin (2013) provides a helpful guide.
18 *The Audience Experience* predominantly addresses audience engagement in a different sense: that of audience 'development', by which artists and companies aim to increase their reach. See also Freshwater 2009: 29–33, and NEF 2010. See White 2013, Bala 2012 and the essays in Kattwinkel 2003 for a discussion of various dimensions of and theoretical perspectives on audience participation. For wider discussion of spectatorship see Freshwater 2009; Balme 2008: 34–46; and the essays in Pavis 2012.

# Chapter 2

# The visible voice (or, the word made flesh)

## Political presence and performative utterance in the public sphere

In the last couple of decades of the twentieth century we observed a turn to testimony in contemporary performance. The wave of individual voices that this released has, if anything, grown more tidal over the first decade-and-a-half of the twenty-first century, as individuals speak across the proliferation of media platforms. It catches up the specific lives and experiences of many different people and groups, and has given new energy to an older form of political theatre – that's to say, theatre that relies on a first-person account, addresses present concerns in the public sphere, and perhaps also develops explicit social and political agendas. It does so by staging the speaking of individuals and groups most immediately concerned with particular topics or incidents. Hence, for example, we have heard from the residents of Crown Heights, Brooklyn, along with civic and religious leaders in Anna Deavere Smith's *Fires in the Mirror* (1992); railway workers and political and commercial officers in David Hare's *The Permanent Way* (2003); or the policemen and women and local residents featured in Gillian Slovo's *The Riots* (2011) – to take three different verbatim-inflected examples. This is also true of the subjects of shows mentioned in the first chapter of this book, albeit that the work is different in form: the immigrants figured in Dries Verhoeven's *No Man's Land*, the individuals touched by war whose stories are featured in Rimini Protokoll's *Situation Rooms*, and Yasser Mroué, the victim of a sniper's bullet, who gives an account of his life in *Riding on a Cloud*. After the withering of an earlier mode of political theatre – drama that dealt head-on *as drama* with overtly political themes – reality-oriented performance has provided a different way of engaging with social and political matters. This development has brought together some diverse strands in late-twentieth and early-twenty-first century culture: the opinionated speaking voice, the feeling body, and the notion of people having a stake in matters of social and civic significance. It also allows us to reflect upon the nature of the 'public sphere' today. I will discuss *No Man's Land* and *Riding on a Cloud* below, along with a public declamation during a demonstration and, differently, an intervention by Rimini Protokoll whose power resides in part in its choice not to speak. These instances are diverse, but they help illustrate dimensions of political utterance through the reality-protocols of contemporary performance.

Physical presence and personal witness are profoundly important here. Witness gives rise to testimony, and in each instance (except Rimini Protokoll's *Annual Shareholders Meeting*, which I include as a counterpoint to the main theme) acts of speaking predominate. Doesn't theatre usually involve acts of speaking? The difference here is that speaking is the starting point as well as the end point of performance. The authorizing source is the individual's voice, prior to the organizing work of the director's plan or the writer's keyboard. The theatrical forms that lie behind this broader tendency – documentary, testimony and verbatim theatre, most obviously, but also reality-trend performance and theatre of encounter – are part of a yet larger and longer-reaching proliferation of vox-pop outputs and scenarios, from radio talk shows to reality TV programmes to self-production through social networking sites, all of which foreground personal utterance in the public sphere.

## The people speak

The incursion of people speaking in public has been marked in theatre by what became known in the US as 'documentary theatre' and the UK as 'verbatim theatre'. Both draw on the testimony of individuals concerning particular events or matters, sometimes (as exemplified in the Tricycle Theatre's tribunal series) deriving such testimony from public commissions. There is wide acknowledgement of the exponential growth of this kind of theatre. Forsyth and Megson's overview addresses 'the remarkable mobilisation and proliferation of documentary forms across Western theatre cultures in the past two decades', and the frequent involvement of audiences as 'putative participants in the public sphere' amid 'the documentary form's ongoing diversification' (2009: 1, 2–3). In a celebrated article that provides an early account of verbatim theatre, Derek Paget addresses selected plays in the UK since the mid-1970s. He locates this work in a broader tradition of documentary theatre that has a number of tributaries, including the social document collation overseen by the Mass Observation movement founded in 1937 by Tom Harrisson, Charles Madge and Humphrey Jennings; the British documentary film movement of the 1930s and '40s; the BBC Radio Features Department, which went on to contribute to the folk revival through the recuperation of English folk songs and recording of local singers; Brecht and Piscator's political theatre, inverting subject positions in order to deal with experience of common people; and Documentary Theatre, based on experiences of 'ordinary' people – including *Oh What a Lovely War!* (1963), developed by Theatre Workshop under Joan Littlewood, and Peter Cheeseman's work at the Victoria Theatre, Stoke on Trent, from 1965 (Paget 1987). As with reality TV and talk radio, which I discuss briefly below, what initially appears to be a distinct form, variously demotic and democratic, has longer roots reaching into the extension of vernacular culture in the wake of popular political movements, evolving archival practices and new broadcasting technologies.

Paget's account reminds us that the genealogy of verbatim theatre mixes social awareness, political agency, formal experimentation, and radical application of new realist principles. In a subsequent essay he is careful to mark distinctions between verbatim and tribunal theatre, and a shift to what he calls 'the *rhetoric of witness*' (2009: 233–4; 235, original emphasis). Witness involves hearing as well as seeing, and a more recent development to verbatim theatre resonates this in an unusual way. Consider, for instance, the work of practitioners such as Alecky Blythe with her company Recorded Delivery in the UK, and Roslyn Oades in Australia, who record the personal accounts of interviewees, with actors then recreating the voices as accurately as possible in performance, synchronous with listening to the recording through an earpiece. The actor's role as mediator is made as transparent as possible, while the originary voice is explicitly the authorizing source.[1]

Verbatim techniques have enabled a renewed 'political' theatre that has wider social and civic reach. Richard Norton-Taylor, the *Guardian* journalist who constructed the text of The Tricycle Theatre's *Justifying War* (2003), observed that 'It was as if theatregoers were screaming for plays with strong contemporary resonance and political relevance' (Norton-Taylor 2003). *Justifying War* focused on proceedings relating to the Hutton Inquiry into the death of David Kelly, who had been revealed as the source of quotations casting doubt on the UK government's case in relation to the possession of weapons of mass destruction by Saddam Husain's regime in Iraq. Verbatim theatre indeed provided a way to explore the tissue of facts and perspectives behind significant public and political events. No less significantly, the form is typically *discursive*, staging diverse articulations in order to enable the spectator to take her own view.

The politics of the personal surface frequently here, increasingly so as verbatim techniques are extended to address textures of experience as well as specific public events or controversies. Consider *Blurred Lines*, presented at the National Theatre in London in 2014, in which eight women speak about a range of experiences around the theme of continuing gender inequality and discrimination. The production was devised by the cast (drawing on elements of their own experience), and curated by director Carrie Cracknell and writer Nick Payne. The playtext returns as the manifest for that which is uttered in the theatre, but its starting point – its authorizing base – is the personal voice (indeed, personal voices), speaking about things that matter to people. This suggests the reappearance of representation, but in a postdramatic way, not dependent upon the fabrications of authored drama but the facticity of authentic speaking. The latter notion will always be subject to challenge: authentic to whom, mediated to what end? I don't mean that speaking in person is always and everywhere truthful, and free of bias or context. 'Authentic speaking' indicates a *discursive* realm, a transactional space of meaning-production where personal experience and perspective is meant to valorize the speech. It's not that suddenly everyone started saying things that were agreed to be accurate and meaningful. Rather, speaking truths became a mode (whether or not the truth was widely agreed to be truthful). Its modality was forged in the fire of personal experience. So while we knew (from postmodernism) not to trust individual truths, we learned (after postmodernism) that any approach to something that might have a claim to truthfulness was likely to be found in the personal. The personal, in this sounding chamber of public discourse, is political. Indeed, for Paola Botham, in verbatim theatre this 'persistent search for intersubjective truth succeeds in taking political drama beyond postmodernism' (2008: 317).

Taken together, not only do the tribunal, verbatim and documentary plays present a plethora of new voices, experiences, positions and perspectives. They resonate with the urgency of having something to say, and they *perform* their speaking as a gestic social act in the public domain. In this sense – as a gathering of discourse about matters of substance and pertinence – verbatim theatre moves decisively beyond postmodernism. It resuscitates political theatre right at the moment of the over-familiarity of the 'dramatic theatre'; and in the midst of routine scepticism with political process, the integrity of politicians, and the trustworthiness of public utterance by political spokespeople. This tension between the greater validity of actual speech, and its slippery nuances of context, editing, production and performance, is also characteristically post-postmodern. Derridean deconstruction held that meaning could not be treated as stable nor even shared, given that language itself, slippery and only ever relative, continuously defers meaning rather than produces it unambiguously. Derrida's dismantling of logocentrism is an attack on the surety of the word – for *logos*, the word, is founded on a typically gendered (male) drive to and assumption of reason, which is seen by Derrida always to be about the assertion of a power founded on untrustworthy premises. In verbatim theatre, however, the *logos* has its place precisely as a bodied and situated phenomenon. The Word is Speech. Reason returns not because it appears in legislature but because it is voiced by a specific speaking body – the flesh itself brings us back to discourse. Verbatim theatre is simultaneously a vehicle of authentic speaking and a performance mode that encourages you to bear witness to (and thereby take your own view of) context and perspective. It is grounded in lived experience, entirely discursive and (by playing out dialectical differences) ascribes meaning to a source, which makes it also typically relativist.

Connected theatrical developments include the use of personal testimony as a resource for theatre production (in particular in feminist, educational and multicultural contexts from the late 1970s onwards), and the growth of autobiography as part of the extension of performance in postmodernism. Indeed, the idea of the authentic voice is widely prized in the creative and performing arts. The voice coach Patsy Rodenburg writes of the 'free and placed voice' – released from tensions, constrictions and blockages – where speaking is produced in relation to listening (Rodenburg 1997: 67–83). The authentic voice is esteemed more widely in late-capitalist culture, as self-help guru Laraine Herring exemplifies when she asks: 'What does it mean to write and live authentically? . . . the crux of them both is the ability to stand in your own body. . . . Standing in your own body helps open the throat for the opportunity to speak with your own voice' (Herring 2007: 21, 23). Speaking with your own voice is held to be self-evidently a good thing, even if it takes a lifetime, or a fortune in therapy, to discover and release it.

This interest in the voice isn't solely the business of theatre-makers or purveyors of personal development programmes. The people's voices have been proliferating for a while. Radio provides an obvious sounding board. According to Seán Street, the term 'phone-in' was coined in the US in 1968, and first heard as a phrase in the UK in 1971. As Street observes, 'During the 1970s, with the growth of local radio, the genre became a staple of output, being cheap and frequently controversial'; the latter not least through the work of the so-called 'shock-jock', whose function is to provoke public participation, often through propagating his own (since shock jocks are usually male) strident and partial opinions (Street 2009: 204). Meanwhile something similar was happening in the USA. Jason Loviglio observes that '[i]n the 1960s, the radio call-in format emerged as the heir to the audience-participation impulse. By the 1970s, talk radio had come into its own as Americans began tuning in the voices of average people talking politics and mediated by professional "hosts" ' (Loviglio 2005: 68–9).[2] The voice of the people was routinely heard (and curated) by the end of the 1990s. In the UK the listener was incorporated as a participant on a national basis in BBC Radio's revamped Radio 5 Live, which relaunched in March 1994 after the network had suffered from a perceived lack of identity following its launch as Radio 5 in 1990 (see Street 2009: 221–222). 5 Live was more determinedly populist in its second coming. Its dedication to the public voice, mainly through phone-ins, marked a form of legitimation of this mode of programming, given the BBC's cultural identity and the nationwide reach of its broadcasting. In 5 Live's case, public engagement was facilitated by a vigorous multimedia activity, with special attention paid to Internet-enabled participation. This is part of what John Corner calls 'a continuing "colloquial turn" . . . and a shift towards greater engagement of the media with everyday terms of living and the varieties of ordinary "private" experience, both pleasant and traumatic' (Corner 2004: 291).

The colloquial turn is nowhere more marked than in reality television, 'the success story of television in the 1990s and 2000s', as Annette Hill has it (2005: 2).[3] By way of evidence, let's consider the UK broadcasting schedules for the first week of June in 1994 (when the Tricycle Theatre staged *Half the Picture*, the first of its series of tribunal plays), and a decade later in 2004 (when David Hare's *Stuff Happens* was presented at the National Theatre, the Tricycle's *Guantanamo* was first staged and Robin Soans's *The Arab-Israeli Cookbook* was presented at the Gate Theatre). I looked expressly for programmes where members of the public are featured as themselves, or where celebrities are featured in private or personal circumstances. I discounted other kinds of documentary, on the basis that this was not a new form of programming, and

I was in any case on the trail of the private person going public; nor did I include shows that featured members of the public but in more consumer- and theme-oriented contexts (as, for example, *Homes Under the Hammer*) or full-on game shows (such as *Hot Property*). I counted 15 programmes for the week of 4–10 June 1994 across the terrestrial broadcast channels, including, for instance, *Right to Reply* (C4), *Through the Keyhole* (ITV) and *Six Go to Europe* (BBC2). In the week from 5–11 June 2004 on the terrestrial channels (now including Five) I counted 59, an increase of over 390 per cent. Programmes included *Building the Dream* (ITV1), *Get a New Life* (BBC2), *The Osbournes* (C4), and one of the most significant reality TV shows of its time, *Big Brother* (C4).

The kind of programming represented here is striking. The incursion of reality TV is largely predicated on people transforming their homes, bodies, prospects or profile. The stakes are often high for the participants, which is no little part of their grounding in actuality. Futures are in the balance. The programmes are often task- or game-based, drawing on dramatic structures that help to provide tension, conflict and eventually narrative closure, while enabling open, spontaneous and immediate action and reaction. Improvised performance here appears to offer insights while also begging questions of 'truthfulness'. Nonetheless, such programmes operate within an economy of actuality. Not all of the programmes depend on 'speaking' in the way that I describe elsewhere in this chapter, but they do promote the notion of the demotic, the everyday, and lived experience, and claim to provide insights into the lives of ordinary people, or the coping mechanisms that might be adopted by any of us. They also frequently ask people to put their bodies on the line.

Misha Kavka argues that we have already seen three generations to reality TV: 'the camcorder generation' (the 1990s), encompassing reality crime pro-grammes and docusoaps; 'the competition generation', which starts with *Big Brother* in the Netherlands (1999), swiftly followed by *Survivor* (2000), whereby the form morphs from game show scenarios to those of self-transformation; and 'the production of celebrity' (here a twenty-first-century reality phenomenon, but of course with a much longer provenance), at which point 'reality TV disengages from its documentary roots and becomes a self-conscious participant in the rituals of self-commodification and self-legitimation that define contemporary celebrity culture' (Kavka 2012: 9–10).[4] This analysis pro-vides a useful way of organizing reality TV as a form with a specific trajectory, although the beginning and end of the generations Kavka suggests are by no means clearly delineated, and tendencies from all three remain in play at the time of writing. Indeed the increasingly mixed modes of reality TV parallel a similar development in theatre, where distinctions between documentary, authenticity, fabrication, celebrity and performance have become increasingly blurred. The substrate of reality TV is that of cultural production more widely, for it comprises the routine mediatization and pervasive surveillance enabled by the incursion of digital technologies; the extension of user- and spectator agency; a notable formal and discursive hybridity; and a fascination with registers of actuality and authenticity. Jonathan Bignell argues that 'Reality TV is a nodal point at which different discourses within and outside television culture have temporarily come together in an unstable conjunction' (2005: 171). The node includes the confessional talk show which, Bignell notes, coincided with *Big Brother* in coming to prominence in the late 1990s and 'has a persistent interest in personal issues with a public dimension' (173). The people speak in and through reality formats across a spectrum from declamation to disclosure.

These developments, including Kavka's arc from camcorder to celebrity, fit with the parallel growth of 'selving' (to use John Corner's term) through social media, which circulates the precepts of celebrity culture and often makes its participants at least temporarily famous, while promoting a sense of unique personhood and private revelation. The extension of media platforms provided by social media marks a final step to the demoticization of communication at the turn of the millennium. The RSS (Really Simple Syndication) protocols of Web 2.0, which enable real-time interactive data sharing (text, images, audio and video files), have facilitated the growth of social networking sites from the beginning of the twenty-first century, including Friendster, MySpace, Facebook, Twitter and Instagram. As discussed in the previous chapter, the principles of social media suffuse a wider range of developments in theatre and performance. For present purposes, it's enough to observe that social media platforms allow individuals to engage in a serial stream of discourse and make repeated personal interventions in public. These are variously bespoke instances enabled by what John Dovey calls 'first person media', the vehicles for a spate of 'subjective, autobiographical and confessional modes of expression' (2000: 1). The modes of expression are a form of performance. They entail the sharing of speaking in public scenarios, even if personal utterance derives from private spaces and settings. The personal becomes also pushed out and public.

## The public sphere(s)

The 'public sphere', as conceived by Jürgen Habermas, has a coffee house quality. Individuals engage in debate based upon, as Habermas says, 'people's public use of their reason' (Habermas 1991 [1962]: 27). This is distinct from what he describes as the 'intimate sphere', which is private and familial. Sociologists and cultural studies scholars have long disputed Habermas's conception of the public sphere.[5] Two developments to this conception in twenty-first-century culture are worth noting here. First there is the incursion of the private as a feature of public discourse – partly due to the privileging of subjectivity in late capitalist culture; and amply demonstrated by the curated selves of social media, tweeting, blogging and Facebooking away. The coffee house has become a series of cafes, kitchens and bedrooms, hosting a set of never-ending conversations. Which brings us to the second development: the growth of plural public spheres, rather than a single regulated space of discursive consensus along Enlightenment lines. As Bohman suggests, 'the Internet and other contemporary public spaces permit a form of publicity that results in a public of publics rather than a unified public sphere based in a common culture or identity.' (Bohman 2004: 152. See also Balme 2014a 174–8; Tully 2013; and Reinelt 2011: 18.) Derridean *différance* is perhaps not so distant, after all. A post-Enlightenment version of the public sphere figures a series of spheres that *perform* difference and a sort of deferral, even as they provide the space by which individuals inhabit their bodies in public and make categorical statements in response to events and activities.

This recognizes that in contemporary western culture (or parts of it) there is space (sometimes) for *dissensus* as a mode, difference as a continuum. You might object that, erroneously for a chapter dedicated to the voice, this particular development is in fact textual, given the flow of words in the new digital public spheres by way of blogs, tweets, text messages, picture captions and text-chat. The shift, however, is towards a discursive mode that *personalizes* communication, which is shaped as conversation or as information–giving and witness-bearing that has the rubric of the spoken word. The voice validates and, through the platforms and devices of digital culture, is textualized. Personal speaking is performed through the platforms of social media, and suffuses new theatre and performance to no less a degree. It's as though a stitch in time has regathered the fabric of theatrical utterance. Lehmann observes that in postdramatic theatre

> the opaque actuality and intensity of the body's visceral presence take precedence over the logos . . . [T]he loss of a central meaning creates a field, a dissemination of possible modes of signifying which in turn calls forward the active productivity of the audience, thus emphasizing once more the situation of the theatre event.
>
> (2007: 47, 48)

This resonates with the idea of plural public spheres and new forms of audience engagement; and it comes close to describing the effects of Web 2.0. Yet we can now suggest that the gathered utterances of social media and postdramatic performance demonstrate the resettling of meanings, the non-extinction of the logos. The words are often banal, but often they are saying something. Speaking speaks *about* something.

The sociologist Nick Couldry remarks that 'we are experiencing a contemporary crisis of voice, across political, economic and cultural domains', compounded by the predominance of the neoliberal market and the pro-liferation of modes of communication that lead towards jangle rather than conversation (2010: 1; see also Wake 2014: 83). More people are saying things, in the theatre, on radio, on TV and across social media. I don't necessarily dispute Couldry's analysis, in which neoliberalism denies 'the value of the voice' (Couldry 2012: 136), but there is also a countervailing tendency. An anxiety to be heard is also an urge to stage one's speaking, and the voice, as an authorizing source, lies behind a range of contemporary cultural production. There are political implications to this development. Personal utterance is increasingly pervasive in the public sphere, and it is possible for it to say something, above and beyond the banal chatter across media platforms. The fact of speaking is, in itself, a marker of presence, witness and perspective. The voice speaks from a body about things that matter to people.

I discuss, below, some instances in contemporary performance situations in which a personal voice speaks, to be re-presented in performance as public discourse about individual experience. The voice speaks *about* something, in a circulation of meanings in the public domain. It does so by way of an encounter with, and in, scenarios defined by reality protocols. The encounter is between the speaker and her context (the set of defining permissions and oppositions that delimit any particular act of speaking); and between the speaker and the witness/listener, who is drawn into an engagement with the wider discursive implications of the act of speaking in a realm of actuality. Lastly, the speaking is staged, thrown into relief precisely through the construction and organization of an act of performance. By way of being performed, the discourse is *made audible*. These three coordinates, *discourse*, *encounter* and *performance*, help to configure the value of voice in a neoliberal scene, and underpin the instances that follow.

## Staging the voice in the public sphere

### Judith Butler | Occupy

The individual voice; a body bearing witness – *requiring* witness; and matters of importance in the public sphere: this compound is figured in an exemplary polemical utterance by scholar and activist Judith Butler at an Occupy demonstration in Washington Square Park near New York University. The Occupy movement mobilized demonstrations in more than 80 countries in response to the financial crisis that affected Western capitalist economies in particular. Occupy Wall Street began in September 2011, Occupy London Stock Exchange the following month. The protests were facilitated and resonated by social media activity, but they fundamentally entailed acts of physical presence and low-tech or improvised modes of public speaking.[6] At Occupy Wall Street the crowd deliberately echoed speeches at the demo, as a way of amplifying and distributing them to people further back who were otherwise unable to hear. Hannah Chadeyane Appel describes the rationale and its consequence:

> Amplified sound requires a permit in New York City for which OWS has applied repeatedly, and been denied. . . . Yet messages still have to be communicated to thousands of people, whether during decentralized days

of small-group work or during the nightly General Assembly meeting at 7pm. The people's microphone is the solution. Perhaps tracing a genealogy to the phrase's use in hip hop, the call of 'mic check!' followed by its response, '**mic check!**' from all who heard, begins what is one of the most definitive experiences of communication at the occupation – the repetition and amplification of one another's voices.

(Appel 2012: 260; original emboldening)

This 'human microphone' produces a peculiar effect of concretization, a *performance* of utterance, solidarity and (re)affirmation. It calls to mind the case that Jan Cohen Cruz makes in her book *Engaging Performance: Theatre as call and response*. For Cohen Cruz, 'engaging performance' (in a UK context we might think of 'applied theatre') responds to 'social controversies' or draws people together in relation to a particular 'social situation' (2010: 1). In either case, engagement operates through 'an ethos of call and response', which describes the exchange between theatre makers and other people who are involved, and the iterative processes of research and performance. The model is optimistic, but understandably so for it seeks to ingrain artistic and aesthetic practices in the weft of social action. As Cohen Cruz suggests, 'An active relationship between actors and community, not only the connection among actors, is at the heart of the work. Call and response brings the fruits of that relationship to the public sphere' (2010: 2).

*Figure 2.1* Judith Butler speaks at an Occupy Washington Square Park gathering

Source: Screen grab of a video uploaded to YouTube by Luke Garai Taylor, 23 October 2011, www.youtube.com/watch?v=rYfLZsb9by4

Butler's speech and its uptake by the crowd in Washington Square Park has something of this relationship between artist and community (Figure 2.1). A transcription of it reads like a poem as well as a polemic:

If hope is an impossible demand
*[Crowd repeats] If hope is an impossible demand*
Then we demand the impossible
*Then we demand the impossible*
If the right to shelter, food and employment
*If the right to shelter, food and employment*
Are impossible demands
*Are impossible demands*
Then we demand the impossible
*Then we demand the impossible*
[. . .]
It matters
*It matters*
That as bodies
*That as bodies*
We arrive together in public
*We arrive together in public*
As bodies we suffer
*As bodies we suffer*
[. . .]
So this is a politics of the public body
*So this is a politics of the public body*
A requirement of the body
*A requirement of the body*
Its movement and its voice
*Its movement and its voice*
[. . .]
But we are here
*But we are here*
Time and again
*Time and again*
Persisting
*Persisting*
Enacting the phrase
*Enacting the phrase*
We the People
*We the People*[7]

Butler has written on the difference between performance (which requires a subject) and performativity (an interactive process). Here she provides an instance of both, with a performance that is itself performative, producing the effects of resistance and solidarity that it describes.

In their analysis of the ways in which the Occupy movement proliferated its action via social media, DeLuca, Lawson and Sun observe that '[a]mid a dizzying array of public screens, the ground of activism has fractured and multiplied into multiple decentered knots creating a cacophony of panmediated social worlds' (2012: 500). This suggests the jangle of utterance that I touched on above, but it's also true to say that the ready mediation of individual voices also helps to preserve their specificity and specialness. Butler's speech is emblematic of the reverberation of speaking in digital culture. It is an act of bodied demonstration, while its posting on YouTube resonates it across geographies, as one among over 90,000 Occupy Wall Street videos on the platform, in a mediascape that saw more than 3.3 million 'likes' of Occupy groups on Facebook pages (DeLuca, Lawson and Sun 2012: 500; Gamson and Sifry 2013: 160). There is a characteristic post-Web 2.0 oscillation between activist presence and viral virtual distribution.[8] The reiterated nature of the latter is peculiarly paralleled in the Occupy demonstrations by the repetition of phrases, as the crowd of protestors itself bodies forth the speech. Interestingly, there is a power here, too, in not speaking. As Adrienne Maree Brown writes, 'another lesson I observed from the people's mic experience at occupy wall street: if someone called for the mic, they were granted it. but if people weren't feeling the statement, eventually they stopped repeating it' (Brown 2012: 84; lower case as in the original). Silence is golden.

## No Man's Land

Whether speaking or deciding not to speak, we are back to the body, in the flesh. There is a connection, in an emphasis on the physical here and now, between Butler's utterance and that of the speaker in *No Man's Land*:

> This is me.
> These are my hands.
> These are my legs.
> This is my face.
> This is not a theatre costume.

The speaker, however, goes on to say:

> This is not my voice.
> This is not my language.
> This is the voice of an actor.
> [. . .]
> But because of the English voice you will regard me differently, listen differently.

> (Verhoeven 2014: np)

Conceived and directed by the Dutch scenographer and visual artist Dries Verhoeven, *No Man's Land* gives a voice to a marginalized community. The piece treats each spectator individually, a mode that Verhoeven has adopted in works including *Thy Kingdom Come* (2003; the spectator encounters a performer of the opposite gender behind glass, with a voiceover providing directions for interaction) and *Trail Tracking* (2005; you move through civic and industrial space in response to prompts on a mobile phone).[9] Adam Czirak observes that Verhoeven's 'pieces – audio walks, gaze dialogues, chat conversations, live-cinema events – operate beyond the representational patterns of theatre or directed stage events and offer opportunities for individual actions' (2011: 78). The actions available to you in *No Man's Land* are fairly constrained. The piece originated in Utrecht in 2008. Featuring 20 immigrants and refugees, it resonates the topic of immigration, a sensitive issue in Dutch political life. It was restaged in Athens with 20 immigrants and refugees living in the city, with the original text reworked a little and voiced in Greek. The translation into a mother tongue deliberately roots the voice in the place of presentation, even as the piece is about dislocation and foreignness.

We gather at Monastiraki metro station in the heart of the city. Each spectator is given a sheet of A4 paper that bears the name of an immigrant who will be your guide for the piece (Figure 2.2). We line up along a wall in the concourse, near the escalators, holding our nameplates like a set of taxi drivers at an airport. Passers by, tourists and commuters look at us quizzically. Characteristically for Verhoeven's work *No Man's Land* has a fixed structure.

*Figure 2.2  No Man's Land*: Awaiting the guides

Source: Stavros Petropoulos

The rule of engagement is simply that you follow your guide, who will take you alone on a pre-determined journey (Figure 2.3). We are wearing headphones attached to an MP3 player. Each spectator's device starts simultaneously and conveys the same soundtrack: a voiceover telling a migrant's story. The text was put together from the accounts of the immigrants in Utrecht, and fashioned to have both a specific and more broadly representative quality:

> I can tell you about a good life, rather plain, but good. That I'm an electrical engineer or that I own a little grocery store.
> [. . .]
> I can tell you about a prison in Spain,
> About the prison in Kirkuk,
> About the prison in Santiago.
>
> (Verhoeven 2014: np)

I am gradually aware of other individuals observing us. They are dotted around at various distances, notable by their stillness amid the bustle of the metro station. Purcell's 'Dido's Lament' plays on the soundtrack. The silent watchers lip-sync to the female voice. We are wearing overt, ear-covering headphones. They have discreet earpieces. It is a curiously powerful moment, a form of neutral confrontation that creates a theatrical moment of interrelation between two different groups, and performs a reversal of gaze. It is we, the spectators, who are scrutinized, held in a moment of vulnerability at a liminal point of entry.

One by one the guides (for of course these are they) collect their respective spectator, stopping a metre or so away and making a gracious open-handed gesture to follow. I am among the last to be approached. Setareh wears Merrell trainers, loose grey trousers, a purple shirt and a turquoise patterned headscarf. I follow her down the escalator to a central pedestrian node in the metro station, where she stops, turns and looks me in the eye as the voiceover plays. This directness is both disconcerting and engaging, a challenge to meet a gaze, make this personal. Setareh's regard is friendly but neutral. Metro travellers stop to watch this peculiar face-off. Setareh closes her eyes and lip-syncs to the voiceover – a dab of performance, and an external affirmation of the speaking in my head.

We move through the busy, narrow streets around Monastiraki, past tourists, cafes, restaurants, shops. The second stop is on a side street, outside what might be a small meeting room. Setareh halts, facing a closed door. There are ecclesiastical posters in the small entrance, and incongruously on the door jamb some graffiti: 'Cunt Club 2012'. Setareh turns to look at me. She lip-synchs to Nancy Sinatra's 'Bang Bang'. This comes over as another piece of performance, albeit utterly discreet, deflected from public consumption by the fact that our soundtrack cannot be heard by anyone else.

Later in the piece, Goran Bregovic's 'Mashala Mashala' plays. Setareh starts to sway as she walks in front of me, waving her arms in time to the music.

*Figure 2.3 No Man's Land*: walking (and listening) through the city

Source: Stavros Petropoulos

The third stop occurs in the middle of a narrow residential street, bathed in the afternoon sun. The voice, I presume from the written translation that I've been given, tells of the rape of the speaker's eldest daughter. Setareh keeps her back to me. A little later, Setareh sways and waves her arms in time to 'Slow' by dEUS. Other spectators come into view, walking behind their guides who are also waving their arms, even though there is now no voiceover or music. We congregate in a patch of waste ground, each spectator standing behind their guide in a line facing 20 beach huts (Figure 2.4). Inside our hut, Setareh gestures me to sit in the only chair, facing the back wall. She stands behind me, takes my headphones from my ears, and sings. In a piece characterized by the intimacy of a voiceover through my headphones, this is the first time that I have heard her voice. The guides each sing a song from their own culture – a personal voice, a song from a biography, a bespoke moment of audience.

Setareh leaves the hut – and her image appears upside down, a *camera obscura* effect on the white wall in front of me. The door to the hut has a small hole with a lens that acts as a pinhole camera. She steps out of view, to be replaced by another performer-immigrant, his face appearing on the wall before me; and then another – actually-present people who are also (as befits the migrant) transitory and fleeting. Setareh returns, and holds up a sign bearing my name. She leaves and a light comes on, the sound within the headphones stops. We emerge from our huts, and are invited to write a comment for our respective

*Figure 2.4 No Man's Land*: a singular destination
Source: Stavros Petropoulos

guide (nowhere to be seen) in a book, as if at a guest-house or a wedding. Verhoeven likes to provide a visitor's book for spectators (Czirak 2011: 81).

*No Man's Land* embeds its participants in both a relationship and a representation. We have access to a biography by way of the spoken account in the headphones, except that, in a characteristic twist of twenty-first century performance, this is partly fictionalized and does not belong to the guide in front of you. All twenty spectators hear the same soundtrack, so the guide is standing in, embodying some larger construction of the immigrant's experience. She is authentically herself – actual to you, and actually an immigrant or refugee – and a performer in a piece comprised of stories, communities, histories. Not untypically in performance within digital culture, the performer is a serial figure, both one and many. I am dependent on her in a witting adjustment of her status. The migrant is often disempowered, yet she has the care of me here.

A similar doubleness characterizes the piece's play with place. The city becomes de-actualized, as the location for a promenade performance that could be presented in many different settings, while the movement through a particular geography creates a reality effect. The *public sphere* involves shared discourse and a movement towards consensus. The *public space* is different, a site for activity in common view. As we traverse public space, we perform a much more private encounter. We stand face to face. We share a soundtrack inaudible to people who might only be a metre away. The show stages a tension between the inhabitation of space on the one hand, and light nomadic travel through it on the other; between what constitutes a public realm and personal belonging; and between intimacy and separation, dependence and detachment.

The voice is foundational. The piece begins with testimonies. These are tributaries for a larger testimony, a sort of Ur-chronicle of the contemporary immigrant to Western Europe. Diverse experiences are reduced to a single narrative, which would be problematic except for the trope of multiplicity ('I might be . . . I could be . . .'), which necessarily fictionalizes the account even while it insists on a basis in experience. The voice, inside your head by way of the headphones, in effect grafts its story onto the individual before you. It is therefore (by association) embodied and also in your own body. When the guide sings in person the piece arrives, not in anything as obvious as a biography, but in a performance that is an expression of self, clinched through the voice as an authenticating personal intervention. The discourse of *No Man's Land* concerns the place and the personhood of the migrant. In this sense, the voice of the piece accords with what Couldry describes as 'the expression of a distinct perspective on the world that needs to be acknowledged. This political use of the word "voice" continues to be useful, especially in contexts where long-entrenched inequalities of representation need to be addressed' (2010: 1). In our one-to-one encounter, the voice and the guide together momentarily redress the balance. The guide is more central than I am (a visitor to the piece), and navigates her journey as a figure in a civic *mise en scène*. And yet she goes at the end – an exit from performance – vanishing into a night and an alien place, a voiceless individual and performatively migrant.

### Riding on a Cloud

In *Riding on a Cloud* (2013), directed by Rabih Mroué, Yasser Mroué sits at a table stage-right.[10] He feeds a series of tapes containing his spoken autobiographical account into an audio cassette, and a series of DVDs into a DVD player. This separation of representations – the co-present performer, the voiceover, the projection of still and moving images and text – emphasizes the composited nature of his story. The text that appears on the large screen upstage explains something of the genesis of the piece (Figure 2.5). Yasser asked to be involved in one of his brother's theatre pieces. A drily comic dialogue ensues by way of the text onscreen. Rabih asks what his brother would do in a theatre show. Yasser replies that he could operate the sound. But I don't use any pre-recorded sound, says Rabih. What would you *like* to do? They decide that Yasser should tell a version of his story – not entirely as himself. 'We agreed that it would be helpful to play this role and learn that in theatre everything belongs to fiction', says the text. 'He [Rabih] agreed that I have to learn what it means to play, to act. These are my words, yet this is not my voice.' This text plays out against an image of Yasser lying in bed. The camera travels slowly up his blanketed body while Yasser onstage stands close to and watches the screen, a composite of identity, representation and fabrication. We will learn that he is paralysed down one side, a consequence of being shot in the head by a sniper as a young man during the Lebanese Civil War; and understand that the mix of videos and soundtracks are fleshing out a personal account that perhaps cannot be voiced live in person.

Yasser's voiceover informs us that between 1990 and 2010 he made 200 videos (in order to help his identification of objects and their representations), and that Rabih as director chose for the show the ones he found more interesting. A motif of music is threaded through the piece. One video segment is entitled 'Piano with 5 fingers'. There is a big close-up of piano keys being played, filmed with deliberateness, the camera closely following – scrutinizing – the fingers. In another sequence, Yasser sings a song to music playing through the audio cassette. 'In intense suffering, the world disappears and each of us is alone with himself.'

We learn of the moment when Yasser was hit in the head by a bullet fired by a sniper in Beirut in 1987. He was eventually moved to the USSR for reconstructive surgery. A sexual encounter followed with a nurse 20 years his senior, just prior to his departure from the hospital. We learn of his aphasia, able to remember some words but not others. The video shows documentation pertaining to the trip, again the camera crawling over the page with a close

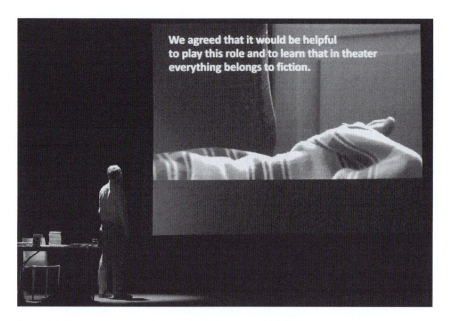

*Figure 2.5* Yasser Mroué, with his audio cassettes and DVDs on the table beside him. In Rabih Mroué, *Riding on a Cloud*, 2013. Performed at The Museum of Modern Art, April 21, 2015, in Projects 101: Rabih Mroué. © 2015 The Museum of Modern Art, New York

Source: Julieta Cervantes

attention that both reveals and obscures, as words and phrases such as 'skull', 'right side', 'medication' come into view. One effect of the injury was that Yasser 'had a problem with representations' – on seeing a photograph, he didn't recognize the image (he gives the example of a pen) – rather, he sees a field of colours and shapes. He stopped going to the theatre because he assumed that everything was real, he 'believed everything'.

The video shows the search for the building where he was shot by a sniper. The window and the balcony where the sniper was located are identified through a series of zoomed images, filmed from the street. The video then shows the point of view of the sniper – to the left, to the right, and along the street that was his main target, beyond a concealing block of buildings. This sequence makes the geography personal, entwining an otherwise ordinary space with the cataclysmic event in a biography.

The closing video silently reprises a dialogue between the two brothers, concerning the making of a show. It starts with Yasser saying that he would like to be involved in one of Rabih's theatre pieces. He could operate the music. But, there is no music in my performances, his brother answers, unless it is played live. The show ends with Yasser sitting on a stool in front of his table. Rabih has come down through the auditorium and squats next to him. Yasser is paralysed down his right-hand side. He plays guitar chords with his left hand. Rabih strums and picks with his right hand, and the pair conjure a flourish of music to finish. It is a fine image of persistence (of memory, desire, individual expression, fraternity), and means that the piece lands in a moment of co-presence, an image of mutual creativity and an act of pure performance.

While it ends with music, this piece, too, begins with the voice. Mroué's testimony is personal, and skates along an edge between lived experience and playful fabrication. It dwells meta-theatrically on its own construction, and the larger construction of meaning where images are manipulable, subject to selection, composition and politicization. This particular voice is knowing and playful. Throughout, however, the fabric is that of lived experience, through an exemplary personal story derived from actuality. It figures trauma, disintegration and fragmentation, along with various kinds of connection and consolidation. To this end the piece fits with Couldry's outline of 'an alternative view of politics that is at least partly oriented to valuing processes of voice' (2010: 3). It shapes a form of quiet resistance, and makes central a Lebanese life, a Lebanese perspective. It goes public in an entirely private way, while giving voice to the texture of marginalization and struggle that characterizes life in the Lebanon.

### Annual Shareholders Meeting

The instances above reinsert utterance at the place where voices appear to be denied, or at least discriminated against. Let's conclude with an example that shows a different sort of witness, and the power of the voice in a negative dimension. In 2009 the Berlin-based company Rimini Protokoll staged *Annual Shareholders Meeting*. Or rather, didn't. As the company's website indicates:

> On the 8th of April 2009 Rimini Protokoll invited theatregoers to one of the most elaborate performances of the season: the Daimler Annual Shareholders' Meeting in the ICC Berlin. This time actual direction was not carried out by Rimini Protokoll but the Investor Relations Team of the Stuttgart corporation.[11]

Rimini Protokoll bought shares in Daimler and transferred the rights of attendance at the AGM to around 200 – what? – theatregoers, who joined around 8,000 shareholders in the International Congress Centre (Figure 2.6). As director Stefan Kaegi observed, his intention was to enable people to see the Daimler AGM as a piece of theatre that dramatized the political hierarchies and ideological assumptions of the company: 'We wanted to watch it as a *mise en scène* and see what was going on – because obviously there's a lot of Shakespeare there'.[12] In other words, the AGM demonstrated in public the sorts of power structures and processes that many of Shakespeare's plays dramatize. The corporation itself had rather different views, as Brigitte Biehl-Missal explains:

> When expressing his greetings to all investors, Chairman Bischoff severely announces: 'You are participating in the AGM of one of the most important industrial companies of our country [pause]. This is neither a spectacle nor a theatre play!' The last part is quoted often in the press and seen as a warning to Rimini Protokoll's spectators.
>
> (Biehl-Missal 2012: 222)

Rimini Protokoll produced a lavish 112-page catalogue and arranged a series of satellite events outside the hall – including, for instance, meetings with a former worker from Daimler, a car seller, an economic journalist, and a lawyer (see Rimini Protokoll 2009). In staging these encounters, the company ensured that other voices were heard beyond those of the corporation's executive team.

And yet one possibility for speaking was left alone. It is possible for any shareholder to take the microphone at the AGM. Biehl-Missal again:

> Among them are representatives of pension funds, shareholder associations, NGOs, activists, employee shareholders and private investors. There is one shareholder shouting out 'confused Christian stuff' (Fanizadeh 2009), and another man beseeching the executive board to put him in charge of the development of a 'revolutionary piston engine'. . . . The debate can be considered the core of Rimini Protokoll's project: the authoritarian style of the meeting is revealed; there is 'no participation, rather reprimand' because 'moral and ethical questions still collide with the profit maximization of a global player' (Schmeicher 2009). Feedback from theatre spectators

*Figure 2.6* Actors on the stage, spectators in the auditorium. Daimler's Annual
Shareholders' Meeting. Rimini Protokoll's *Annual Shareholders Meeting*

Source: Barbara Braun

revealed that the style of managers was considered 'cynical', 'authoritarian',
'condescending' and 'evasive'.

(Biehl-Missal 2012: 223)

According to Kaegi, the Daimler corporation tried to stop the theatre company
from attending the AGM, before ascertaining through legal process that the
shareholders indeed could not be kept away. Clearly the managers feared some
gesture of public utterance. On the day, Kaegi and his colleagues in the hall
merely watched. Here, then, is an ingenious inversion. It puts one in mind of
the outing of closet gays by more radical members of the gay community. The
theatrical nature of the event is made more evident by the staging of
spectatorship. This 'theatring' of the business proceedings of Daimler – and
we could say the same of Deutsche Bank in Rimini Protokoll's *Situation Rooms*
– makes a drama of corporate process. Political presence is manifested twice
over, first by way of the new appearance of the corporate machine as theatre,
and second by virtue of the disturbingly silent witness performed by the theatre
company and its facilitated spectators. The decision *not* to speak performs
(indeed articulates) a political position by way of a subversive reserve, a
dissensual presence that marks critical reflection rather than compliance, and
*could* be given voice at any time. You could argue that it also performs the

only sort of presence that neoliberal corporatism leaves us; our participation tolerated where it is not overly disruptive. Even so, in arranging witness and constellating other sorts of speaking in its satellite meetings, Rimini Protokoll enabled different voices to be heard – at least by those who chose to hear.

## Epilogue

In *Why Voice Matters* Nick Couldry describes five general principles concerning the voice as a process:

> Voice is socially grounded.
> Voice is a form of reflexive agency.
> Voice is an embodied process.
> Voice requires a material form which may be individual, collective or distributed.
> Voice is undermined by rationalities which take no account of voice and by practices that exclude voice or undermine forms for its expression.
>
> (excerpted from Couldry 2010: 7–11)

The four instances above indicate some ways of having your voice heard and making your presence felt in the public domain. None of them quite fit with the genres and modes that I outlined earlier in this chapter: documentary theatre, reality TV, voxpop radio, or social media chat. Nor should they, for they mark a still-evolving scene of speaking, as part of a wider return to the voice and an extended sense that the voice matters. Each belongs to the broad set of reality-protocol performances that suffuse contemporary culture. They exemplify the first four of Couldry's principles, and take a tilt at the fifth. Performance here is socially grounded, and addresses a specific history, experience or perspective. It asserts its own agency by virtue of framing an utterance, presenting a testimony and staking a claim to corporeal witness. There is a sharpened sense that we see and hear the act of a particular body or set of bodies, here in this space and this moment. The voice is present, and belongs to its respective body, each with its biography, its reason and its context. Each of the instances echoes a feature of network culture by proliferating utterance while in full possession of presence. The voice of the witness, the *testifier*, speaks one way or another about issues of social and civic inequality, irresponsibility and discrimination. This marks a return of representation, underpinned not by a dramatic mode, nor by textual authority (so ably dismantled by deconstruction and post-structuralism) but by the multiple bodied voices that produce their respective texts. Performance then *theatricalizes* – indeed *medializes* – acts of looking and speaking in modalities of the real. In so doing it re-performs collective and individual intervention in today's multiple public spheres.

# Notes

1  See Wake 2013 and 2104 on 'headphone verbatim' theatre. The growth of 'audio theatre', where you listen and respond to a commentary on headphones, usually in some sort of a walking tour, is related to the developments discussed in this chapter, while also participating in wider shifts towards immersion, site responsiveness and spatial dislocation. See Balme 2006. For an article on three instances of earphone/headphone theatre and issues of authenticity, see Taylor 2013. For a set of accounts by and interviews with makers of verbatim theatre, including David Hare, Nicolas Kent and Alecky Blythe, see Hammond and Steward 2008. For an essay addressing the divergent strategies of post-9/11 verbatim dramas, see Claycomb 2012. See Martin 2006 for an overview of documentary theatre, in a special edition of *TDR* devoted to the form; and Martin 2010 for a collection of essays and texts addressing and exemplifying the form more broadly.

2  The 'intimate public' of Loviglio's book is that represented in radio broadcasting in the US in the 1930s.

3  As Hill observes, 'Reality TV . . . is located in border territories, between information and entertainment, documentary and drama' (Hill 2005: 2). See also Hill 2007. For a collection of essays addressing reality TV, see Taddeo and Dvorak 2010. For a discussion of *Big Brother* in relation to theatricality, see Lavender 2003.

4  For a discussion of the celebrity-reality nexus as a manifestation of (late) consumer capitalism, see Marshall 2006: 634–644.

5  See Loviglio 2005 (xix-xxii) for a brief overview. See Calhoun 1992a for a collection of essays addressing Habermas's conception of the public sphere, including one by Habermas in which he reviews and reasserts his original thesis. See Emden and Midgley 2013 for a collection of essays considering new applications for it. In their edited volume, Roberts and Crossley note four key factors that, for Habermas, compromise the notion of the public sphere: a blurring of delineation between state and society; the professionalizing of debate; public opinion as an object for control rather than an organic expression of consensus; and the commodification of mass media (2004: 4–6). Each of these factors is now normative in western societies, although there remain opportunities for and instances of resistance and exception. See Bunz 2014 (82–94) on the 'digital public'. See also Calhoun 1992b for an account of Habermas's thesis and its controversial nature; and Reinelt 2011 for a recalibration of Habermas's notion of the public sphere in favour of a more global (rather than Europeanist) conception, recognizing 'a plurality of . . . publics' (18). See Balme 2014a (5–21) for a detailed account of Habermas's conception of the public sphere and changing conceptions of it in theatre and performance studies. Balme 2014b provides a condensed summary. See Levin and Schweitzer 2011 for a brief consideration of issues arising from performance in the public sphere, introducing a special edition of *Performance Research* devoted to the topic. For a discussion in relation to verbatim theatre productions, see Botham 2008.

6  There is useful information about Occupy at http://en.wikipedia.org/wiki/Occupy _movement. See also Schrager Lang and Lang 2012, and Van Gelder *et al.* 2011. On social media in relation to the Occupy Movement, see DeLuca, Lawson and Sun 2012, and Gamson and Sifry 2013 (introducing a special section on Occupy in *The Sociological Quarterly*). For a blog on the theatricality of Occupy, see Mirzoeff 2012. For a broader account of the Anonymous movement and digital activism, see Coleman 2014 (317–35 includes discussion of Occupy in New York City).

7  Speech by Judith Butler, www.youtube.com/watch?v=rYfLZsb9by4 (posted by Luke Taylor, 23 October 2011). See Butler 2011 for a discussion of embodied collective protest, persistence, the re-functioning of space, and the contested nature of public and private.

8 This is figured in the protest movements that sprang up in the 1990s and early years of the twenty-first century in response to, for example, ecological issues, financial summit meetings of the G8 countries and the International Monetary Fund, and the wars in Iraq and Afghanistan. For a pre-Occupy analysis of public mobilization and protest, see Hardt and Negri 2004; Chvasta 2006; and O'Neill 2004. Post-Occupy, in a commentary posted in March 2013, Manuel Castells addresses a mobilization process that cuts across actual and virtual spaces (www.guardian.co.uk/commentisfree/video/2013/mar/25/manuel-castells-political-cyberspace-video; posted 25 March 2013). This resonates with Castells' broadly optimistic analysis elsewhere of the 'Internet Galaxy', whose 'communitarian source' provides 'a new form of free speech' (Castells 2001: 55).

9 Verhoeven's website is at www.driesverhoeven.com/en; details of *No Man's Land*, including a video trailer, are at www.driesverhoeven.com/en/project/no-mans-land. For an interview with Verhoeven on principles of spectator engagement, see Czirak 2011.

10 For a brief account of the piece by Rabih Mroué in a promotional video made in relation to its premiere in the Rotterdam Schouwburg on 5 March 2013, see www.youtube.com/watch?feature=player_embedded&v=AAAzv22DH3U.

11 www.rimini-protokoll.de/website/en/project_4008.html. For an account of predominant techniques and principles in Rimini Protokoll's work, see Malzacher 2010.

12 Interview with the author, 18 February 2010. See Biehl-Missal 2012: 211 for references to writing that addresses the theatricality of corporate events. Biehl-Missal's article provides an excellent insider account of the event.

# Chapter 3

# In the mix

## Intermedial theatre and hybridity

## Towards hybridity

Writing about a 'mélange of genres' in contemporary art, Jacques Rancière points to 'the idea of a hybridization of artistic means appropriate to the postmodern reality of a constant exchange of roles and identities, the real and the virtual, the organic and mechanical and information-technology prostheses' (Rancière 2009: 21). He suggests that this idea can lead to some 'stultification' by way of banal performance outputs. Nonetheless, Rancière articulates a notable trend: the apparent hybridity of processes, forms and media in twenty-first-century performance. Hybridization provides an increasingly pervasive mode for cultural engagement.

The concept of hybridity in the arts is not entirely straightforward. Erika Fischer-Lichte has been a principal voice of caution in relation to theatre studies. She suggests that 'ultimately the notion of the hybrid which is transferred from biology assumes that we are dealing with elements that do not belong together "originally" or by their very "nature" but have been linked arbitrarily. So I am avoiding the terms "intercultural" or even "hybrid theatre" in order to circumvent such notions and connotations' (Fischer-Lichte 2009: 399). In a keynote lecture in 2010 Fischer-Lichte observed that the term 'hybrid' properly referred to the conjunction of different and often unlike species in biology, suggesting that its application to cultural processes was therefore inappropriate. Hence the turn to 'interweaving' (in the title of the Interweaving Performance Cultures research centre that Fischer-Lichte directs), a term drawn from textile crafts, to indicate the interrelation but distinctness of plural strands (Fischer-Lichte 2010).[1]

If we interpret hybridity metaphorically, however, it applies more comfortably to various sorts of mixing in contemporary theatre and performance. As Isabella Pluta observes, 'the effect of hybridisation mines the characteristics of different systems and places them in new configurations, either fused or remaining in tension' (Pluta 2010: 187) – and indeed tense relations can be as productive as actual fusions. In spite of – or, I shall suggest, because of – its application in life sciences, hybridity is very useful as a concept for discussing postdramatic, digital and immersive performance, and indeed a wide array of work in popular culture. More pressingly, hybrid processes and practices have now become commonplace. They help structure our engagements as creators and consumers in cultural production. In order to address the 'new configurations' that arise, I shall explore different understandings and applications of the term; then, by way of example, focus on the work of dreamthinkspeak, a British company that extensively hybridizes production processes, cultural spaces, intertexts, media, and spectator engagement.

## Horizons of hybridization[2]

In September 2010 the art magazine *Frieze* ran a cover feature entitled 'What is "super-hybridity"?' Its author, Jörg Heiser, writing in the wake of postcolonial debates concerning hybridity (more of which below), suggests that 'the cultural techniques of hybridization [have become] ubiquitous, accelerated and diversified'. Pointing to the effects of the Internet, globalization and diverse engagements with identity and tradition, he argues that 'hybridization has moved beyond the point where it's about a fixed set of cultural genealogies and instead has turned into a kind of computational aggregate of multiple influences and sources' (Heiser 2010). Heiser coins the term 'super-hybridity' to indicate this routinely hybridizing cultural sphere.

Historians and social anthropologists have employed the term 'hybridity' without Heiser's perhaps unnecessary prefix. In *Cultural Hybridity*, published in 2009, the historian Peter Burke addresses a broad sweep of hybrid formations by way of artefacts, practices and peoples. In his overview Burke suggests that 'A preoccupation with the topic is natural in a period like ours that is marked by increasingly frequent and intense cultural encounters of all kinds. . . . it is difficult to deny that what we see, hear and experience . . . is some kind of mix, a process of hybridization that assists economic globalization as well as being assisted by it' (Burke 2009: 2).

Burke doesn't mention the following theatre and performance organizations that have embraced the term explicitly as part of their identity, although they would fall within his purview. New York-based Hybrid.[Theatre].Ensemble describes itself as 'an up-and-coming theatre company exploring the collisions of various cultures and societies, dance and theatre, realism and non-traditional theatre, and poetic text and gestural movement' (Hybrid.[Theatre].Ensemble). Hybrid Theatre Works, also based in New York, is 'a growing network of theatre artists, scholars and activists dedicated to deepening the role of theatre in peace-building efforts internationally and within our own communities' (Hybrid Theatre Works). The company's response to the oil spill in 2010 in the Gulf of Mexico manifested in a YouTube posting featuring 14 short videos, showing dance, music and performance routines.[3] Rather differently, but again mixing artistic forms and civic engagement, Hybrid Arts, based in Warwickshire, England, works with schools to provide creative opportunities to 14–19-year-olds. According to its website, 'Hybrid Arts meld the technological with the analogue – these [*sic*] can include sonic dancing with bicycles and the cultural identity of gardening' (Hybrid Arts).

Hybridity here entails a fairly rampant eclecticism. It also has currency as an experimental artistic praxis, as indicated by the Ars Electronica festival, based in Linz, Austria, which offers a prize in its 'Hybrid Art' category.[4] The winner of the 'Hybrid Art' prize in 2011 was the French company Art Orienté Objet for its project *May the Horse Live in Me*, which the festival's website described as 'a bio-art project and an example of extreme body art. Via blood plasma injection, an animal organism (a horse in this case) is crossed with a human organism. . . . This staged blood-sisterhood raises the question of the boundaries separating different species.'[5]

This points towards a biogenetic understanding of hybridity, which takes us back to the term's roots in the natural sciences. That said, Art Orienté Objet's horseplay is not representative of the category as a whole. *Hotel Medea*, Zecora Ura Theatre Network's adaptation of the Medea myth, for instance, was awarded a Hybrid Arts 'Honorary Mention' in the same year. The show (which I discuss in the next chapter) is a site-adapted immersive production that runs through the night, mixing ritualized performance, staged dramatic scenes and video mediation, all involving its spectators in various ways.

The companies and artists mentioned above have in common a deliberate mixing of artistic forms as a means to refunction the familiar, and engage with civic and cultural concerns (for example eco-protest, community-building and explorations of bio-science). They all aim to make *more than* theatre or live performance. I take this functional reach, this *going beyond*, to be part of the hybridity that is claimed by the respective practitioners. We see here not only the mixing of media, but a mediality that makes for something that we might call 'theatre-plus'. The hybrid is a product of the simultaneous use of different artforms or distinct media. It also expresses a wider kind of mixity between cultural forms, processes, situations and agendas.

As we know, the term 'hybrid' refers us to bioscience, and blending at the level of genetic reconstitution. Andrea Bonnicksen gives some useful definitions in her book *Chimeras, Hybrids, and Interspecies Research: Politics and Policymaking*.[6] In mapping the territory of her study, Bonnicksen notes a distinction between a chimera and a hybrid, both of which give rise to ambiguities in scientific and artistic fields alike:

> A scientific definition of a chimera can be this: an organism with cells from two genetically different sets of parents in its body. A social definition can be this: an animal with cut and pasted body parts reminiscent of the Greek chimera.
>
> (Bonnicksen 2009: 9)

The latter is a combination of lion, goat and serpent whose body parts none-theless do not fully combine. They are juxtaposed to make a single creature, but each part retains its distinctness. In biological terms, the cells of the new chimeric organism remain separate just as, in representational terms, do the body parts of the mythical chimera. Hybridity is different. As Bonnicksen suggests, 'Technically, a hybrid is an organism resulting from fertilization of the egg of one species with the sperm of another. Under this definition, true hybrids are rare'. (2009: 59) They do nonetheless exist. An example is the mule, the result of the coupling of a male donkey and a female horse – the donkey (with 62 chromosomes in its cell nucleus) and the horse (with 64) are different species.

If true hybrids are uncommon in the animal kingdom, they are rather more plentiful in the botanical world. Plant cells can be fused if their cellulose walls are stripped away (thus making them permeable). The new plant can then regenerate cell walls and reproduce itself, thereby ensuring that the hybrid is sustained – a process discovered in the 1960s, leading to a proliferation of botanical hybridizing.[7] The fuchsia provides an example. The genus, fuchsia, contains separate species that can be hybridised (and are, routinely, by flower producers). It is possible not only to cross species with each other to create new hybrids, but also to cross species with hybrids, and hybrids with hybrids. As might be expected, a rubric of classification has been formalized to control this blooming economy (Boullemier 1985: 13).

The fuchsia and its annotated array of hybrids appear to bear out Fischer-Lichte's concerns in relation to arts practices. The hybrid is categorically a mixed being, comprised of cells from unlike sources in which genomes appropriate to each may simultaneously be present. If we seek to describe hybridity in media processes, then, are we saying that separate media should 'fuse'? This makes no sense, in that the characteristics of digital video, for instance (involving the capture of light and shade by way of coded information on a chip) is quite distinct from that of, say, dance (the movement of a body or bodies over time and in a particular space). Different media are ontologically distinct, and rely on different technological apparatuses, production processes and cultures of use. And yet we can watch dance on video, and dance that takes place alongside or in relation to video projection. We understand what is meant when we think of a hybrid dance-video project (along the lines of work by, for instance, Shobana Jeyasingh, Keith Khan or Meredith Monk). We know that the word 'hybridity' betokens adaptation and refunctioning. This is our key to its use in theatre and performance. There is a prompt to such an approach elsewhere.

The concept of hybridity is important in postcolonial studies, and some of its usages and problematics in this sphere are instructive. One of the main narratives of postcolonialism concerns the reshaping of cultures, whether deliberate or otherwise on the part of those who find themselves reshaped, and the emergence of new (or newly complicated) identities and power relations. Unsurprisingly, in addressing such shifts, the question of boundaries has consistently preoccupied theorists of hybridity – as, later, it would preoccupy theorists of intermediality. Ien Ang provides a deft perspective in her broadly positive account of hybridization in relation to diasporas: 'Hybridity . . . is a concept that confronts and problematises boundaries, although it does not erase them. As such, hybridity always implies [. . .] encounters at the border . . . [H]ybridity is a heuristic device for analysing complicated entanglement' (Ang 2003: 149–50).

In a similar vein, in his account of the 'post' in postcolonialism (or indeed postmodernism and postfeminism) Homi Bhabha addresses the demarcation between one territory and another. In Bhabha's analysis, the prefix does not indicate historical sequence – a time before and a time after – but suggests what we might call 'beyondness', a space in which new configurations concretely take shape. As Bhabha observes, 'It is in this sense that the boundary becomes the place from which something begins its presencing' (Bhabha 2004: 7).[8]

This view of presencing can be applied to hybridity in both its literal and metaphorical sense. Hybridization denotes the creation of something new from elements that are unalike. The newly-formed something (a culture, a plant, a theatre production) displays various characteristics of its component parts but as a blended phenomenon exists *differently*, across a boundary, in a new configuration. In this sense the hybrid is not a freak of nature or circumstance. It is simply *beyond* that from which it derives. If this suggests that the hybrid is an outlier found at a margin, Bhabha's notion of 'presencing', with its evocation of temporal and spatial locatedness, is a useful corrective. The hybrid appears to us in its here and now.

The notion of beyondness in relation to postcolonial border crossing resonates with Deleuze and Guattari's celebrated concept of 'becoming', which has a more phenomenological aspect. In *A Thousand Plateaus* Deleuze and Guattari describe 'becoming' as a state of being in itself rather than a mode of transition from one determinate state to another:

> To become is not to progress or regress along a series. . . . Becoming produces nothing other than itself. We fall into a false alternative if you say that you either imitate or you are. What is real is the becoming itself, the block of becoming, not the supposedly fixed terms through which that which becomes passes.
>
> (Deleuze and Guattari 2004: 262)

This idea is developed, for example, in relation to becoming-animal, typically rendered as a noun ('the becoming-animal'). Deleuze and Guattari's concept of becoming is useful in that it allows us to see a phenomenal certainty and distinctness to what might otherwise be thought of as liminal or 'in between' states. A scenario of alteration is itself concrete and distinct.[9] As a Deleuzean example: Jennifer Parker-Starbuck proposes as a 'metaphoric structure' for her analysis of multimedia performance the figure of 'the cyborg, created through an intertwinement and negotiation between organic and non-organic materials, the body and technology' (2011: xiv). Parker-Starbuck's 'cyborg theatre' is one in which bodies and technologies are subject to 'mutually dependent intersecting' (8), to the point where 'the organic/synthetic binary' (11) is better understood as a compound – a continual becoming – rather than as categorically separate entities. Whether becoming-animal or becoming-cyborg, the resulting figures are phenomenally distinctive.[10]

This brings us finally to multimedia and intermediality in relation to the apparent hybridising of media. We can unpack this briefly with reference to the two volumes produced by the Intermediality in Theatre & Performance working group of the International Federation of Theatre Research.[11] In its first volume, *Intermediality in Theatre and Performance* (2006), the group addressed intermediality as a relation between media that figured an 'in-between'. As the editors noted in their introduction, 'Our thesis is that the intermedial is a space where the boundaries soften – and we are in-between and within a mixing of spaces, media and realities. . . . intermediality is an effect performed in-between mediality, supplying multiple perspectives and foregrounding the making of meaning by the receivers of the performance' (Chapple and Kattenbelt 2006: 12, 20). By the time of the second volume, *Mapping Intermediality in Performance* (2010), the position had changed. Dissatisfied with the categorical imprecision of the 'in-between', which suggested a no-space as much as a space, we turned to more committed formulations of media convergence and interrelation. As Robin Nelson observed in the book's Introduction:

> we now seek to mark the concrete effects of being definitively multiple and interrelational. We have come to see that detailed attention needs to be paid to the range of 'inters' in 'interrelationships' . . . we have come to think that the compound 'both-and' better characterises contemporary performance culture.
>
> (Nelson 2010: 17)

The phantom in-between was replaced by the phenomenal actuality of conjunction. This returns us to the hybrid – not literally, as some sort of mutant spawn of technologies of presentation, but as an *effect of becoming* enabled by blended processes and forms. Manovich dates the process of media hybridization from the late-1970s (2013: 161–198). Digital culture has accelerated this development, merging protocols of reality and representation in the process. As Benford and Giannachi suggest, 'the nature of mixed reality and of performance is complex and hybrid, involving multiple spaces, shifting roles, and extended time scales, all of which are connected in multiple ways through diverse forms of interface' (2011: 1, 7).[12] More broadly, we are now so routinely in a domain where media interrelate that it may be better to talk simply of hybrid mediality: the work and effects of blended media, whatsoever they be, and howsoever (inter)related.

Vittoria Borsò provides a useful perspective: 'Hybridity is a questionable term. It means the crossing of plants and, metaphorically, of cultures. However

. . . [t]here is no other condition of culture but a "crossing" condition' (Borsò 2006: 40). This condition applies no less to media within culture, which are now plurally determined, and implicated in a wide array of underpinning technologies, production processes and presentational strategies. We see this in many spheres, including factual and news production; the political messaging of governments; social networking by individuals; and not least contemporary theatre and live performance. This might not lead to actual fusions of ontologically distinct media. It does mean that we go towards and beyond the hybrid.

Facilitated by developments in nuclear physics (fusion), botany (plant hybridization), biogenetics (species development), cultural studies (in particular postcolonialism) and arts and media production, a lexicon of terms has entered into circulation. Blending, fusing, hybridizing, mixing: all have wide applications to contemporary theatre and performance. Borsò notes that 'hybridity' can be defined 'not as an ontological property, but as an epistemological tool' (2006: 41). In both its literal and metaphorical meanings, the term 'hybrid' gestures towards a becoming, and a beyond. The 'becoming' is processual, and involves new states or arrangements, enabled by mixity – what Hannerz calls 'an organization of diversity' (1996: 106).[13] The 'beyond' is contextual, and concerns the way in which artistic formations refigure the particular scene that they inherit and inhabit. Hybridization creates a new scenario. It suffuses the theatres of engagement discussed in these pages. We will be concerned with the nature of this scenario – culturally, artistically, affectively – at the moment that it appears. To explore this further let's consider blended Chekhov, and dreamthinkspeak's production *Before I Sleep*.

## Blending and beyond: an immersive instance

dreamthinkspeak describes its work as 'site-responsive', as distinct from site-specific (dreamthinkspeak [a]). It develops productions in relation to particular locations and settings. The pieces can then be remounted elsewhere. This means that they are situated and contextual, but do not depend entirely on the location in which they begin. They normally require spectators to move through the event according to a more or less defined route. They sometimes draw on different texts for the same piece. And they feature a number of media, including film, live performance and architectural or scenic installation. They are thoroughly hybridizing.

The company was founded in 1999. It is based in Brighton on the south coast of England, and has been associated over the years with the Brighton Festival, whose support has helped dreamthinkspeak develop an international profile. In 2001 *Who Goes There*, adapted from Shakespeare's *Hamlet* and presented in Brighton and at the Toneelschur Theatre in Haarlem, Holland, was a promenade piece blending film and live action. The company approached *Hamlet* from a different perspective in *The Rest is Silence* (2012), commissioned by the Brighton Festival in association with LIFT (London International Festival of Theatre) and the Royal Shakespeare Company. This time the promenade principle was reversed. The audience was shown into a rectangular space, and stood surrounded on all four sides by a series of rooms of different sizes, all of which were behind Perspex. The rooms presented various spaces appropriate to the action of the play, including Claudius's office, Hamlet's bedroom, a receiving room in the palace, the sleeping quarters of the boat in which Hamlet is transported, and so on. On one hand the show explored a form of scenographic authentication, developing a naturalistic depiction of these various settings. On the other hand, the serial nature of the spaces, the detachment produced by the Perspex separating performers from spectators, and the clean intercutting between different rooms, continually foregrounded the unorthodox spatial arrangement.

*Don't Look Back* (2003), derived from the myth of Orpheus and Euridice, was a promenade piece that included several film sequences. Premiered at the Brighton Festival, it subsequently toured to venues 'including the labyrinthine former Treasury building in Perth Australia, a vast disused print factory in Moscow, and the abandoned Majestic Hotel in Kuala Lumpur' (dreamthinkspeak [b]). *One Step Forward, One Step Back*, presented at Liverpool Cathedral as part of the city's European Capital of Culture 2008 programme, was a response to Dante's *Divine Comedy*, drawing additionally on Milton's *Paradise Lost* and William Blake's epic poem *Milton*, in which Blake and Milton journey together in search of both literary and personal meanings. The piece entailed a meandering exploration of the Cathedral's interior with, occasionally, views of the external world and the Cathedral's civic environment (Gardner 2008).

*In The Beginning Was The End* (2013) features similar shifts of perspective – spatial, dimensional and temporal. The production takes its spectators through workshops, offices, corridors and basement spaces at Somerset House, a grand neo-classical building in central London. Inspired by Leonardo Da Vinci's drawing 'A Cloudburst of Material Possessions', it draws additionally on themes from the Book of Revelation. It presents the variously ingenious and malfunctioning machines and staff of a fictional company called Fusion International. In one performance sequence a group of office workers strips naked and ascends a spiral staircase in slow motion. A film installation shows three colleagues at a meeting, who casually don oxygen tanks and goggles just before the table at which they are sitting slowly submerges in water. (The scene is rhymed in a model in an adjacent room.) In another room we look out of three large windows to see two performers, on harnesses, in slow-motion suicidal falls outside the building.

In each of these pieces classical (indeed canonical) source material is revisioned through contemporary frames of reference. The production process includes architectural recalibrations of the built environment; model-making for installations; filmmaking; rehearsal and performance of live theatrical scenes;

and the organization of the spectator's journey in immersive and promenade settings. Without a continuous blending of intertexts and a mix of techniques, processes, technologies and media, the work would not achieve its coherence or its affective force.

*Before I Sleep* (2010) was presented in a disused department store, and became the biggest-selling production in the Brighton Festival's history. It was remounted in an office block in Amsterdam as part of the Holland Festival 2011. Both locations provided a series of separate but interconnected spaces of varying sizes, a sense of scale, and a pervasive atmosphere of dilapidation or commercial functionalism. The show itself was a melancholic reflection upon Chekhov's *The Cherry Orchard*. In his programme note to the Brighton iteration, director Tristan Sharps observes that:

> [a] key influence in our piece is the Co-op building itself and the local area that surrounds it. In the basement areas, where we have deconstructed some of the interiors of a re-imagined Cherry Orchard house, we have been influenced by local, rather than Russian architecture. . . . Areas of the basement that stubbornly refuse to be hidden, we have simply left in view, as if a more recent world has already crashed into the past. As with all our work, we strive to design spaces that respond to and sit within the host site as if they have always belonged there.

Artistic creation here is situated, contextual and relational. It blends historical and actual space with metaphoric and intertextual reference. It conceives of space and setting as palimpsestic, accumulating different layers of function, meaning and aesthetic presentation. Space is defined partly by the manifestation of its history, and partly by the opportune set of circumstances that give this site, now, its evocative features. These defining features mark a shift in theatre practice towards the contextual and the felt – the fact of performance situated in a particular time, place and culture, produced for people with their own relationship to history, the present and (re)presentation. To that end, dream-thinkspeak's work echoes that of other immersive theatre companies that work in site-responsive ways. Clifford McLucas, co-artistic director of Welsh performance company Brith Goff, for example, suggests that 'The real site-specific works that we do, are the ones where we create a piece of work which is a hybrid of the place, the public, and the performance' (in Kaye 2000: 65). The respective companies have different civic agendas. Nonetheless, blended aesthetics are similarly in play. We can turn to some of the scenarios and encounters of *Before I Sleep* to reflect on the strategies of hybridization in this kind of theatre, and the ways in which these facilitate engagement on the part of the spectator.

Selected motifs from *The Cherry Orchard* were figured repeatedly, such as the cherry orchard itself, the figure of the elderly butler Firs, and the taking of tea.

*Figure 3.1* dreamthinkspeak's *Before I Sleep*: taking tea (Ulrika Belogriva, Mihai Arsene)
Source: Jim Stephenson

In one space, for example, the audience found itself in what appeared to be a rather faded living room, looking through a window to a patio on which a couple in smart nineteenth-century dress are drinking tea (Figure 3.1). It's not necessary to know *The Cherry Orchard* to enjoy the piece, but it adds various dimensions if you do. We might imagine that we watch Madame Ransvskaya and Gayev. She reads, he 'pots' an apple with his stick. The performance is durational, in that the actors sustain the scene while spectators pass by individually and in clusters. The actors here are playing a mode – something between casual civility and ennui – rather than a specific narrative unit from the play.

The piece features a number of small-scale models. One showed a manor house, alone in the middle of a snowy landscape of fir trees and, behind it, a cherry orchard (Figure 3.2).

We passed a table on which was a forest of half-burnt-down candles, with a couple in miniature at a table in the middle, and a butler figure towards the edge, as if moving towards them (Figure 3.3). This may have been the couple from the patio. We understand that the butler is Firs. It is Firs who leads you into the piece, in groups of four or five, speaking in Russian before leaving you to make your way onward. As Sharps' programme note says:

> Tragic-comically abandoned at the end of the play, while the orchard and the old world that he represents is being destroyed, he is one of the key

figures in *Before I Sleep*. Our piece playfully re-imagines him lingering in the long-abandoned house, trying in vain to go to sleep or perhaps to die, but being constantly interrupted by the influx of new audience members, who could be prospective purchasers, and the rapid arrival of a new century.

(dreamthinkspeak 2010: 1)

Firs, then, has a fleeting relationship with the spectators of the piece, whom he talks to directly, although not in any highly specific or personalized way. He appears at various points through the piece, looking vaguely absent and distractedly busy; variously guide, servant, seeker and lost soul.

Some rooms housed life-size installations rather than miniature models. One such was an expanse of white: a snowy scape, with a wooden path running through it, lit only by storm lanterns every few yards on the floor, and a wind soundscape playing – a rendition of bareness. The effect was bleak and beguiling, an evocation of outdoors inside the space. This was one of an accumulating series of scenes that sketched references to Russia and the imagined landscape of *The Cherry Orchard*, and generated a bleak mood for the piece. Scenes of encounter such as this are affective, through the striking impression on first entering the space, the visceral nature of a scenography that evokes sensations (wind, temperature) and thematic motifs (isolation, fragility),

*Figure 3.2* Model Chekhov: the manor house and orchard

Source: Jim Stephenson

*Figure 3.3* The forest of candles

Source: Jim Stephenson

and the experience of being *within* a playworld. The scene has a specific effect, but also operates metonymically by way of its place within the journey through the piece as a whole. We will later encounter a scene that provides a drastic counterpoint to this one. The *experience* of accessing the representational schema of the piece is facilitated in a layered way through a range of encounters (models, installations, films, performances).

One floor was given over to a recreation of a Russian department store, 'Millennium Retail', gesturing towards both the provenance of Chekhov's play and the former function of this particular venue in Brighton – although in a nod to the globalization of commerce, the shop assistants (and the performers playing them) were multinational – French, German, Italian, Japanese, Russian.

The forest of candles, smart now, appeared again as a display item in the store, complete with the ubiquitous butler as miniature model (Figure 3.4). This part of the event offered a form of interaction. You could be fitted for a dinner jacket, or talked through the furniture on display as if you were considering a purchase. The sign 'Closing Down Sale' was projected in different languages. Given the rather staid items on offer, the earnest friendliness of the staff, and a soundtrack of ambient string chords, the whole arrangement evoked a time-period now faded. Firs reappeared, this time in his nightshirt, as if condemned perpetually never to find rest (Figure 3.5).

After the department store, we entered a room that was occupied by cosy beds, and we took the opportunity to lie down. In a damp-smelling room, later on, we came upon a dusty bed, the same sort as the one we had previously sampled in pristine form, but now long neglected. In this way the piece layered time, and evoked transience.

Motifs of impermanence and loss accumulated their effect across media. One room featured simply a very wide-screen video showing Firs in the forest, approaching a couple at a table (Figure 3.6). This is the couple that we have seen in series throughout the piece, as live performers, miniature models and, here, on film. Ignoring him, the couple leave, slightly staggering towards the camera and moving out of shot. Firs comes to the table. He looks around. He is carrying a cup and saucer. The film shows a top shot of Firs as he collapses slowly on the forest floor, holding the cup and saucer. The shot zooms out to reveal that he is within a small patch of wood on a small island in the middle of the sea.

Towards the end of the piece, set aside in its own roped off space, is a cherry tree in pink blossom, surrounded by grass (Figure 3.7). It is a potent image, the literal figure of that which, in *The Cherry Orchard*, is so productively metaphorical. In a final room we walk through a floor of decapitated tree stumps and wood chippings, a suggestion of industrialized rendition (and Lopakhin's termination of the orchard) that makes a grim rhyme with the virginal snowy forest floor that we encountered previously. It is as if we have been tricked by time again, with the present and the past, the metaphor, its figure and its future all in rapid juxtaposition.

*Figure 3.4* Millennium Retail: candles (and butler) on display

Source: Jim Stephenson

*Figure 3.5* Firs (Michael Poole) adrift, with shop assistants (Ocean Isoaro and Francesco Calabretta)

Source: Jim Stephenson

*Figure 3.6* Firs (Michael Poole) in the woods: film as installation

Source: Jim Stephenson

*Figure 3.7* The cherry tree

Source: Jim Stephenson

*Before I Sleep* is made through miniature models, large-scale installations, architectural adaptation, performance, sound design and film. It is intertextual – continually referencing both Chekhov's play and the former Cooperative department store in which it is located. You might say that Chekhov infuses this piece. Yet it is also very situated. The production strategy is one of systematic blending, folding the play into the models, an outer world into the interior, the past into the present, the dramatic fiction into the lived life of a local shop, and separate media into each other. It then imbricates its spectators in its spaces, and through a series of encounters with mixed modes of presentation.

What is the work of the director or designer, here? The programme has a list of collaborators under the title 'Associate Designers and Makers'. Pre-eminent here is Tristan Sharps, credited for 'Direction, Film and Design Conception'. According to Sharps, 'It was only in the mid '90s I realised I could marry visual art, architecture and theatre. It was like a neon sign – "Of course! That's what I'm about!" – and I was off' (Meakin 2012). There is no designer or scenographer indicated – rather, there are credits for a scenic artist, individuals responsible for modelling, costume, graphics and sound designers, and a master carpenter. The system is one of distributed creativity, not unlike that of cinema production. The process helps to secure the *efficacy* of the piece, technically (by achieving often quite complicated media interrelations and spatial arrangements) and aesthetically (by exciting us with ways of arranging and sharing information and meaning that we may not have seen or experienced before). This is key to the apparent hybridization of *Before I Sleep*. The deliberate interrelations achieve hybridity's characteristic mode of becoming, and figure the 'beyond' of a newly discrete performance iteration. The work of direction and scenography is not so much in the rehearsal room as spread across a series of spaces required by the creative process, including the modelling studio, film set and of course the site itself.

If *Before I Sleep* engages with the past (the setting in Russia, late-nineteenth-century modernism, the former department store) it also stages a Deleuzean becoming. Film gives onto the theatrical present, the (beyond-cinematic) extra-wide screen rendering video as installation. Theatre scenes become part of an immersive environment, unmoored from linear sequence. Acting is a matter of establishing mode (the performance of theme rather than incident) and mood (anxiety and ambient ennui). The beyond that is figured here is beyond-Chekhov; beyond *The Cherry Orchard*, the department store, even *Before I Sleep* itself. It is the concrete expression of the plural as an entity – presenting theatre as a place of felt encounter, configured by textual sources and social and cultural frames, to produce a site of spectatorial engagement. The affect of the piece is to do with experience in the face of its hybrid mediality. For example, the point at which the film refigures variously the models that we have seen, the live actor playing the butler and the scenic arrangement of the tea party, all of which metonymically respond to *The Cherry Orchard* – in a filmic space that is also an event within the installation – is a point at which hybridization coheres. Immersion becomes not so much a matter of personal interaction, but of being situated in a sensorium that has blurred chronology, linear time, consistencies of space and diverse intertexts. At this moment we, too, are being blended in.

## Notes

1 In the mix: intermedial theatre and hybridity. Fischer-Lichte's position on hybridity has shifted over time. In conversation with Rustom Bharucha, she discusses a culturally and stylistically mixed production of *King Lear* by the Singaporean director Ong Keng Sen that premiered in Japan in 1997, finding it 'not just a hybrid performance based on a variety of performance traditions, but one that reflected on the very concept of hybridity, on so-called hybrid identities and passages' (Fischer-Lichte and Bharucha 2011).
2 Ien Ang talks of 'the unsettling horizon of hybridisation' in Ang 2003: 152.
3 www.youtube.com/watch?v=7yWU6ENHOpA.
4 The prize is adjudicated by way of submissions made in advance. The winner presents their work at the festival in the year in question. See Ars Electronica website at www.aec.at/prix/en/kategorien/hybrid-art/.
5 http://prix.aec.at/winner/3043/, accessed 29 May 2011.
6 The book addresses early genetic research involving combinations of genes and embryonic stem cells across human and non-human species (for example, in the use of pig valves in human hearts).
7 See Ringertz and Savage 1976: 8, 290. The book summarizes the methodology of cell fusion in biological and botanical contexts.
8 Bhabha problematizes the cultural and political value of hybridity. In his analysis hybridity may be imposed by colonialism; or appear in colonialist discourse as the emergence of a disavowed Other. In terms of artistic and media processes, my concern is with the 'metonymy of presence' and 'peculiar "replication"' that Bhabha observes in hybridization (2004: 164, 165). See also Heidemann and de Toro 2006: 9–17; and, on cultural intersection and complexification, Kwok-bun 2012.
9 I don't want to press the point too hard. *A Thousand Plateaus* is informed by – and written against – psychoanalytic theory. Deleuze and Guattari are less concerned with the operations of particular media or artforms, let alone their interrelation.
10 For related discussions of cyborg theatre and, more broadly, multimedia performance as a blended phenomenon, see Giannachi 2004; Dixon 2007; and Klich and Scheer 2012.
11 I declare an interest here as a member of the group, and as its co-convener from 2010 to 2013.
12 See Benford and Giannachi 2011: 42–52 for an account of hybrid spaces in mixed reality performance, drawing on discussions in media studies, human geography, architecture, computing and cultural studies.
13 Hannerz observes that 'A complex culture . . . has to be seen as a moving interconnectedness' (1992: 167).

# Chapter 4

# Feeling the event

## From *mise en scène* to *mise en sensibilité*

### Beyond *mise en scène*

There is a moment in Punchdrunk's children's show *The Crash of the Elysium* (2011–12) that raises the young heartbeat and a few questions about theatre.[1] We are in a corridor within what we understand (within the drama) to be an alien spaceship that has crash-landed. We have just left a control room, full of screens and gadgets of dubious age. We are on a mission to save Doctor Who, the eponymous hero of the long-running children's television series. Matt Smith, the actor then playing the Doctor across the franchise's various outlets, has appeared in a video message to request as much, warning us to look out for 'escaped art'. We have glimpsed the art in question: a stone statue, one of the Weeping Angels – an alien lifeform that will kill you if don't keep your eyes on it. For the conceit concerning this monster is that the angel cannot move if it is watched. Blink and it approaches.[2] Now, in the corridor, we gather before a locked door as our facilitator, 'Captain Solomon' of the British Army, tries to open it. Other than the light from a couple of torches, we are in darkness. An Angel is revealed in a blast of illumination at the other end of the corridor. It goes dark again. Another shaft of light, and the angel has come closer to us along the corridor. Again it goes dark. The Angel is revealed again almost upon us. And just in time, Solomon has opened the door and through we go. We find ourselves in a holding pen. Its walls rise, to reveal an outdoor space (within this interior installation): a straw-covered floor, surrounded by faded fairground stalls and entrances to attractions. A single figure awaits – a performer playing Dolly, a fairground artiste from the year 1888.

What is afoot here, theatrically, in this transitory moment? The corridor is a place of passage between two scenographically rich spaces. The production includes a number of connecting spaces, some of which we traverse in a crouch, passing industrial corrugated metal, swathed black cloth, across concrete floors and through a lot of dry ice. In this instance we are not supposed to notice the space – rather, its critical encounter. The performers playing Solomon and two other soldiers are the only human actors, for the Angel is a scenic item, moved through some sleight of stagecraft. And yet we too are actors – in a scene that simultaneously depends on the trope of spectatorship (we are instructed not to look at the Angel, which on the other hand is precisely the action the staging has us do) and the denial of sight (we are deprived the continuous eye-contact that, diegetically, will save us). A scene, too, that is otherwise bare of scenography, as is amply counterpointed by the designed spaces either side of it. The scene isn't for watching. It is to be lived in. *The Crash of the Elysium*, as with *Before I Sleep* and, I shall suggest later, *Hotel Medea* and *The Drowned Man*, join with other immersive, site-responsive and participatory pieces to exemplify a turn in contemporary performance from scenic presentation to evental experience.

We can assess this by starting with the concept of *mise en scène*, previously a cornerstone of film and theatre aesthetics. The term, literally 'placed on the stage', is usually left in French in anglophone theatre studies. As with the terms *mise en événement* and *mise en sensibilité*, which I discuss later as part of a trajectory for engagement, the compound construction featuring the past participle indicates human agency – something was *arranged* – along with a *process* of construction. In an Anglophone context the foreign language also provides an evident code-function. The term *mise en scène* has fallen somewhat from fashion although, as Fischer-Lichte says, it remains 'undeniably fundamental' (2008: 182).[3] It is continually pertinent in addressing how theatrical work appears to people and the organizing principles by which it is manifested. However, it has become inadequate as a means by which to describe certain kinds of theatre production. We shall need different frames of reference to explain how performance works for those who visit, witness and sometimes participate in it.

*Mise en scène* is to do with the organization of the performance space for spectating. In film studies it denotes everything that, coming in front of the camera, is captured by the filming apparatus and shown within the frame of the screen. As Bordwell and Thompson observe, *mise en scène* in film typically involves consideration of '[s]etting, costume, lighting, and figure expression and movement', determined by spatial and temporal coordinates (1990: 141). In this classic usage, the term betokens a predominantly visual field that is subject to artistic preparation. The authors suggest that 'In controlling the mise-en-scène, the director *stages the event* for the camera' (127, original emphasis). Here is a familiar turn to *mise en scène* as the province of the director, along with a nod to the rubrics of the proscenium theatre in the notion of staging. That said, *mise en scène* can also be decoupled from the ostensible decisions of the director, cinematographer and other contributors. It can refer to the visual and spatial structures of any particular shot, whether or not deliberately worked. Placement within the frame of the camera or, in theatre and performance, the playing area, betokens an effect of presence as much as an act of organization. Of course such presence in film is recorded, but that doesn't change the fact that we observe the configuration of things and people as they appear to us through the realization of the artwork. To that end, *mise en scène* is an arrangement of space, presence and appearance that produces an effective figuration for the spectator. It is, to use a term drawn from transport (that other medium of communication), a *manifest*.

In both cinema studies and theatre studies, *mise en scène* is an aesthetic system that engages the viewer in the act of viewing. This doesn't mean that, as far as the theatre is concerned, *mise en scène* is simply the arrangement of images, people or objects on the stage. A *mise en scène* can feature various elements of the medium, including the rhythmic and spatial dynamics of exits, entrances and movement within scenes; the architectonic nature of space – more or less open, confining, sweeping, shadowy and so forth; the visceral qualities of textures and colours that in themselves produce a felt response to space, bodies and action; and the fact that the features of a space can change over time. *Mise en scène* can also involve that which is heard, as arranged by the sound designer, composer, director or indeed the writers and actors who shape spoken utterance. Sound is a scenographic element that both takes and creates space. Nonetheless, while the list above is to do with the theatre in its three-dimensionality and duration, *mise en scène* is most readily to do with spatial and scenic organization for spectating.

Patrice Pavis has undertaken the most extensive theorization of *mise en scène* for the theatre. His scholarship has shifted over time, and provides something of a map of developments in critical perspective. Pavis moved from a semiotic account of *mise en scène* as a signifying practice (what the things on the stage mean) to a more culturally inflected account (how social and cultural expression is negotiated) to a phenomenological analysis (how staging elements work more broadly on those perceiving them). His work forms a bridge between the dominant poststructuralist discourse of the 1970s and the late-twentieth-century interest in embodied aspects of performance. A brief survey of Pavis's writing allows us to track the term *mise en scène* from a terrain of literary signification, concerned with playwriting; towards a wider landscape of performance; and perhaps to its resting ground as a concept overtaken by the different demands of contemporary theatre production.

In 'Towards a Semiology of the Mise en Scène?' (1982), describing himself as an 'unrepentant logocentrist', Pavis argues for a semiological approach that focuses on 'the relationship between text and performance'. The performance text realizes, interprets and indeed 'questions the dramatic text' (139). *Mise en scène* is contingent and never complete. It can always be remade and made differently, but it is nonetheless a 'concrete enunciation' of the dramatic text, which is thereby changed through a process of interpretation within a signifying practice (142). Pavis conceives of text and performance as 'an ambiguous *couple*' (136, original emphasis). It appears that there is a pecking order, with the text coming first, as one might expect of unrepentant logocentrism. A shift of authority is nonetheless prefigured in this criticism, from the luminous origin (the playtext) to the illuminated realization (the production) – a shift that would gather pace over the final couple of decades of the twentieth century. The tension figured in this writing in the early 1980s will rupture in the 1990s.

Indeed by 1992 the balance has changed. In *Theatre at the Crossroads of Culture* Pavis observes that '[w]e no longer attempt to analyse a performance on the basis of a pre-existing dramatic text' (Pavis, 1992: 2–3). The adherence to a 'semiotic point of view' remains, but it is now at the service of intercultural critical procedures, for whom '[m]ise en scène is a kind of réglage ("fine-tuning") between different contexts and cultures' (6). Meanwhile, the audience enters. In 'From Page to Stage: A Difficult Birth', adapted from a piece written in 1988 and published in 1992, Pavis defines *mise en scène* 'as the bringing together, or confrontation, in a given space and time, of different signifying systems, for an audience' (1992: 24). Here again Pavis is interested in the oscillation between text and performance, but this time the point is perception. *Mise en scène* is 'an object of knowledge, a network of associations or relationships uniting the different stage materials into signifying systems, created both by production (the actors, the director, the stage in general) and reception (the spectators)' (1992: 25). The pertinent transaction here is not so much from page to stage as from stage to auditorium. To that end Pavis increasingly emphasizes the particular attributes of performance over those of the text.

In 1996 Pavis argues that 'mise-en-scène is by definition a synthetic system of options and organizing principles' (2003 [1996]: 8). Such principles now concern the '*metatext*' and the 'performance text'. The former is 'an unwritten text comprising the various choices of a mise-en-scène that the director has consciously or unconsciously made during the rehearsal process' (8).[4] Pavis glosses the latter as 'the mise-en-scène considered . . . [as] an organized ensemble of signs' (8–9). *Mise en scène* is understood here as the concrete realization of staging, whether or not deliberately produced; and as that which is 'read' by spectators.

As Shepherd and Wallis indicate, semiotics and phenomenology are distinct critical systems that are 'opposed, but necessarily interconnected' (2004: 239). In his latter work Pavis attempts to make the connections stronger and clearer. In *Contemporary Mise en Scène* (2013 [2007]) he focuses on ways in which to extend the conception of *mise en scène* in order for it to work for new sorts of production. He relates *mise en scène* to developments in media practice, intermediality and postdramatic performance, along with contemporary performance scholarship. This line of analysis informs his essay 'The Director's New Tasks', and it is here that he tracks the term *mise en scène* to its endgame. As Pavis observes, '*Mise en scène* as a semiological sign system, overseen by a single pair of eyes, has died out' (2010: 395). The eyes were those of the director. The change, Pavis suggests, is to do with cultural predisposition (in the wake of postmodernism we are no longer wedded to the idea of the single authority figure) and the freer interpretative range accorded to the spectator. If the conventional operations of *mise en scène* are unsustainable, what then? Pavis argues that 'we should complement the notion of *mise en scène* with the Anglo-American notion of *performance* . . . [which] considers theatrical perform-ance as the accomplishment of an action, and not as "stage writing"' (2010:

400, original emphasis). There is a tension here, between an interpretative view of *mise en scène* as the (signifying) domain of drama, and the postmodern position that performance does not need to signify but simply exist (affectively). Pavis asks whether we should 'find another word, and thus another theory, for a *mise en scène* that does not represent an already-written text but which works with silence and non-verbal signs (be they visual or musical)' (407). The challenge (which might equally apply to already-written texts, in some productions) is worth taking up.

This much is clear as soon as we consider dreamthinkspeak's *Before I Speak*, as discussed in the previous chapter. The production features scenes on a series of stages, as well as models, installations and films. We can talk of the *mise en scène* within the model, or the *mise en scène* that arranges a model within an installation, or the *mise en scène* that configures an installation within a larger set of spatial coordinates through which the spectator travels. What's more, we are sometimes within the piece as participants – as when we find ourselves in a 'staged' version of a department store floor (on the actual floorspace of a former department store) and are invited to try out products or talk with shop assistants. We walk through the piece, broadly speaking in our own time, where we mingle with other spectators whose pace and reactions become part of the texture of the event, and where we observe others observing and sometimes participating. Something similar is happening in pieces like *No Man's Land* and *Situation Rooms*, as mentioned at the beginning of this book. In these instances, are we watching *mise en scène*, or helping to realize a *mise en scène*? Or do we need a different term to describe what has been figured for us, with us and by us?

## Through *mise en événement*

In *Before I Sleep*, *No Man's Land*, *Situation Rooms* and *The Crash of the Elysium*, the work of the theatre practitioners is no longer to realize a text or 'complete' a staging, but to oversee the audience's engagement with the production in its several spaces. This requires them to cohere the different zones and places of passage that make up the spectators' multiple encounters of the event. In which case we can talk not just of *mise en scène* but *mise en événement*, since we are interested in something broader than simply the staging of performance. *Événement* is the French term for 'event': something that happens, that takes place. It can also refer to a 'happening' in the sense of a more or less spontaneous performance, a usage that emphasizes the here-and-nowness of the event. The uprisings in France of May 1968 are known as '*les événements*', while the Algerian war of independence is '*les événements d'Algérie*', which indicates a civic and political reverberation to the term (Allain *et al.* 2006: 382).

In Anglophone theatre and performance studies the term 'event' has gained wide currency since the 1990s, where the notion of the 'theatrical event' in particular has provided a way of assessing theatre's engagements with its spectators. It has enjoyed considerable attention in philosophy for a much longer period, with philosophers since Aristotle exploring a variety of considerations. These include means of describing events in language; the nature of events, for example to do with their relation to space and time, and singularity and repeatability; their structure; their relationship to causation and change (does the event always entail an alteration of some kind?); and their relation to perception.[5] Rather than dwell upon matters of categorical definition, my interest here is with a pair of interrelating concerns: the *representation* of the event (in the face of history and aesthetic mediation); and the event as an affective *transaction* between its occurrence (or theatrical presentation) and its experiential basis (or theatrical reception and indeed participation). On the face of it, these two concerns are schematically distinct.

Let's start with the adequacy or otherwise of representation. The problem here concerns the drastic reach of events both in their historical import and their profound significance to individuals. As Hayden White observes:

> The notion of the 'historical event' has undergone radical transformation as a result of both the occurrence in our century of events of a scope, scale, and depth unimaginable by earlier historians and the dismantling of the concept of the event as an object of a specifically scientific kind of knowledge.
>
> (White 1996: 22)

White lists 'holocaustal' events such as the Great Depression, the genocide in and around Nazi Germany, and widespread poverty linked to a growth in world population (20). Written around five years before 9/11, White's essay considers the representation and mediation of trauma in relation to modernist aesthetic strategies of rupture, discontinuity and anti-narrative – strategies that are perhaps formally well-matched to their topic. The problem is one of dealing decently with history, creating representation that is adequate to the thing that is represented.

This challenge appears unsurprisingly just as acute in the volume *Ritual and Event: Interdisciplinary perspectives* (2007), published just over a decade after White's book, amid the ongoing reverberations of 9/11. In his introduction, Mark Franko notes that:

> 'the event' took on a new shape in the wake of World War II. Since the bombing of Hiroshima and Nagasaki and the discovery of the camps, what happens became historically aligned with what is socially impossible to process, culturally and psychologically unabsorbable, and highly resistant to linguistic, visual, and/or performative symbolization. . . . In the wake of 9/11 the event has taken on a new immediacy.
>
> (Franko 2007a: 1)

Franko's volume adds the appearance of Abu Ghraib in media (re)presentations, and the HIV/AIDS pandemic to the list of 'unabsorbable' events. The volume takes a long-modern view of the event in relation to history, experience and cultural production, particularly insofar as the event both expresses and gives rise to ritualized cultural performance.[6]

In his own chapter, Franko notes that twentieth-century 'aesthetic activism' produced a sense of event *in* and *through* the artwork, which was often interdisciplinary in nature (enhancing its eventness) – but that the drastic irruption of 9/11 challenges such constructions of the event in aesthetics: 'Because the performative event has been turned against itself as the disaster, has not its instrumentality for performative positioning been indefinitely suspended? How can performance respond to events while abandoning the essential engagement to itself as an event?' (Franko 2007b: 125–6). The latter question really breaks into two. It has indeed proved difficult for performance to respond to events that appear to be 'unabsorbable'. However, if anything performance has more routinely, since 9/11, presented itself *as* event – of course not in the history-making sense, but in the extended ontological mode of eventness, something that in and of itself marks a moment and shapes an engagement. There is not necessarily any 'performative positioning' here in relation to historical circumstances or political agendas. Instead certain sorts of performance, including those discussed in this chapter, produce a sense of eventness, experienced as such, that is part of what we find pleasurable. Perhaps the answer to Franko's question lies in revisiting his use of the term 'performative', which here suggests something that belongs to performance rather than the term's linguistic derivation meaning a speech function that itself effects an action or a change in social process.[7] Precisely because it is more difficult for it to 'speak', the performative event is instead constructed in order to be experienced *as* event. Its eventness overtakes its referentiality.

Franko's perspective is informed by Foucault's theory of the 'discursive event', which is worth revisiting here as it opens out the relationship between the structure of the event and how we might relate to it. Foucault treated the event as a cornerstone of his larger project, the analysis of discourse. He notes that:

> the material with which one is dealing is, in its raw, neutral state, a popu- lation of events in the space of discourse in general. One is led therefore to the project of a pure description of discursive events as the horizon for the search for the unities that form within it.
>
> (Foucault 2002: 29–30)

For Foucault, the event (as discursive formation) marks difference. It is part of a structure. It appears within time, so therefore by virtue of its emergence inherently marks a departure, a new scene. An 'archaeological' procedure that deals with such events is mindful of sedimentary layers, simultaneities, discontinuities and ruptures, non-linear processes. For the event must also be understood in relation to a longer historical view of events in series, sequence or interrelation. Foucault partly defines it by way of what it is not. As he suggests:

> Naturally the event is neither substance nor accident, neither quality nor process; the event is not of the order of bodies. And yet it is not something immaterial either; it is always at the level of materiality that it takes its effect, that it is effect; it has its locus and it consists in the relation, the coexistence, the dispersion, the overlapping, the accumulation, and the selection of material elements. It is not the act or the property of a body; it is produced as an effect of, and within, a dispersion of matter. Let us say that the philosophy of the event should move in the at first sight paradoxical direction of a materialism of the incorporeal.
>
> (Foucault 1981: 69)

It is tempting, now, to think of the evental incorporeality Foucault describes as being also always corporeal. That's to say, if the event takes its effect at the level of materiality, this includes the minds and bodies of those wrapped up in or touched by it, such that the effect is also affective. To finesse this: in relation to a theatrical conception of the event, which involves the spectator/participant in its present moment, there is a bringing into experience of that-which-is.[8]

The critics and philosophers, above, consider ontological aspects of the event, which are to do with structure, duration and distinction (what separates an event from that which surrounds it). They point us towards historical process; and civic, social and personal consequence – what the event *does*, and what it *means* to people. They suggest that if we cannot be sure that we can really *express* the event, we can certainly *create* and *experience* it. In this respect there is a more localized sense of event that is relevant to our interest in these pages: the use of the term in theatre and performance studies since, broadly, the 1990s.

Here, too, the notion of 'event' has been well mined. Part of this labour was undertaken by a working group of the International Federation of Theatre Research, called 'Theatrical Event: Production, Reception, Audience Participation and their Interrelationships'.[9] Willmar Sauter, the group's leading figure, proposes a bipartite model of theatrical communication in his book *The Theatrical Event: Dynamics of Performance and Perception*. On the one hand there is *presentation* in performance by way of actions that are deliberately exhibitory, embodied and encoded (Sauter refers to aesthetic norms or learned behaviour). This is theatre as it is given to us. On the other hand, there is *perception* by way of reactions on the part of spectators. These reactions include affection, pleasure, evaluation, identification and interpretation. Theatrical communication is configured by time and occurs across artistic, symbolic and sensory levels – that's to say, the aesthetic arrangement of the piece; what it might mean to you; and how it feels to watch it (Sauter 2000: 6–11). Sauter (not unlike Pavis, as we have seen) proposes a paradigm shift from the idea of theatre as a work of stage art towards an understanding of it as a communicative event: 'theatre manifests itself as an event which includes both the presentation of actions and the reactions of the spectators, who are present at the very moment of the creation. Together the actions and reactions constitute the theatrical event' (2000: 20). Every instance in which a performance is presented to an audience can be thought of as a theatrical event. And in this case, as Sauter says elsewhere, 'Our concern is the "event-ness" of theatre' (Sauter 2004: 11).

Informed by reception theory, Sauter's analysis is part of performance studies' engagement with phenomenology in the 1990s and thereafter. His notion of 'event' is strategic in shifting focus from the text and its reception (its landing in *meaning*) to a larger sense of *transaction* between a production and its audience. Sauter makes it clear that he is interested in 'theatre as a playing culture', instances of which he finds prior to the classical Greek drama that is held up, he notes wryly, as the beginning of '[t]he canonized history of theatre'. The theatrical event, in Sauter's account, is to do with 'the amusement and pleasure of watching' (Sauter 2004: 4), which has a yet longer provenance. If this marks a movement beyond the more semiotic considerations of playtext and production analysis, such a move had already been anticipated from within reception studies itself.

In her influential book *Theatre Audiences: A Theory of Production and Reception* Susan Bennett discusses 'The specific encounter of the spectator with the theatrical event' (1990: 133). Bennett's analysis exemplifies a growing attention among scholars to private experience as a component of this theatrical encounter; the merging of private and public spaces; and the facilitation by theatre events of personal engagements that are also experienced as communal. As its title suggests, Bennett's book is grounded in reception theory and semiotics, where meaning is located in the spectator's understanding, and it is concerned with cultural production, ideology and the institutions of theatre. For all that, Bennett remarks upon 'The enormous growth over the last twenty years of theatre groups who work non-traditionally . . . Above all, the event has been decentred both as occasion and place. Performances are no longer tied to traditional spaces with a fixed audience-stage relationship' (1990: 110). She considers festivals, non-traditional spaces of performance and unorthodox performance durations, with reference to work by practitioners including The San Francisco Mime Troupe, 7:84, Ariane Mnouchkine and El Teatro Campesino. This is a diverse field, but together Bennett's examples point to theatre as both event and encounter. Both Bennett and Sauter, at either end of the 1990s, indicate that a fuller understanding of the theatrical event will mesh performance analysis, reception studies and phenomenological considerations. It requires not only attention to what the production means (in a reception/cognition paradigm) but also how it operates in specific situations, by way of the *experience* of its audience.

Two German scholars help us to round out this critical journey through evental encounter. Erika Fischer-Lichte attributes three key features to the nature of performance as event: 'the feedback loop's autopoiesis', by which she means the mutually-informing relationship between the performance and its in-the-moment reception by its spectators; 'a destabilization, even erasure, of binary oppositions' such as subject and object, art and reality, the aesthetic and non-aesthetic; and 'situations of liminality that transform the participants of the performance' (2008: 163).[10] By participants, Fischer-Lichte means those who witness a performance as much as those who present it. Indeed her model seeks the dissolution, 'even erasure', of distinctions between stage and auditorium, construction and consumption. This analysis is part of Fischer-Lichte's larger project: to propose an aesthetic scheme that in effect reconciles semiology, reception theory and phenomenology, whereby the *experience* of the aesthetic can lead to what Fischer-Lichte terms 'reenchantment'. The constituents of a performance event in this scheme can be summarized using slightly different terminology. They include a mutual and reciprocal charge between actors and spectators; a hybridizing of effects and affects; and the experience of transformation (we might say transfiguration). In such a scheme, we have moved quite a distance from the *cognitive* figurings performed by *mise en scène*.[11]

The point is not that we are considering competing schemes. Rather, that there is a development from production grounded predominantly in *mise en scène* to production in which *mise en scène* is contingent upon a larger sense of 'eventness'. Pavis recounts Lehmann's formulation of 'eventlike' *mise en scène*, in which 'the stage is presented as an event that owes nothing to a reading of the text, but provides a configuration or an installation, a situation characterized by the co-presence of production and reception, of actors and spectators' (Pavis 2003: 214–15). Lehmann's use of 'eventlike' is intended to describe a *mise en scène* without a dramatic text (more strictly, perhaps, without a playtext) – but it also implies a sense of specialness to the performance. The event is *experienced* as an event precisely because it is unusual, unorthodox, or requires commitment (if only of time) on the part of the spectator. Lehmann gives the example of the 22-hour reading of Homer's *Iliad* presented in Vienna by Angelus Novus in 1986 (Lehmann 2006: 147). To this we can add a number of instances of *longue durée* productions including Peter Brook's nine-hour-long staging of *The Mahabharata* (1985–9); *Gatz*, the full reading of F. Scott Fitzgerald's *The Great Gatsby* staged over eight hours by Elevator Repair Service (2005–12); and, as I discuss below, the all-night production of *Hotel Medea* by Zecora Ura Theatre Network (2009–12). We might also include the multi-part productions, typically lasting around six to nine hours, by Robert Lepage, such as *The Dragon's Trilogy* (2003–7) and *The Blue Dragon* (2008–12). Each entails dramatic mediation that derives from or (in Lepage's case) is subsequently recorded as text. And each requires an unorthodox commitment on the part of the spectator that contributes to the sense of attendance at an 'event'. *Mise en scène* is *incorporated by* the event, rather than the other way round.

Lehmann zooms out further to discuss a 'postdramatic theatre of events'. He sees this as part of a trajectory away from the political commitment and 'demand for changing the world' of the modernist avant gardes (2006: 105) and towards instances of more gratuitous disruption – as exemplified by Squat Theatre's work in the late-1970s in which an audience watches actors performing in a shop window that has a view onto the street, where passers-by can also watch the performance and its interior audience. The event, here, marks the fact of its encounter with its observers. As Lehmann suggests, this is 'theatrical communication . . . as the production of situations for the *self-interrogation, self-exploration, self-awareness* of all participants' (2006: 105; original emphasis).

Such pronounced personal inflection (all that business around the *self*) might be thought increasingly apposite to late-capitalism's consumer culture and its emphasis on individual agency and gratification. This does not necessarily cancel out the effects of textuality or those of dramatic representation. I suggest a slight reformulation: we are interested in the production of evental situations that produce *experience*. These might involve self-interrogation or self-awareness. But they might equally entail heightened experiences of dramatic mediation, indeed of engagement with the issues and import that the event stages.

The journey taken by postdramatic theatre isn't necessarily the departure from the dramatic that Lehmann envisaged when writing his book in the 1990s. Lehmann depicts a shift towards eventness and a simultaneous swing away from mimesis, narration and representation. Nearly twenty years later, the immersive work that you might think would sustain this trajectory suggests a more complicated picture. *Before I Sleep*, *The Crash of the Elysium* and *Hotel Medea*, for instance, draw intertextually on the 'meaning of the text' and certainly the meaning of the intertext (the 'Chekhovian'; the world of Doctor Who; the Medea myth). They depend, structurally, on the coherence provided by texts and intertexts in presenting their own no less cogent worlds. They stage scenes of mimetic representation, albeit framed overtly within evental production. While there is an emphasis on the *process* of viewing, and an *openness* by way of their multi-perspectival mode, there is also a drive to closure and conclusion. In these instances the production is rendered as a complete entity, a 'finished result'. If these works are postdramatic, they are so in a way that recuperates the dramatic. The event mediates the material that it contains. The spectator experiences the event in its event-ness, while enjoying its dramatic mediations (its *mises en scène*). To explore this further, let's look more closely at *Hotel Medea*.

## In the event: a night at *Hotel Medea*

*Hotel Medea* is an interpretation of the myth of Medea, who marries Jason, is betrayed by him and in an act of revenge murders their children. To call it a 'show' doesn't really do it justice. This really is a theatrical event. It is durational (starting at midnight and finishing at dawn) and to varying degrees throughout intermedial and immersive. Its ambition and achievement makes *Hotel Medea* a compelling instance of the twenty-first century's theatre of engagement. This tale from a hot place is presented by the Anglo-Brazilian company Zecora Ura Theatre Network (since renamed as ZU-UK), based jointly in London and Rio de Janeiro. The company develops intercultural and cross-disciplinary work, with a deliberately hybridizing agenda.[12]

In 2011, in collaboration with LIFT (London International Festival of Theatre), Zecora Ura curated *BR-116*, presenting work by English and Brazilian artists in venues across London including the Theatre Royal Stratford East, Royal Festival Hall and Trinity Buoy Wharf (see Prior 2011). The following year the company's *Humble Market: Trade Secrets*, programmed by the London 2012 festival (as part of the cultural Olympiad) and FACT (Foundation for Art and Creative Technology) Liverpool, was a performance-exhibition in which visitors were encouraged to 'experience the hustle and bustle of the Rio de Janeiro carnival from a Brazilian taxi, lie back on the grass . . . and discover what happens when the impersonal automated voice on the telephone suddenly gets very personal indeed'.[13] Brazil's status as host nation of the Olympics in 2016 provided the link that motivated the piece.[14]

Zecora Ura's work hybridizes event and experience. It is performance-based and routinely features diverse media. The activity here is as much to do with producing and facilitating as it is with the creation of specific productions – a meld of entrepreneurship and entertainment that characterized *Hotel Medea*. In London (2010 and 2012), Rio de Janeiro (2010) and Edinburgh (2011) *Hotel Medea* became something of a phenomenon, selling out in spite of what might initially appear to be the unconducive offer of an immersive theatre experience that lasts the whole night. For the members of Zecora Ura, 'Hotel Medea is an act of resistance'. It is not the kind of theatre that

> starts at 8pm and can be preceded by a 'pre-show dinner' and followed by an 'after-show drink' . . . [It] offers a 'dramaturgy of participation' to the audience member which involves risk, intimacy and collective action in a way which sets out to re-write the 'unspoken contract' with the audience not as consumers, but as collaborators.[15]

As it turned out, audiences had a taste for the show's innovations; and word-of-mouth reports and reviews endorsed its distinctive qualities.[16]

There is a relaxed confidence to interactions with the audience that has something of the carnival about it. In a preamble to the first section, in the bar where people have gathered prior to the show, six members of the company each carry a large ring, held by supports on their shoulders, from which is draped a circular curtain of coloured ribbons. We are encouraged to enter the curtains randomly, crowding into one then another. In one 'tent' the performer holds a tea bag, a feather, a stone, and a bag marked 'gold dust'. 'How is your heart?' she asks. 'Feather or stone?' 'Keep it moving!' calls Jorge Lopes Ramos, the show's director and animateur, who is wearing a sun-hat and flip flops. This taster sets a carnivalesque tone: it is eccentric, involving and motional. It deterritorializes the theatre space from the outset; and mixes spectators with performers and scenography in an eccentric set of encounters. As with dreamthinkspeak's *Before I Sleep*, we cannot straightforwardly attribute scenography to a single individual. Artistic direction is by Jorge Lopes Ramos and Persis-Jade Maravala, DJ Dolores and Nwando Ebizie provide the soundtracks to the respective sections, and there are costume and lighting designers and a software programmer. No set designer is named in the credits for the creative team.

## Part I: Zero Hour Market

We enter a room suffused with dry ice. I am directed to a sign on a stand: 'Station 3'. Once we have gathered at our stations, Jorge announces, in an exaggerated Portuguese (Brazilian) patois, 'You have the training people to train you how to make interactive theatre . . .' We are taught a basic dance that entails forming a circle and taking three steps in one direction, then three steps the other way. We learn a variation, then a vocal response in song to a musical accompaniment. Jorge tells us 'Now you can participate in this participatory theatre!' As if it were that easy. And yet, it is. Part of the success of this show is its balance of sudden involvement, where there is nothing else for it than to be within the action, performing under instruction; and the graduated chain of involvements including this brief rite of preparation, easy and unthreatening, that is made less daunting by the possibility of sitting out anything at any time. The integration of the spectator into the event is, as Boenisch suggests, 'careful and caring' (2012).

Part 1 of the trilogy begins. We are in a loose formation around the edges of the room. The Argonauts enter at one end, bare-breasted (both men and women), in helmets, with torches and guns. James Turpin as Jason wears a black leather jacket, a belt of bullets and carries a baseball bat, a mélange of masculine, military and urban American indicators. Persis-Jade Maravala as Medea enters at the other end of the room. There is a DJ on a platform at one end of the space overseeing the dance music. Medea's court dances, unfurling orange and red streamers. Jason and Medea meet, and Jorge translates their dialogue into English.

The spectators dance their easy steps left and right. We are now amidst – performing – a carnivalesque sequence that includes a brief enactment of the shooting of the sheep with the golden fleece, Medea's dismissal of Jason, and Cupid's firing of an arrow into her heart so that she falls in love with her suitor.

The men and women in the audience are separated by a black curtain across the middle of the space, in preparation for the wedding of Jason and Medea. Jason stands on a small box. To an easy beat, the men dance in their circle, left and right, around him. I can see, at the edge of the screen, that the women are also in a circle, dancing. A simple chant starts up. Some of the spectators join in.

Jason is undressed by members of his retinue. After being washed, he is sprinkled with fragrance, dressed, and garlanded with beads (Figure 4.1).[17] It is easy to participate, en masse, within a dramaturgy that places us as watchers, endorsers. The audience provides a visual volume to the *mise en scène*, helping by our very involvement to make it more communal, ritualized and of the moment.

Jason is blindfolded with a white bandage. The screen across the middle of the room is removed. Medea has been prepared in a bridal gown. Jorge calls: 'You can marry each other if you can find each other!' They are spun round by their respective attendants, then freed to mingle through the audience, feeling faces as they go. Popcorn and tickertape are thrown when they eventually touch (Figure 4.2).

A circle is formed that mixes spectators and cast members. Members of the cast take it in turns to recite a snatch of verse, and audience members begin

*Figure 4.1* Jason (James Turpin) is prepared for marriage

Source: Ludovic des Cognets

*Figure 4.2* The spectators celebrate the wedding
Source: Ludovic des Cognets

to join the main phalanx of dancers, in an unforced process of integration. The dance is inclusive, not coercive. Spectators participate by invitation, imbrication, implication. The action has narrative drive, in relation to the depiction of a wedding. It is loud, energetic, yet focused.

Jason makes to leave. This sequence too becomes a dance, in which Jason and Medea are hemmed in, not allowed to depart with the Golden Fleece, the spoil of a previous adventure. Medea trades a poisoned kiss with her brother and three members of her court, who come together to die, blood spilling from their mouths. She cuts her brother's hand from his wrist, in order to take away the case holding the Fleece and leaves her homeland with her new husband.

An interval follows, during which tea and juice are available. We are free to ponder how this happened – this integration of our own bodies into the weft of a wedding, along with our witness, from within, of a drama that enacts courtship, marriage, murder and flight.

## Part II: Drylands

This part is played three times over, with the spectators experiencing each iteration from different places (hence different subject positions). Medea's bedroom is depicted by way of a large double bed on a dais (Figure 4.3), surrounded by a semi-circle of twelve bunk-beds, evoking the beds of Medea's children. Each bunk contains a member of the audience, dressed in pyjamas, covered with a blanket, holding a teddy (Figure 4.4). I am one of around 24 spectators sitting on stools inside the semi-circle, around the double-bed. The Nurse asks questions of individual spectators, circling around fancy, feeling and fidelity. Have you had a broken heart? How was it, falling in love. Are you single? The sequence playfully, briefly, turns the play outwards, asking spectators to place their own voice and testimony into the thematic weave of the drama.

Jason enters. He undresses and goes to bed. Medea makes her way around the bunkbeds, kissing each incumbent on the forehead, saying goodnight to her children. The couple goes to bed together. Jason receives a call on his mobile phone. 'I love you too', he says. His wife, we understand, is asleep. He departs. The Nurse leaves his phone on the bed. It rings. Medea answers, the caller rings off, and Medea investigates what's in the phone.

Iteration Two: I am led outside and line up in a corridor. I am asked to practice a handshake and a 'look' for a meeting with Jason. As we file forward, everyone has her or his photoshoot moment with Jason, who wears a politician's practised smile for each click of the camera (Figure 4.5). We are led into a media room that contains a bank of TV screens. The screens show a mix of news, reality TV, and a considerable amount of film of Jason in civic

*Figure 4.3* Medea (Persis-Jade Maravala) in her bedroom

Source: Ludovic des Cognets

*Figure 4.4* A spectator in bed
Source: Ludovic des Cognets

*Figure 4.5* Posing with Jason (James Turpin)
Source: Ludovic des Cognets

and political mode, meeting people, waving at the camera. We are interpellated as a focus group. We complete a questionnaire: 'How did Jason make you feel? What does it mean to be a real man? Jason's campaign manager is a voice in the headphones we have put on, going over a schedule for an election campaign. There is a live link with the bedroom scene I witnessed previously. There are images of other politicians. We understand that the election takes place tomorrow.

The direct questions again help bind Euripides' ancient Greek drama with contemporary notions of gendered performance and mechanisms of political presentation and efficacy. Our part in the drama here is as extras within the image-system of political power, meta-theatrically presented as a matter of stage management for media circulation.

Iteration Three: my group is taken back into the bedroom, which is strewn with toys. This time I am led to a bed, and invited to put on a pair of flannel pyjamas. My bed has a small cuddly toy. The Nurse reads us a story – it is a picture-book version of the Jason and Medea myth, with comically inappropriate graphics of Medea chopping up the limbs of her brother. We are each served a mug of hot chocolate. The scene in the bedroom plays out again, as if we, the children, are asleep. The drama is viewed from within. This time, instead of finishing at the point when Medea discovers Jason's phone, the scene continues, filmed live and relayed on the wall behind the bed and on the side walls. Medea wears a nightshirt, Cupid's arrow of Act One arrow lodged in her breast – she tries and fails to remove it – in a piece that mixes hyper-real staging devices with choreographic, metaphorical and symbolic materials.

There is a different rhythm to this act in comparison to the first. The repetition of action enables a more staccato pace, but also moments of reflection and near-repose. We are pressed into situation and action, and disported around diverse places of spectating across different media. We have been interpellated as wedding guests, members of the public meeting a political leader, a focus group, children.[18] The section is beautifully paced.

It is 4am. My eyes feel tired. I feel a little cold, so put on my jumper. I am glad of the hot chocolate and biscuits in the interval. There is a buzz of conversation. Some audience members are slumped against walls.

## Part III: Feast of Dawn

The third act is set initially in a nightclub for women. (The men are given wigs to wear, as if 'in disguise'.) A series of vaudeville-style acts expand on themes of the piece. The club is then broken up by a military intervention. We learn that Medea has been raped – we watch as, splayed across a shopping trolley, she is made up and 'distressed' by her female attendants. Headlines and text are projected across the back wall.

The piece ends with the audience gathered in a large space that contains the shrines of Medea's children – whose bodies are represented by two

*Figure 4.6* Spectators play Medea's children in death

Source: Ludovic des Cognets

members of the audience, lying still *in situ* (Figure 4.6). They are wearing earpieces that play a soundtrack just for them, so that they too continue to be sensorially engaged. At the front of the space, Medea kisses audience members as if they were her children. She reads a night-time story that tells of her wanting to inflict pain on Jason, and always seeing him figured in her children. We understand that she has killed them.

The mood is very somber. We file out, and are led downstairs to a long line of trestle tables, containing bread, jam, fruit – breakfast (Figure 4.7). Medea sits at the head, the Maid at the foot, audience members all around. Medea asks: 'Do you think it was too much?' We are facilitated to join hands in a circle. The hands are dropped, and we eat.

### Encountering the event

What aesthetic strategies and techniques are in play here, and how do they illustrate a move from *mise en scène* to *mise en événement*? First, spectators are *interpellated* as participants – we are not just involved in closer proximity to the action, but positioned as players in it. The positioning is partly functional (we stand in particular places, observe from selected perspectives, as appropriate to

*Figure 4.7* Breakfast is served. Persis-Jade Maravala as Medea, Thelma Sharma as the Maid

Source: Ludovic des Cognets

our 'role' at the time) and partly verbal (our function is named). We are variously members of Jason's retinue, Medea's court, members of a focus group, spies in a nightclub, Medea's children. We are not required to perform in these roles – to 'act' as if we are the figures of the interpellation. It is as if instead we are painted in, placed (in our own personae) as dramaturgically coherent figures in a theatrical narrative. The fact of being called something – 'my child', 'colleague', 'you', 'we' – produces an affect of affiliation that becomes part of the experience of the event.

The dramatic narrative is thereby differently *figured*. It is played out for us, but also populated by our own bodies. The separation between actor (specialist to be watched) and spectator (amateur and observer) remains valid but is nonetheless blurred. We are in the midst of what Boenisch describes as 'a complex interference of representation and presence' (2010: 171).[19] We understand dramatic action not least as it is filled out by other spectators who figure in the respective *mises en scène* of, for instance, party, bedtime or nightclub performance.

The production is thereby structured by way of *multiple perspectives*, more overtly than might be the case in a theatrical arrangement that places the performance in one place and the spectators in another. This is so in two senses. First we are encouraged to take the subject positions of different characters at different points (protagonists, children, hangers-on). Second, we understand that there are other people like us watching (experiencing) the drama from over there, or in another room – living the same piece a little differently. Multiplicity of position is staged as part of the procedure of this form of *mise en événement*. The performance is thereby more contingent than in other modes of presentation – contingent upon subject positions, places of spectatorship, affective moments that may be distinct from one spectator to another.

In this particular show (and this may be less true of other instances of immersive theatre) there is a tendency to *ritualize* the spectator's encounter with the event. This is most evidently the case in the extended wedding scene that provides much of the focus of Section I. It is also true of scenarios in which a bedtime routine is played out, a rape is evoked and its aftermath presented, mourning is performed, and finally breakfast is shared. Through such ritual encounters we are integrated in dramatic mediation that tells a particular story, expands on its significance, and embeds us in its theatrical scenario of affect.

The event is not just watched or received, but *encountered*. And the encounter is one of bodily engagement. Through each of the means above the production produces sensation, activity and experience. This is the case not only with immersive theatre but a range of other cultural productions: different kinds of live performance, sports matches, video games and, sometimes, social media interactions. I don't want to say that we are quivering sensators at all turns. It seems clear, however, that the production of experience is a key feature of contemporary performance culture. In that case, *mise en événement*, as a concept to do with the creation of an event, will only take us so far. In moving from *mise en scène* and the arrangement of the stage, we are really interested in the arrangement of experience: *mise en sensibilité*. In Chapter 8 I look more closely at the notion of an experience economy and various ways in which spectators are enaged. At this point, it will suffice to reflect upon the notion of *mise en sensibilité* as a new coordinate for the mediation of performance.

## Towards *mise en sensibilité*

The French term *sensibilité* means 'sensibility', as in artistic sensibility or sensibilities that are offended (Allain *et al.* 2006: 903). It has connotations of sensitivity, sympathy, feeling, emotion and affiliation. It captures the oscillation between the deliberate and the unwitting in our relationship to art and culture – between unconsciously formed tastes and a talent (or otherwise) for awareness and choice.

Any recourse to 'sensibility' puts us in mind of the term's appearance in mid-eighteenth-century Europe, as it applied to the work of writers including Goethe, Rousseau, Sterne and Wordsworth, and widely across literary genres. Janet Todd notes that:

> 'Sensibility', an innate sensitiveness or susceptibility revealing itself in a variety of spontaneous activities such as crying, swooning and kneeling, is

defined in 1797 by the *Encyclopaedia Britannica* (3rd edn) as 'a nice and delicate perception of pleasure or pain, beauty or deformity' . . . 'In France where 'sensibilité' translated the English sensibility, a new term 'sensiblerie' developed to distinguish sensibility from the debased and self-indulgent quality.

(Todd 1986: 7–8)

The latter quality is sensibility's close cousin sentimentality, which denotes cheap and mawkish displays of emotion – to be avoided in any age. As the mention of swooning and kneeling indicates, however, there was a sense that some emotions simply could not be contained. The eighteenth-century notion of sensibility 'appears physically based, a quality of nerves turning easily to illness and described in contemporary medical treatises in terms of movements within the body' (Todd 1986: 7–8). The effects of sensibility, then, were also affects, physically evident and nothing if not embodied.

This feature of the mid-eighteenth century – its interest in and expression through embodiment – is echoed by scholars in more recent publications, and resonates with a focus upon encounter and experience towards the beginning of our present millennium. Paul Goring opens his 'Preface' to *The Rhetoric of Sensibility in Eighteenth-Century England* with the observation that '[t]his is a book about bodies – about the eloquence of bodies and their capacity to express symbolically the values of a particular culture. The "rhetoric of sensibility" under scrutiny here, then, is a bodily rhetoric' (2005: ix). By way of illustrating this, Goring discusses Aaron Hill's *The Art of Acting*, published in various versions over a twenty-year period from 1733: 'Hill advances an acting technique in which the performer should attempt to *feel* the emotions which the fictional character would feel in the various situations engineered by the playwright' (2005: 3, original emphasis). As Goring notes, this is different from Diderot's account, which cautions against emotional extremes in acting style, indicating some of the tensions not just in approaches to acting during the period but in the construction of what it was to be 'sensible'. Goring nonetheless notes a wide engagement in the eighteenth century 'with the human body as an eloquent object' (5), and thereby with public modes of disporting the body. In this corporeal economy, knowing how to act is as important as the appearance itself. This is a matter of judgement as well as physical disposition. In this schema, as he observes of Hill's acting theory, 'Sensibility is essential to proper dramatic expression . . . but in order for it to be truly affecting, it must be managed and refined within an aesthetic code' (2005: 138).

The task here is to meld appropriate judgement, behaviour and expression, while acknowledging that feelings will be felt. Jerome McGann's *The Poetics of Sensibility* takes the same tack. McGann aims to recuperate the eighteenth-century lineage of sensibility, affective not least in and through language, from the pejorative judgements applied by literary modernism, represented principally by T. S. Eliot. As he suggests, the 'literatures of sensibility and sentiment . . . assume that no human action of any consequence is possible – including "mental" action – that is not led and driven by feeling, affect, emotion' (1996: 5–6). This opens into questions of cognition. McGann argues that eighteenth-century sensibility is not to do with a split between thinking and feeling, but a turn to ingrained and embodied knowledge: 'thought began to imagine itself not as a set of concepts or ideas but as a cognitive process' (1996: 23). Thinking itself is a corporeal (indeed neural) act, bound up with bodiliness.

It is perhaps no coincidence that this reappraisal of eighteenth-century sensibility should occur in the wake of the renewed interest in phenomenology in theatre and performance studies, which reaches from the work of States, Wilshire and Garner to the writings of scholars including Fischer-Lichte, Lehmann and Pavis, as suggested above. As Stanton Garner puts it in *Bodied Spaces* (his account of phenomenal aspects of the work of playwrights including Chekhov and Beckett): 'actuality continually pressures representation/fiction/ illusion with the phenomenal claims of an experiential moment' (1994: 41). Artistic production, then, *lands* in sensation in the present. That which is seen (read, watched) is also by definition experienced. In a work also published in the early 1990s, Deleuze and Guattari argue for an inherence between the artwork and its reception in and through the senses:

> What is preserved – the thing or the work of art – is *a bloc of sensations, that is to say, a compound of percepts and affects.* . . . Sensation is not realized in the material without the material passing completely into the sensation, into the percept or affect.
>
> (1991: 164, 166–7; original emphasis)

In a rather different vein, Lehmann addresses postdramatic theatre's apparent taste for incoherence and its detachment from direct political commitment, as noted in Chapter 1. He arrives at a formulation that resonates with those above:

> Theatre can respond [to disconnected images] only with a *politics of perception*, which could at the same time be called *an aesthetic of responsibility (or response-ability).* . . . it can move the mutual implication of actors and spectators in the theatrical production of images into the centre and thus make visible the broken thread between personal experience and perception.
>
> (Lehmann 2006: 185–6; original emphasis)

Here again, then, the link between percept and affect. Lehmann is concerned to find a social, indeed ideological, dividend to what might otherwise seem to be a theatre that has emptied itself of civic engagement. The call for any sort of 'politics of . . .' suggests as much. The procedural engagement of actors and spectators in the *same act* is a part of what connects this analysis to wider phenomenological currents, and, not least, to the increasingly blurred boundary between acting and spectating that the present volume in part explores. Lehmann's account pre-empts the growth of participatory and immersive theatre, but it seems all the more perceptive given the subsequent advance of this form of theatre. For Lehmann, 'the mutual implication of actors and spectators' is not solely a matter of aesthetic description but also of purposive social engagement in and through theatre. As he suggests, 'It will increasingly become an important task for "theatrical" practices in the widest sense to create playful situations in which affects are released and played out' (2006: 186). The sentence is portentous. In moving from a predominant grounding in *mise en scène*, where the play took place on stage (over there), new theatre has moved to a playground in which *mise en sensibilité* predominates, where the event takes place with us inside it. The arrangement of affect, which I explore more closely in Chapter 8, is not simply a question of aesthetic organization, nor even one of effective event production. It implicates the *matter* of theatre – what it is about, deals with, dramatizes – with its *mediation*. When we are within mediation, as participants or immersants, we are differently response-able. It is tempting to suggest that with response-ability comes power, but that would oversimplify things. The power at stake here is a mixture of agency, authentic feeling, witness from within and – not least – the power to withdraw, not to participate. It is not always easy to make our own choices, but that too should remain a possibility.

## Notes

1  The show was created by Felix Barrett and Tom MacRae, written by Tom MacRae, based on an original idea by Steven Moffat, directed by Felix Barrett. It premiered at the Manchester International Festival, 1–17 July 2011 and was presented in Ipswich 15 June–8 July 2012. I saw it at Ipswich on 7 July 2012. Details of the production are at http://punchdrunk.com/past-shows/article/the-crash-of-the-elysium.
2  See Lavender 2013 for a discussion of the Weeping Angels in relation to statue performance.
3  Erika Fischer-Lichte notes that the earliest reference to the expression '*mettre sur scène*' 'can be found in Diderot's *Salons* dating from 1765 where it refers to painting' (2008: 215, n. 3).
4  For a discussion of metatext see also Pavis 1982: 149–153.
5  See Casati and Varzi (1996) for a collection of essays that consider key aspects of the event as described and discussed in philosophy. See also Schneider 2005.
6  In his introduction Franko traces critical perspectives including those of Freud, Peirce, Bateson, Fanon, Sartre and Schechner.
7  See Austin 1975 (1962).
8  Writing a little before Foucault, Hannah Arendt provides another approach to conceiving the affective nature of the event. See Arendt 1998; Barder and McCourt 2010: 137; and Vázquez 2006: 51–2.
9  See Cremona *et al.* 2004, which gathers work by a number of contributors.
10  For Fischer-Lichte's analysis of the three key features, see 2008: 163–80.

11 The term *mise en scène* nonetheless remains important to Fischer-Lichte, and she devotes a section to it (2008: 182–90).
12 The company's website is at http://zu-uk.com/.
13 www.youtube.com/watch?v=QmYXEW2D2RM&feature=youtube.
14 See https://driftprojectinternational.wordpress.com/.
15 www.hotelmedea.co.uk/#!vstc9=clockcontact/vstc0=about.
16 *Hotel Medea* was presented at the Arcola Theatre, London, as part of LIFT2010; the Oi Futuro/TEMPO Fesival in Rio de Janeiro; Summerhall as part of the Edinburgh Fringe Festival in 2011; and the Hayward Gallery, London, in 2012. A website for the project is at www.hotelmedea.co.uk/; for videos of performances, see http://vimeo.com/hotelmedea. I saw the show at the Summerhall in Edinburgh, 13–14 August 2011.
17 The images are from the production of the show in London in 2010.
18 In Louis Althusser's analysis (1970: 11), subjects are interpellated by being explicitly positioned – 'hailed' – in relation to social processes and structures that are always already ideological. In recognizing herself as she is named (customer; trouble-maker; mother; lawyer), the individual likewise acknowledges her place within a power structure, and the work of ideology is thereby sustained. For an account of Althusserian interpellation, see Nguyen 2004: np.
19 Boenisch writes here about productions by Katie Mitchell, Frank Castorf and Chris Goode, which are not immersive but entail 'an act of encounter' (171).

# Chapter 5

# Sincerely yours

## From the actor to the persona

Between the mid-1980s and mid-1990s the notion of 'character' in performance underwent what appeared to be a fatal crisis. Philip Auslander's *From Acting to Performance*, a collection of essays written over this period, traces the upheaval. Auslander looks at shifts in theatre and performance – and in ways of writing about these disciplines in the aftermath of deconstruction and post-structuralism – in an historical trajectory from modernism to postmodernism. In his introductory essay, Auslander notes Richard Schechner's resonant declaration of 1992 that 'The new paradigm is "performance," not theatre' (Auslander 1997: 2). Auslander takes a more nuanced view, suggesting that 'Performance Studies appears to be a new articulation of the Theatre Studies paradigm, not a revolutionary new paradigm' (3). Nonetheless, he is clear that a significant shift has taken place. Whichever position you take, the rise of Performance Studies – with its interest in behaviour, social efficacy and a wide variety of modes of performance – marks the separation between representational drama (let's say fictionalized storytelling) on the one hand and performance as presentation (rather than the pretence of stage acting) on the other. Auslander describes this turn as 'a progressive redefinition of theatrical mimesis away from "character" toward "performance persona," with consequent redefinitions of the function of the performer's self in relation to performance' (1997: 6).

The distinction is useful, although vexed. In *The Death of Character*, published a year before Auslander's collection of essays, Elinor Fuchs discusses a transition in western theatre from modernism to postmodernism, observable through changes in the concept of character in dramatic presentation. Fuchs takes a long view, tracing the shift back to modernist forms including symbolism and expressionism at the turn of the twentieth century, and finding it figured in aspects of the work of Ibsen and Chekhov. The death throes of character are nonetheless felt in postmodern theatre practices, where Fuchs discusses work by Peter Handke, Liz LeCompte, Richard Foreman and Cindy Sherman. She suggests that 'a cultural "death of character" [is] . . . shorthand for an explosion of doubt about ontological grounding' and that it 'necessarily brings about an expansion of the theatrical term' (Fuchs 1996: 14). The doubt is to do with shifting constructions of (or problematizing of) the self, gathering pace through the twentieth century as new discourses and critical strategies questioned the stability and trustworthiness of individual identity. The expansion concerns different forms of representation in the theatre, including symbolist, allegorical and ironic treatments. This leads Fuchs to describe 'a new poetics of theater' that marks a departure from character archetypes in favour of more indeterminate dramatic figures; and entails diverse modes of theatrical presentation. As Rebecca Schneider observes, 'Fuchs explicates . . . the postmodern turn in drama as a "literalization" where "the artists of performance theater don't merely haunt presence-structure with trace-structure, they directly stage the traces"' (1997: 541). In other words, the constructed nature of character becomes more apparent: the 'being' of a character is overtaken by the formal marks that she leaves. And character is more contingent on the means by which she is mediated.

This analysis resonates with that of Hans-Thies Lehmann in *Postdramatic Theatre*, published in German in the same year as Fuchs's book came out. Fuchs wrote a stinging review of Lehmann's monograph, observing that the ideas Lehmann presents were in any case in wider circulation. This is true in terms of broader thematic connections between some of the arguments of *The Death of Character* and *Postdramatic Theatre*. While he does not focus on characterization *per se*, he traces a shift from the dramatic, founded on playtexts in which characters appear in narratives, to the postdramatic, in which theatre moves towards sensorial arrangements and reality-effects that privilege the present person and her body over the imagined character.

Auslander (without at this point referencing Lehmann, whose book had not yet appeared in English nor impacted on the Anglophone theatre studies scene) expands on the kind of acting associated with the postdramatic, in a discussion of Willem Dafoe's performance in the Wooster Group's *LSD (. . . Just the High Points . . .)* (1984–5). The production – an icon of postmodernism – includes self-referential material on the creation of the piece, and presents a profoundly ironic reading (or rather, rendering) of aspects of Arthur Miller's *The Crucible*. As Auslander notes:

> Dafoe's performance persona is at once his presentation of self to the audience and his image of himself performing. There is a certain frankness to the approach; the performed image is generated by the activity of the moment, by what the audience sees him doing under the immediate circumstances. Task/vision, vision/task; 'The perfection of a persona is a noble way to go.'
>
> (Auslander 1997: 45)

The closing phrase is like a mission statement for much that has come afterwards. In similar vein, consider John McGrath's account of the work of Dafoe's colleague Ron Vawter:

Vawter was a key collaborator in a series of Wooster Group works, much admired for his ability to create an extremely complex performance without seeming to 'act', without, that is, attempting to create a coherent character or present a history other than his own. In pieces such as *Frank Dell's Temptation of St Anthony*, Vawter would often stand downstage centre, muttering into the microphone, redefining the audience's under-standing of charisma. Vawter's seemingly direct presence was, however, always mediated. The microphone was rarely absent; the performance took place within a complexly ordered structure of mechanical effects, video and sound recording.

(McGrath 2004: 151–2)

I recall the controlled yet throwaway panache with which Vawter placed his foot in front of him, in order to strike a pose before speaking into the microphone as Vershinin (from Chekhov's *Three Sisters*) in The Wooster Group's *Brace Up!* (1991). This was a performance of striking presence and studied dramatic disruption, as the character of Vershinin was both conjured through a pose and renounced through Vawter's insertion of himself between the text and its theatrical reproduction. McGrath's account makes clear both the 'presence-structure' and 'trace-structure' of Vawter's performance, evidently mediated while also unique and originary. And it accords with the sense that drama is subsumed to the presence- and sense-effects of performance. It marks the replacement of characterization with charisma, indeed persona.[1]

You would think that this shift has now become an orthodoxy if you look at productions by directors such as Richard Maxwell, Marianne Weems (artistic director of the Builders Association) and John Collins (artistic director of Elevator Repair Service) in New York, or Frank Castorf, Christoph Marthaler, Roderigo Garcia, Christoph Schlingensief and Romeo Castellucci in western Europe. All employ(ed) strategies that stop you empathizing with the 'Character Named Character' (Fuchs 1996: 21). Consider, too, work by companies such as Blast Theory, Ontroerend Goed and Rimini Protokoll, discussed elsewhere in this volume, who in different ways have done away with those pretending figures that we once called actors. Yet you could be forgiven for wondering what the fuss was all about, if you think of celebrated television characters such as Detective Jimmy McNulty in *The Wire* (HBO 2002–8), played by Dominic West; or Detective Inspector Sarah Lund in *The Killing* (DR 2007, 2009, 2012), played by Sofie Gråbøl. In the theatre, West's performance as The Man in Jez Butterworth's *The River* (2012) conveyed (in *Guardian* critic Michael Billington's account) 'profound sadness, insecurity and sense of loss'.[2] Johnnie 'Rooster' Byron, played by Mark Rylance, appeared as a priapic embodiment of a disjointed Britain in Butterworth's play *Jerusalem* (2009). Rylance won Olivier and Tony Awards for Best Actor for his performance as this partic-ular central character. Indeed the work of actors such as Rylance, West, Juliette Binoche, Cate Blanchett, Kevin Spacey, Ian McKellen and Simon

Russell-Beale across theatre, film, television and radio demonstrates that in-depth, well-worked characterization remains a core component of contemporary drama in different media. What is the real trajectory here? Did character really disintegrate in the shockwaves of postmodernism and postdramatism? Or did it keep going regardless? Perhaps Character never died at all but emerged from postmodernity with a new twinkle in her eye.[3]

What do we understand by 'character', after all? We mean a figuring of a self; the presentation of personhood by way of actions that allow us to envisage an individual. Even where character is very archetypal or caricatural, as with the modernist figures of the Cashier in Toller's *From Morn to Midnight*, or Strindberg's Julie; or (to take more recent examples) Jeffrey Skilling in Lucy Prebble's *Enron* (2009) and Nick in Elevator Repair Service's *Gatz* (2004), we can flesh out from the performance an imagined Other, shaped by subjecthood. The binary split envisaged by theatre and performance scholarship before the turn of the millennium – in which fictional character is replaced by a 'performance persona' – may not be quite so stark. Ridout reminds us that it is always a 'suspect permission' to grant 'the existence of such a person as "the character"' (2006: 74). Who could disagree, given that we all know that characters are always only constructions? Yet theatre frequently hinges on this suspect permission. The postdramatic persona brings with it tropes of characterization that have proved difficult to do without – personhood and individualized behaviour on the part of the persona, and affiliation and attribution on the part of the spectator.

The term 'persona' suggests something person-like, a figure or being. It already conveys a tinge of performance, derived from its etymology: it means 'mask' in Latin. One can adopt a persona, or present a persona – be something or someone a little different from one's usual state. If persona can mean something more *actual* than a character, it also evokes an appearance that is *different* from one's normative self. This is expressly the case in Jungian psychology, where the term is used to indicate a mask that is both contextual (depending on situation) and concealing (of inner self). As Jung suggests: 'Fundamentally the persona is nothing real: it is a compromise between individual and society as to what a man should appear to be. . . . The persona is a semblance, a two-dimensional reality, to give it a nickname' (1966: 158; see also Stevens 1999: 42–3). Jung does acknowledge that there is 'something individual' in the way the persona is delineated. Nonetheless, the performance aspect predominates. The persona is 'a mask that feigns individuality, making others and oneself believe that one is individual, whereas one is simply acting a role through which the collective psyche speaks' (157). Auslander's turn to persona in 1997 posits an originary non-pretending personhood; Jung's posits performance as an essential aspect of the term.

The distinction, then, between character and persona is not necessarily straightforward, for 'persona' itself is a slippery term. It suggests a radical departure from character, but also a means of sustaining some of the attributes of character (appearance, difference, personality type) within any given presentation. I will address this further by way of the sorts of persona presented by three machines and two magicians.

## Persona Ex Machina

The Belgian artist Kris Verdonck creates installations and performance pieces that feature human performers, machines and objects.[4] Each of these figures are 'actors' in the sense of putting action (and sometimes inaction) into play. Verdonck's pieces present distilled scenarios in which individual figures, or sometimes pairs or groups, are pinned in a (re)presentational scheme as if butterflies for gallery-style observation. In *In* (2003), for instance, a fully-dressed performer stands submerged in a glass tank full of water, like a pickled artifact in a museum. He breathes through a miked-up tube running out from the tank, thereby providing an amplified soundscape to his incarceration. Briefcase in hand, he is an ordinary working man in suspended animation, a figural capture of the everyday, in a trope of pure presence and presentation. (Verdonck has also presented the piece with a female performer.) In *Heart* (2004), a woman holding a bag stands in front of the audience in a studio theatre. We can hear the amplified beating of her heart. After 500 beats the woman is mechanically yanked upwards and backwards to a crash mat against the back wall. On landing, she returns quickly downstage, looking out wordlessly to the audience before being pulled back again on the appropriate heartbeat by her unseen harness. In *Duet* (2005), a male figure is fixed (again invisibly) to a device that holds him in mid-air and turns him slowly through 360 degrees in front of us. He is in a clinch with a female, who shifts her position in order to remain suspended as the pair rotate, clasped in an emblem of attraction or adherence. In *Stills*, which I discuss in Chapter 9, living figures appear trapped within the walls on which they are projected by video.

Verdonck's pieces are conceptual, framing a scenario; but also affective, prompting visceral reactions in response to elemental qualities of water, light, fire and breath, for instance, and images of discomfort, dependence or abjection. If these themes are worked with human performers who are subject to mechanical constraints and processes, they also apply to objects for which Verdonck creates a sort of personhood. *Actor #1* (2010) provides a good example.[5] It includes three elements, so that the spectator moves through a series of spaces in order to take in the piece as a whole. The first, entitled *Mass*, is a swirling mist inside a rectangular container (not unlike a portable swimming pool), around which the spectators stand. The mist has, as it were, a life of its own, gaining and diminishing in density, moving in undulations in a brooding, threatening manner. The second, *Humanid*, features a small mannequin dressed in a suit and tie. The face of an actor speaking a text by Samuel Beckett is projected onto the mannequin, creating a peculiarly unstable effect of presence, personhood and irreality. The third element is a bouncing piston entitled *Dancer*

*#3*. The installation as a whole is completed by a short film in which, as Verdonck's website indicates, 'the philosopher and mathematician Jean-Paul Van Bendegem outlines the history of the homunculus in his own inimitable fashion.'[6] The website goes on to say that *Actor #1* presents '[t]hree variations on the metamorphosis from chaos to order.' The metamorphosis in which I am interested for present purposes is that from object to persona. This is exemplified by *Dancer #3*.

We enter a room in which there is a robotic figure inside a cordoned–off space, like a small guy in a boxing ring (Figure 5.1). In appearance the figure is constituted of a spring inside a steel frame, affixed to a square base, powered by a hydraulic piston that acts as a jumping foot. A number of cables run from the machine to the grid overhead. They provide electrical power, connect the device to a computer (at once a semi–remote brain and master), and hoist up the figure when it falls over, which happens inevitably once its bouncing tips it off balance. This is a performance in real–time, for we cannot know at which point the object will topple. There is an element of serendipity. Once it has fallen, its pistonic foot sometimes performs a few more spurts like an unwonted death–twitch. It is difficult not to ascribe personality to the machine by way of adverbial accumulation. It bounces cheerfully or wearily, falls pathetically or heroically, is lifted cruelly or maternally, recommences blithely or gamely, caught in a cycle of activity and failure; life and death.

*Figure 5.1* Ready for action (again). Kris Verdonck's *Dancer #3*

Source: Reinelt Hiel

In his discussion of chatterbots (software programmes that engage in conversation with human interactants), Auslander observes that 'chatterbots are themselves performing entities that construct their performances at the same time as we witness them. . . . They perform live, but they are not a-live' (2002: 20). Likewise *Dancer #3* performs live. It invites immediate connection with its titular predecessors. Verdonck's *Dancer #1* (2003) presents an L-shaped piece of tubular steel suspended from a motorized disc. When the disk turns, the shape performs a jig that becomes more or less frenetic depending on the speed of gyration. Towards the end of the routine it emits smoke from its 'head'. The whole presentation lasts for about a minute, and comes over as a pure piece of performance by an object that seems characterized by obedience, effort and a form of wild abandon. *Dancer #2* (2009) places a combustion engine on a plinth, inviting the onlooker to admire (or otherwise) the brutish accumulation of sound and energy as it inexorably accelerates to a smoking crescendo. The machine is both extraordinarily potent and comically redundant, roaring away on its immobile white stand not unlike the sort of chuntering bore that my Scottish friends refer to as a 'blowhard'. There is something deliberately Beckettian to all these performances of earnest effort, constraint and enforced recommencement.[7]

In her text on the company's website, dramaturg Marianne Van Kerkhoven remarks that:

> Kris Verdonck's actors, his characters, . . . are the transition between man and machine. They are near-cyborgs. But their tragedy consists precisely of this 'near'. They are intermediate creatures, in full transition and suffering from the fact that they are neither the one nor the other.
>
> (Van Kerkhoven: nd)

Kerkhoven paints these 'actors' as people. Verdonck's turn to the term 'dancer' – normally someone so lithe and agile – invites this humanizing move. Further, he conceives his objects' anthropomorphism in a theatrical paradigm. As he suggests:

> Objects are the perfect tragic heroes. Much like the protagonists of Greek Antiquity, they set out to achieve a certain aim and they will keep ploughing away at it until it kills them. The analogy is perfect. [. . .] Both the object and the tragic hero will do everything it takes to accomplish their aim. [. . .] So I think of objects as the perfect actors. They are able to create a level of theatrical tension that is real. [. . .] Plus objects do not pretend, for the simple reason they are unable to. They are what they are. I am a great fan of this sincerity of objects. In addition, we entertain an emotional connection with objects.[9]

The object, here, has a persona. But the persona is not 'put on' in the sense that a Jungian subject might present a version of the collective unconscious;

or a postmodern performer might ironically assume a version of herself. It derives from the ineffable 'sincerity' of the object. By this means, the object becomes characterized as an individual.

In their 'Introduction' to *The Rhetoric of Sincerity*, a volume that considers sincerity in and in relation to performance, van Alphen and Bal propose that sincerity can be conceived separately from subjectivity, and considered 'as framed by media, so as to become a media effect instead of a subjectivity effect.' Hence it is 'an issue of rhetoric' (2009: 5). The separation of sincerity from an 'inner self' is helpful. Sincerity can obtain without revealing some deep foundation of personality. In his discussion of amateurism in nineteenth- and twentieth-century theatre, Salvato notes both the endurance of ideas of sincerity as a guarantor of certain sorts of authenticity and engagement; and the emergence of sincerity 'through careful regulation' by way of controlled performance (2009: 71–3 [73]). It is, then, a matter of controlled communication and shared understanding of cultural codes. This helps to explain Verdonck's observation about the sincerity of objects. If sincerity coalesces as an effect of mediation, it does so in ways that are affective – that's to say, ways that produce feelings and responses in subjects. It is an effect of actions that accrue an affective charge in context. The vehicle of mediation in the case of Verdonck's *Dancer* series is, purely, action within situation. The context, here is most immediately spatial, rhythmic, material – to do with the speed at which things are done to the object, the reactions that are played out in it, and the object's movement from rest (stasis) to reaction (energy). The theatricality of the object is postdramatic in a primary sense of Lehmann's term – to do with sensory charges and spatio-visual presentation rather than narrative drive. And yet the *fact* of sincerity – the seriously present, not-playing, always responsive aspect of the object – helps to underpin its associative persona as it accrues the 'ideas, percepts and emotional experiences' (Stevens 1999: 32) that we read off its presentation.

Peter Eckersall sees *Actor #1* as an engagement with what it is to be an actor in a mediatized performance landscape, observing that the piece realizes '[t]erms and ideas connected to processes of acting, such as "character", "agency", "expression", "truth" and "pretence"' (Eckersall 2012: 72). It does indeed throw questions of acting into relief. To consider these further, we can look back to a celebrated formulation of the actor's work. Denis Diderot's *Paradox of Acting*, written in 1773–7 and published in 1830, proposes that in order to move the audience, the actor must remain unmoved. That's to say, the actor's task (task/vision, to follow Auslander) is to show rather than to be (see Gebauer and Wulf 1995: 174–85). Diderot articulates, from within the eighteenth century, a relationship between performing and being in which the business of the actor is to create *effect* for the spectator rather than to 'live' the character in the manner that would come to be associated with Stanislavski (at least in some readings of his work) and Strasberg over a century later. As Gebauer and Wulf observe, Diderot's thinking is 'wholly indebted to the rhetorical tradition in establishing effect as the goal' (1995: 177). We might now often say that the purpose of the effect is not necessarily to present a position (rhetorically) but to produce *affect*. Given what happened to 'character' in the late-twentieth and twenty-first centuries, as noted above, the paradox seems resonantly postmodern, even if it departs from Diderot in being connected more with abjection and reception than representation. Effect is often to do with the offering up of the performer, and the feeling responsiveness of the spectator, at least as much as it is with recognition and realization in the rationalist sense. Its thrust concerns the *work* of the actor – the business of being a technician of expression, someone who is in control of presentation without an overly messy personal immersion. It also concerns the work of the spectator, who is subject to feeling through the perception of that which is presented, irrespective of anyone else's (the actor's) emotional engagement. *Dancer #3* perfectly represents Diderot's paradox in a postdramatic domain. How can a piston have feelings? We know this is impossible. And yet the piston *produces* feelings. It does so through *mise en scène*, *mise en sensibilité* and action, in a postdramatic scenario of affect, by appearing to be a persona. Not a pretending persona, simply something that has personal characteristics. In her discussion of the body/bodies in Verdonck's work, Sarah Bay-Cheng observes that:

> the body is powerful only so far as it makes mistakes: greatest of all is its potential to die. Looking at Verdonck's performing bodies, then, is to observe bodies caught in a moment of transition, stretched almost to the breaking point between technological determinism and biological breakdown.
>
> (Bay-Cheng 2012: 72)

She ends her essay with the observation that Verdonck's forthcoming pieces (at her time of writing) replace human actors with robots, and wonders 'whether objects can take on the vulnerability of the human' (2012: 72). *Actor #1* suggests that they can. Notwithstanding this, the actor in Diderot's terms is 'self-controlled' (Gebauer and Wulf 1992: 179) – able to shape and calibrate that which s/he presents. This clearly cannot be the case with the piston, whose control rests entirely with external agents (the fabricator, the director, the operator, the computer). The paradox is thereby intensified. Characteristics appear wholly through context and construction, rather than the personable inhabiting of character.

## Showmen and sincerity

To explore this further, let's consider two manifestations of the showman-magician. You might think of this figure as being nothing if not insincere and inauthentic. Not unlike *Dancers #1, 2* and *3*, however, the American magician David Blaine and his British counterpart Derren Brown present personae that trade heavily in contemporary forms of authenticity and sincerity. In *Above the*

*Below* (2003), Blaine spent 44 days and nights apparently enclosed in a plexiglass box suspended 30 feet above the South Bank of the River Thames in London, next to Tower Bridge, surviving only on water.[10] This was one of a series of endurance stunts, following *Buried Alive* (1999), in which Blaine was sealed underground in Manhattan in a plastic coffin for seven days, with only a hand buzzer for emergency use connecting him to the world above; *Frozen in Time* (2000), in which he was encased in a block of ice for 63 hours in Times Square, New York City; and *Vertigo* (2002), in which he spent 35 hours standing atop a 100-foot-high and 22-inch-wide pillar erected in Bryant Park, also in New York City. Other acts of endurance have followed.[11] This work is alluring partly because of the concatenation of the biophysical feat of endurance with Blaine's persona as a high-calibre trickster and magician. The latter is part of Blaine's performance identity following the broadcast of his shows *Street Magic* (1997) and *Magic Man* (1999). There are repeated cries of 'How did you do that!?' from the onlookers to Blaine's street magic, as some implausible trick or other is performed. A young man chooses a card, for it to be revealed stuck into his waistband underneath his t-shirt ('Spoof 1'); three women shriek as Blaine levitates in front of them ('Levitation'); a couple look on awestruck as Blaine puts his hand through the glass window of a jeweller's shopfront to retrieve the wristwatch on display, that we understand he has only a minute ago spirited from the woman's wrist ('The Jewelry Store'). Confronted by such demonstrations of the impossible, there can surely be nothing trustworthy about the feats of endurance. And yet they display the paraphernalia of authenticity. In a number of these stunts Blaine is permanently visible. He is also placed as an object of medical concern. Blaine was, we understand, taken directly to hospital after *Frozen in Time*. He apparently 'entered an agreement with doctors from Yale University to monitor him in order to study the human physiological reaction to prolonged submersion.'[12] A 600-word paper addressing Blaine's physical condition at the conclusion of *Above the Below* and studying 'the effects of refeeding after prolonged fasting' was published in the peer-reviewed *New Journal of Medicine*, with Blaine as one of the credited authors (Korbonits *et al.* 2005: 2306). We have every appearance of sincerity.

I am less interested in the facts of these matters – whether (or how) Blaine put his hand through a glass window or how (or whether) he fasted for 44 days in a glass box – and more in the performed tension between actuality and appearance, truth and fabrication, in a culture that continually produces this tension amid ubiquitous mediation, the theatricalization of political process and an aesthetic interest in the phenomenological self. The magic turns are effectual because we know that surely the things that we witness cannot truly have happened as they appear. This is the age-old delight, part of a long tradition of illusionism as entertainment. We are in the face of an act of virtuosic deception, enjoyable precisely insofar as it transgresses the bounds of possibility. The endurance stunts are not dissimilar, for they involve a visit to a border (of behaviour, norm, human capability) and a transgression of orthodox limits.

It may well be possible to endure in the terms established by each respective challenge. Each stunt, however, has an added frisson due to the persona of the performer: David Blaine, illusionist, in splendid isolation as talented magus, a man of literally super-human (indeed supernatural) capability. The fact that Blaine *is* Blaine – an individual with a biography, and an alluring combination of showman and shaman – provides added potency to the performance.

In her discussion of the work of the American magicians Penn and Teller, Susan Kattwinkel addresses an oscillation between mystery and demystification:

> Apparent revelations turn out to contain further mysteries, and one is always left wondering at what point the two men have told the truth. . . . This manipulation of truth and fiction unbalances the spectator, engaging them mentally by putting them in a position of continuous interrogation.
> (Kattwinkel 2003: 90)

Kattwinkel considers Penn and Teller's work as the pair debunk spiritualism, expose fake psychics and uncover different sorts of fraud. This arguably civic agenda goes hand in hand with the shows themselves, which reveal aspects of their magic tricks while always keeping something (metaphorically, if not actually) up their sleeves. Kattwinkel describes the routine, for example, in which Teller accidentally drops a rabbit and his arm in a shredder. He comes onstage later to demonstrate that all is well, albeit that 'he carries a rabbit clearly different than the one apparently thrown in the shredder' (Kattwinkel 2003: 92) – a joke about gratuitous trickery and the dispensable nature of rabbits. Teller's still-intact arm (rather less dispensable), meanwhile, indicates the likely safety of his unwitting assistant.

The entertainment values here are also cultural values that help explain the popularity of Penn and Teller's work, along with that of magicians like Blaine and Brown. They depend on a negotiation between illusion and inauthenticity on the one hand, and transparency and actuality on the other. This makes for a peculiar construction, the apparently-actual, clearly fabricated and palpably present. The structure of the apparently-actual underlies a good number of con-temporary performance manifestations, and is at the heart of the unresolvable tension between being a character and presenting a self.

When I saw Derren Brown's show *Svengali* in the Novello Theatre in London's West End (13 July 2012), it was with a view to considering this boundary between fakery and authenticity. Brown has been treading this line since his first television show, *Derren Brown: Mind Control*, in 2000. More shows and series have followed, including *Trick or Treat* (2007), *Derren Brown: The Events* (2009), *The Experiments* (2011) and *The Great Art Robbery* (2013). They feature Brown performing illusionist stunts and tests involving a mix of traditional theatrical mesmerism, remediated for television, and psychological manipulation. Brown has also presented solo-based theatre shows, includ-ing *Derren Brown Live* (2003), *Something Wicked this Way Comes* (2005), which won the UK theatre scene's Olivier Award for Best Entertainment, *Enigma* (2009–10) and *Svengali* (2011–12).[13]

As it turned out, the latter was in many respects a traditional encounter. Its set and poster evoke the theatrical illusionism of the Victorian theatre, and the show is in part a straightforward sequence of illusionist turns. The first half features a series of routines, often involving audience members. The second introduces an automaton. Brown claims this is the original (in its restored form) used in performance by a Hungarian illusionist who modeled the figure on his deceased six-year-old son, thereby setting up a small reverberation between a stage dummy and an actual historical figure. This sequence is followed by a series of numerical predictions involving different members of the audience. And there is a turn in which Brown appears to hypnotize a good many of the audience, one of whom comes up on stage to suffer a needle being put through his hand, bloodlessly, in a nod to the presence-structures of extreme body performance. In Brown's work (as in Blaine's), the camera is used as a witness and an apparent guarantor of the actuality of that which we watch. We know that the camera often lies, but in the close-focus work of both *Street Magic* and *Svengali* it is interposed ostensibly as a device for truth. Mediation, in this instance, is authentication, even while we know we are being misled in this conjuring of the apparently-actual.

*Svengali* presents Brown as the show's eponymous all-powerful trickster but also as a version of the bloke next-door, accessible and convivial. A fuller development of Brown's persona – as both person and performed presence – is played out in the programme sold to accompany the show. The first article, on page 3, is entitled 'Please allow me to introduce myself'. This is not so much a biographical account as a brief description by Brown of the process by which he, his writing partner Iain Sharkey and the production team create a show. It is a mix of informal commentary and behind-the-scenes detail: 'My flat becomes strewn with sheets of A4 containing half-baked routines as well as snippets of ideas and key words which might suggest scenarios or "moments" we hope might work.' The next article, 'Ten years of showmanship', lists Brown's now prolific set of TV series, one-offs and theatre productions, dating from his first TV show for the UK broadcaster Channel 4 in 2000. The article is subtitled 'I am often dishonest in my techniques but I'm always honest about my dishonesty.' The next is entitled 'Advice to a young mentalist: From an email to a budding mentalist finding starting out difficult.' The email from Brown to his young peer is reproduced. It includes the following, which bears reasonably lengthy quotation:

> in order to perform convincingly, what comes out has to come naturally from the inside. It applies to voice, persona, everything. This means that you already have the answer. And when you find it you know it'll be the right one because it won't feel like a character. The moment anyone getting into this area starts talking about 'I could be this or this sort of character',

then I know they're not going to really get it, and there'll be no depth to their performance. There are no real choices for you at this level – because YOU are the character, and all you have to do is give a few theatrical tweaks to make YOU work as a performer on stage. . . . So if you're 18, BE 18. If you try and pass yourself off as a goateed master of the mysterious you're going to seem ridiculous, because you're plastering on a character from the outside. It has to come from within.'

Brown, no less than Verdonck, is an advocate of actuality, authenticity, sincerity. He discusses the line between honesty and fakery in his book *Tricks of the Mind*, when he explains his performance as a 'mentalist' – a magician who appears to work on and with the minds of others, with apparently psychic abilities: 'now I clearly frame both live and TV shows as that mixture of psychology and trickery, and concentrate on making them as entertaining as possible while avoiding any direct claims that are untrue' (2006: 18–21 [19]). As Brown suggests, with this kind of magic 'personality is paramount' (2006: 18). The next three pages of the programme for *Svengali* sustain this framing. They contain a selection of questions asked by members of the public, answered here by Brown:

If you could have any superpower what would it be and why?
*Jodie, Huddersfield*

Maybe to read minds for real. Would make all of this a lot easier.

This is followed by 'Extracts from the blog' sustained during the run of Brown's previous theatre piece, *Enigma*.

April 27, 2009 at 10.58am

Yesterday managed to make it to Debenhams here before early Sunday closing: just in time to have a very sweet member of staff at the till recognize me in a blushy, lovely way, while I knew I had then to pay for a bunch of pants I'd just bought.

An advertisement on the facing page, in pastiche mid-Victorian style, promotes Brown's Twitter feed. The programme also includes a biographical excerpt from Brown's book, *Confessions of a Conjuror*, a series of observations by Brown on hypnosis; an account of the creation of one of Brown's portraits (he is a talented artist); 'Ten little known or cared for Derren Brown facts'; and 'My top ten influences'.

This is a post-postmodern compendium: a mix of celebrity, biography, confession and conversation, carried out across platforms that include theatre, television, print publication and social media, involving professionals, collaborators and members of the public. There is a candid acknowledgement that *Svengali* is a production, a pretense; alongside the insistence that for it to be properly produced it depends on an originary self, the YOU that is the real core, the unique and personable performer. As Hill observes, 'Brown creates mind traps with his audience where he appears to go beyond the concept of magic – "it's not a trick", "it's just him" ' (2011: 138).

The personae of Blaine and Brown draw on their status as celebrities. Studies of celebrity show how different cocktails of fame, stardom, affection and notoriety are enabled by the spread and workings of the media (see Boorstin 1992 [1961]; Rojek 2001; Turner 2004). In this sphere of cultural production celebrity is, as Turner notes, '*a genre of representation and a discursive effect*' (Turner 2004: 9; original emphasis). Celebrity is produced and performed. It is part of discourse around desire, efficacy and ideas of value. The allure that surrounds celebrities has a non-linear relationship to their achievements in specific fields of action. Some achieve fame as a consequence of special capability. Others are famous for being famous – in Boorstin's pithy construction, '*The celebrity is a person who is known for his well-knownness*' (1992: 57, original emphasis). And fame can attach both to a person and a persona. Andrews and Jackson contrast the 'fictive identities' of TV and film stars (who are known in part through their characterizations) with the apparent authenticity of sports stars (who appear to be '*real* individuals participating in unpredictable contests') (2001: 8, original emphasis). The personae of magicians such as Blaine and Brown fall somewhere in between, as showpeople appearing in a routine who nonetheless perform as themselves in scenarios that appear to be open to failure. They inhabit the zone of Diderot's paradox. The work that they do, not unlike that of sports stars or indeed actors, requires task-based (super-) competency. It also depends upon the mixed associations that attach to the idea of the street magician–cum–magus – a man of the people, a showman, a conjuror, a medium of the paranormal. Performance here is an *act* designed to create effect for the spectator, produced by a person with a biography.

The persona appears to signal a specific self, a being at the borderline between characteristic originality (the things that make one different from anyone else) and characterful fabrication (made-upness precisely for presentation). This return to a self that is somehow sincere and always also fabricated is a backwash from the tide of postmodern performance, which appeared to sweep away the tainted procedures of dramatic characterization. That's to say, in the middle of our personae, we really are also characters, in a hybridizing of self, character and persona. This accords with broader principles of digital culture, not least as demonstrated through social networking, where we curate ourselves in order to present an originary persona that is nonetheless shaped for public consumption. Likewise, the turn to verbatim performance and reality TV promotes authentication by way of actuality – the lived lives of its subjects and the experience testified to by its speaking voices – even while, as we have seen, both formats are subject to the shaping work of dramatization, editorial selection and sometimes more deliberate plays with pretense.

Persona, then, is a matter of selective characterization. Character, in the analysis above, is not so much an agent within a narrative (although it might also be that) as a continuous figure within a cultural *mise en scène*. Character is a counterbalancing accompaniment to the Self of performance and spectatorship. It takes on new life as a construct through which we relate to, experience and inhabit performance events in a postdramatic landscape of the awesome, the affective and the somatic. If reality incurs, it does so through tropes that humanize our relation to it – through its personable presence.

## Notes

1 I take Auslander's point regarding his 'concept of noncharismatic performance' where 'what is at stake is a critique of presence in which the charismatic performance is accompanied by its own deconstruction' (1997: 67). Of course, the performance is charismatic for all that. Kirby (1984) addresses a spectrum from 'non-matrixed performance' (the presentation of self) to 'complex acting' (immersion in character) that I suggest we can view differently by way of a mingling of attributes.

2 Billington, Michael, 'The River – Review', www.theguardian.com/stage/2012/oct/27/the-river-jez-butterworth-review.

3 For a cautious reassertion of the validity of the concept of character in relation to plays by writers including Barker, Churchill, Crimp and Kane, see Blattès 2007.

4 For details of Verdonck's company and work, including video excerpts, see www.atwodogscompany.org/en/. For an essay addressing ways in which 'Verdonck's mediated and technological bodies suggest a new status between wholly mediated representations and immediate live bodies', see Bay-Cheng 2012: 68.

5 I saw the piece at Huis aan der Werf in Utrecht in 2011. See Eckersall 2012: 72–5 for a discussion of it. See Vanderbeecken (2010: 363–5) for a discussion of Verdonck's *I/II/III/IIII*, a performance installation that also operates as a series, featuring four suspended live performers.

6 www.atwodogscompany.org/en/projects/item/154-actor-1?bckp=1. A video of *Dancer #3* can also be viewed at http://vimeo.com/8260258.

7 The 'text' entry to 'Humanid', an accompanying piece in *Actor #1*, notes that 'The script of Humanid was inspired by Samuel Beckett's Lessness.' There are other references to Beckett in the company's website. See www.atwodogscompany.org/en/projects/item/172-huminid?bckp=1.

8 Van Kerkhoven, Marianne, 'text', www.atwodogscompany.org/en/projects/item/158-dancer-1?bckp=1 (follow the link to 'text').

9 'Kris Verdonck interview', trans_digital, http://transdigital.org/archive/articles/kris-verdonck-interview.

10 http://davidblaine.com/video/2003-above-the-below-brief/, accessed 21 July 2012. Blaine's website is at http://davidblaine.com/.

11 http://en.wikipedia.org/wiki/David_Blaine#Above_the_Below lists Blaine's work, with accounts and links.

12 http://en.wikipedia.org/wiki/David_Blaine#cite_note-cnn.com-44. In a TED talk Blaine describes a challenging regime of training in order to control his breathing and hold his breath (http://davidblaine.com/video/2010-how-i-held-my-breath-for-17-minutes/; accessed 21 July 2012).

13 Brown's website is at http://derrenbrown.co.uk/. See Hill (2011: 134–49) for a discussion of Brown's work, in particular addressing his use of psychological strategies. See Wilson (2005) for a short interview in which Brown discusses psychological techniques in relation to illusionism. See Brown (2006 and 2010) for partly autobiographical volumes addressing principles and systems of magic and mentalism.

# Chapter 6

# Me singing and dancing
## YouTube's performing bodies

A version of this chapter is presented as an e-resource on the product page for *Performance in the Twenty-First Century*, on routledge.com. If you read it online you can click on the hyperlinks as you go, most of which take you to YouTube videos.

When my daughter's friend Lily was 15, early in 2013, her other friend Izzy (also 15) presented her with an unusual birthday present. Lily opened a small box, inside which was a piece of paper on which was written a link. The link took Lily to a YouTube channel containing seven short videos, recorded over the week leading up to her birthday. In one video, Izzy drew their friendship, speeding up the doodles to make an action animation. In another she drew Lily's name in Circular Gallifreyan (the 'first' language of Doctor Who, the eponymous alien protagonist of the children's television series). In others she read chapters from books that Lily liked, and sang covers of songs playing her guitar and ukulele.

This might sound precocious, but it is also an emblem of today's digital body. Izzy put herself out there. She communicated through the social (but also very intimate) medium of YouTube. She performed to camera. She was both herself, and a performing version of herself. She was digitally enabled, although in one sense she was unproduced. This was Izzy in person without the assistance of anyone else, mediated by the camera but in a way that was meant to be as direct and transparent as possible. This seeming transparency – the appearance of a person *in person* – is a feature of social media and has helped change the way we think about performance and the bodies in performance.[1] In this chapter I will look particularly at the performing bodies presented on YouTube, the video-sharing platform that has helped change the viewing and performing habits of a generation.

## YouTube, creation and consumption

YouTube was launched online on 14 February 2005 as a platform for video sharing.[2] It has been a subsidiary of Google since 2006. Its slogan from 2005 to 2012, 'Broadcast Yourself', indicates YouTube's gearing towards solo dissemination – the creation and uploading of content by individuals, and the publishing of often banal or everyday minutiae concerning the lives of its contributors. As Henry Jenkins observed in 2006, 'YouTube has emerged as a key site for the production and distribution of grassroots media – ground zero, as it were, in the disruption in the operations of commercial mass media brought about by the emergence of new forms of participatory culture' (274). By the end of that year, YouTube enjoyed a footfall of 13 million visitors a day (Snickars and Vondereau 2009: 10). It had become the most popular entertainment website in the UK by November 2007 (Burgess and Green 2009: 1). By 2012, according to its press page YouTube had over 1 billion users each month, watching over 6 billion hours of video, with 100 hours of video uploaded every minute.[3] Richard Grusin sees this sort of statistic as part of what he calls 'the YouTube sublime' (after Kant's 'mathematical sublime'). As he suggests:

> this sublimity is expressed in various permutations of the following sentence: 'The video of X attracted more than Y million views on YouTube.' . . . [T]he mind is unable to conceive the immensity of the YouTube universe even while it is empowered by the experience of an affective awe in the face of such immensity.
>
> (Grusin 2009: 60–1)

Much of this swirl of online video emanates from individuals viewing and uploading from computers in their bedrooms; much of it is produced by corporations and commercial companies, not least by way of licensing deals between YouTube and the likes of the BBC, CBS, Universal and Warner (Uricchio 2009: 28). These bigger beasts, familiar from the jungle of commercial mass media, are visibly present by way of postings of videos concerning performances by, say, Def Leppard, and competitions managed by the likes of Sony/BMG; and invisibly as in the case of the poignant but ultimately posturing lonelygirl15 (see Burgess and Green 2009: 29; Salvato 2009: 70; and Suhr 2012: 61–68). While you cannot always trust the provenance of that which you watch, this very uncertainty results from a notably hybrid model of creation and consumption. Participants (individuals, groups, companies, corporations) of utterly diverse scope and aims share their outputs in a single continuum of exchange. Grusin argues that while Henry Jenkins 'proclaims YouTube as the fullest embodiment of convergence culture', he fails to see that 'the hypermediacy of YouTube also produces a *divergence culture* that is fragmented, niche-oriented, fluid and individuated' (Grusin 2009: 65–6; original emphasis). There is merit to both cases, and they take us into the heartland of YouTube's affordances: it is a marketing and distribution vehicle for commercial organizations, an engine for self-publication and social exchange, and an archive that jangles with documentary, testimony, lived experience and entertainment.

The first video to be posted on YouTube was uploaded by one of its three co-founders, Jawed Karim. Entitled *Me at the zoo*, it is a 20-second clip showing Karim in front of the elephant enclosure at San Diego Zoo (www.youtube.com/watch?v=jNQXAC9IVRw, at time of writing, over 16.8 million views).[4] The video already demonstrates some of the key signatures of YouTube performance. Karim looks directly at the camera and engages in direct address to the spectator. The camera is fixed in position and focus. The video presents a single unedited take. It celebrates the everyday (albeit that this is a day out). It is suffused with an off-hand irony. 'Um, cool thing about these guys is that they have really, really, really long trunks, and that's cool', says Karim. The video gives the sense that the person addressing us is authentic and is, in a peculiar way (given that this is a short film), unmediated.

Strangely, there is also a text box that appears briefly at 14 seconds, that says 'can you hear the goat? MEEEEEEEEEEEH!!' which references a possible long bleat in the ambient background noise. Here, then, is a layer of additional mediation, a scripted text from an editor or filmmaker, pointing extra-diegetically to the fuller actuality of the scene. The text indicates that the format is adaptable, subject to irreverent intervention; and that it is fulsomely communicative. Given his foundational place in YouTube's history, further irony is provided in the detail that, according to his online profile, Karim appears to have posted only this single video.

YouTube facilitates onward viewing – by way of sidebars in which you can see other videos uploaded by the same individual (although not in Karim's case); the end-frame that shows a grid of title slides for other videos; links in the comments section; the Featured Videos section; and, not least, the length of the videos – often very short – which is conducive to serial viewing. As Uricchio notes, while YouTube is fragmentary in the diversity and multiplicity of its content, it includes 'initiatives that seek to restore notions of collectivity', such as the comments feature, a collaborative annotation system (marking likes and dislikes), and the platform's facilitation of interest groups and sub-channels (Uricchio 2009: 34). This ecosystem of fluid engagement means that YouTube conforms with Burgess and Green's suggestion that 'Media consumption . . . has moved away from being a "read-only" activity to becoming a "read-write" one' (2009: 48). It also means that onward viewing is open-ended, a metonymic run of videos within a shared-but-splintered culture of commentary, comparison, copying and compositing.

Among the title slides in the end-frame to Karim's video is one tagged 'Noah takes a photo of himself every day for 6 years' (www.youtube.com/watch?v=6B26asyGKDo). There is something haunting – certainly in the somber, pulsing piano music that plays over the video, but also in the serially reiterated gaze out from the frame – in Noah Kalina's video *everyday*, a compilation of portrait photos. Kalina took a photo of his face staring at the camera every day over a six-year period (11 January 2000–31 July 2006), joining these together in a riff of changing hair arrangements, clothes and backgrounds, but always with a melancholic stare at the viewer. For all that this is a monomaniacal gaze, it shows a double-edged self, one that is both private and public, actual and virtual, exposed and contained, available but unreachable. This is what our body becomes in digital culture, a performing thing of blurrings, doublenesses and indeterminacies, all of which are shared.

Kalina's video has received over 25 million views. In 1968, that year of revolutions, Andy Warhol observed that 'In the future, everyone will be world-famous for 15 minutes'. He wouldn't have thought to add 'or through 24 million views'. YouTube has proved Warhol to be correct – being world-famous is now within reach of almost anyone, given the viral nature of video sharing. Warhol's comment also suggests the ephemerality of pop culture. That's true of much of the content on YouTube, but the digital body is also a preserved, pickled body, permanently available. You *fix* yourself on YouTube. As Burgess and Green observe, YouTube is 'evolving into a massive, heterogeneous, but for the most part accidental and disordered, public archive' (2009: 89). I'd like to add 'but also deliberate' to this list of adjectives, for you can search YouTube for the historical record – for videos that capture, say, sporting moments, public events and significant instances of performance – placed there by individuals or organizations interested in making information available. While YouTube presses the future with its waves of new uploads, it contains a growing sea of material, an archive of digitized clips and movies that reaches back into history and across cultural production.[5]

## The archive of digital bodies

Digital culture has allowed us to *share* our bodies more diversely than ever before. Such sharing has a theatrical dimension, and we can think of the performing body, specifically in relation to its distribution on YouTube, in at least three different ways.

### 1. The body in performance, digitally archived

By way of example, consider this video of the butoh artist Kazuo Ohno in *The Dead Sea*, from around 1980 (www.youtube.com/watch?v=ZUjhQLB0h XY). The clip comes from a documentary on butoh made by Edin Velez in 1989 (www.youtube.com/watch?v=2gqukIxf8oM). This is not a digital per-formance – that's to say, the performance was made in a pre-digital culture, and initially not intended for dissemination through any other medium than the theatre. Nor is there a sense of any compromise or adjustment made for the presence of the camera that, here, has an archival function. The performance is as originally conceived and presented – this is butoh in the raw. When Velez put together his documentary, Ohno's performance was preserved for posterity but (in contrast with online archives) not made drastically more accessible. The video would have to have been replicated, ordered and despatched by mail, or purchased at a specialist outlet, or viewed by way of broadcast or festival screenings. The fact that you can now search for this performance and view it online within a couple of clicks of the mouse makes it much more easily available. As a consequence the performance itself endures differently – it has been revivified. Kazuo Ohno becomes newly discoverable, sharable. The concentrated technique of his idiosyncratic, auteurist mode of performance is permanently preserved by way of its storage online, yet rendered less exotic as it becomes more consumable. The immediate responsiveness of the archive stands in for the immediacy of theatre and brings (often bite-sized, emblematic) moments closer to us all. The same is true of sporting moments – great goals, saves, wickets – which make sporting history and its moments of definition recoverable. This is one way in which digital culture has reordered our experience of time – the now-moment of transient events and entertainments are continuously resonant in a parallel echo-chamber. Performance – once a thing definitively of its own present – is now always with us. This applies to performance in both senses of the word: high achievement, as witnessed in elite sport, and putting it out there, as seen in some of the amateur videos I describe below.

## 2. The body in performance, digitally distributed

The archive looks backwards. It exists as a place to go to reach the past. One logic of the growth of the YouTube archive, however, is that new performance comes into a proper being in the present precisely by way of its online manifestation. The difference between archiving (collecting and depositing) and distributing (releasing and pushing out) is blurred, in that digital distribution in and of itself creates archivable products – the repository is live. Consider the case of the South Korean pop star Psy. His video accompanying the song 'Gangnam Style' (www.youtube.com/watch?v=9bZkp7q19f0&hl=en-GB&gl =GB) became the first YouTube video to gain more than 1 billion views after going viral shortly after its release in July 2012.[6] His subsequent single, 'Gentleman M/V' (www.youtube.com/watch?v=ASO_zypdnsQ), had notched up over 1 billion views on only the fourth day after its release.[7] As Wikipedia reports (in this instance citing a range of sources):

> As of 31 July 2013, the video has been watched more than 500 million times on YouTube. It has set YouTube records for most views in its first 24 hours, most views in any 24 hours, fastest music video to reach 100 million views, fastest overall video to reach 200 million views, and 300 million views.[8]

We are truly in Grusin's territory of the YouTube sublime. Psy's success was subject to a range of preparatory marketing activities and expectation-raising features within the online landscape, not least the self-fulfilling anticipation of whether 'Gentlemen M/V' could outdo the phenomenal success of 'Gangnam Style'. Nonetheless, both videos are created to be viewed by a community of fans and others who will access them online, and then tweet, repost, blog or send messages that serially reiterate viewing opportunities.

The dance moves of both 'Gangnam Style' and 'Gentleman M/V' – laddish and irreverent, quirky and peculiarly unexpert, original and easy to copy – are comfortably suited to their place on social media. The videos are shot to be effective in the small-screen formats that typify this viewing milieu (from computer monitors to phone screens), with its mix of close-up shots, body filling the frame, short and complete scenarios within the video as a whole, group dance routines, and bodies in relation to iconic objects or spaces in popular culture. Psy, to his global audience, is nothing if not an Internet phenomenon, but he is an exemplar of the wider tendency towards performance made for multi-social mediation.

While Psy's brand of K-Pop appears entirely oriented to the mass market of pop culture, the viral popularity of 'Gangnam Style' made the piece a useful vehicle for political expression. The Chinese artist Ai Weiwei performed a pastiche in which he sporadically wields a pair of handcuffs, interpreted as an oblique reference to his house arrest by the Chinese government (www.youtube.com/watch?v=n281GWfT1E8). The British sculptor Anish Kapoor performed a similar routine in 'Gangnam for Freedom', in tribute to Ai Weiwei and as a demonstration in favour of freedom of expression, after Ai Weiwei's video was blocked by the Chinese authorities (www.youtube.com/watch?v=tcjFzmWLEdQ).[9] While this material now exists in YouTube's archive, it was originally circulated as commercial product (Psy), political pastiche (Ai Weiwei) and interventionist protest (Kapoor). This series of videos is iterative, replicative and morphs through different frames of reference. The body in performance, digitally distributed, can be expert, inexpert, innovative, populist, a body in protest – sometimes all at once.

### 3. The body performing as itself

This is perhaps a sub-set of the category above, but it is substantial enough to warrant close attention. The performance presents a self that is more textured, more present, and more promiscuous than was the case before the advent of Web 2.0 from around 1999, which facilitates dynamic interaction and sharing of content. (Salvato, indeed, describes YouTube as 'a synecdoche of Web 2.0 technology more generally' [2009: 68].) This is the self that speaks, dances and sings to camera, forming the accumulating gallery of short videos that is such a signal feature of YouTube specifically and digital culture more broadly. Here lies the new performance. It is to this category, and its blurring of the authentic and the presentational, that this chapter now turns – in particular by looking at its manifestation on YouTube by way of singing and dancing.

## Me dancing

Dancing alone while performing to others is a familiar spectacle on YouTube. Consider Sam Sadler dancing to 'Gangnam Style', in a video entitled 'Me dancing to Gangnam style- PSY' [*sic*] (www.youtube.com/watch?v=QZn Pkb2r-fA). A presumably teenaged, bespectacled young man gives his version of Psy's dance as the song plays in the background. Everything about the video speaks of amateurism. It is shot indoors, in front of a doorway to what might be a kitchen in the background. The fixed framing, showing a light switch, open door behind and external door beyond, presents a decidedly quotidian, non-composed backdrop. Peters and Seier describe this kind of 'home dance' on YouTube:

> a certain aesthetic randomness is apparently accepted easily: this randomness contrasts profoundly with the thoroughly designed video clips to which the performances refer. But it is precisely this lack of self-consciousness that leads to considerations that not so much emphasize the amateur status of the YouTube video, but makes their very mediacy the center of attention. (2009: 192–3)

Sam Sadler's dancing fits this template: it is a jerky copy of Psy's routine, in which the amateur simultaneously inhabits a cultural phenomenon, the medium of dance, and a space inside digital mediation. He concludes with a verbal sign-off, as if speaking to fans. He will be back – and the sidebar indicating videos entitled 'Me Singing Flo Rida Whistle', 'Me Doing Skrillex Bangarang' and 'Me Singing call me maybe!' attests to a serial showman. Sam Sadler's digital body is metaphorically viral – it is infected by popular culture. It carries a foreign body, that of Psy, which it copies and reiterates. This 'reenactment', to use Peters and Seier's term, is a means of *embodying* a social scene. It is differently meaningful in that it is shared. Suhr discusses hybrid cultural operations that draw on processes associated with the commercial music industry and those of DIY consumers and creators: 'Overall, YouTube is a major purveyor of a new type of culture, which is neither mainstream nor underground but which combines both in an indefinable way' (2012: 70). Kirsten Pullen provides a form of definition for this mélange, arguing that YouTube facilitates 'counterpublics'. She defines these (after Michael Warner) as 'groups who are aware of their subordinate status but claim public space and enter public debate through the same mechanisms as those groups generally recognized to be part of "the public"' (Pullen 2011: 146). In similar vein, in her discussion of swing dance and digital media, Carroll argues for 'the *cooperative* or *consensual* notions of "community" and cultural practice' facilitated by YouTube as a platform for shared discourse arising from shared dancing (2008: 200, original emphasis). Sam Sadler doesn't have the political edge (entering public debate) that Pullen ascribes to some counterpublic activity.[10] Even so, a cultural transaction is taking place. This isn't just some teenager dancing solo in his hallway to a song playing in the background (akin to the air guitarist of an earlier era). This is a performer pimping a pastiche body in a safe space of cultural exchange.

The meme of 'me dancing', and its reach from the personal to the public sphere, is differently illustrated by Matt Harding's 'Where the Hell is Matt?' dance videos. An erstwhile video game designer from Connecticut, Harding spent some time travelling in South East Asia. According to his website:

> A few months into his trip, he and his friend, Brad Welch, were taking pictures on the streets of Hanoi when Brad said 'Hey, why don't you stand over there and do your stupid dance. I'll record it.' Matt did it, and he thought it looked pretty funny, so he kept on doing it everywhere he went.
> (www.wherethehellismatt.com/about)

Harding initially posted the videos on his blog. By his account, a compilation was uploaded on YouTube in 2005 by an individual pretending to be Harding, with views of the video passing the one million mark. (For the first video, made in 2003–4 and posted in 2005, see www.youtube.com/watch?v=7Wm Mcqp670s.) Harding himself was offered sponsorship by an American chewing gum brand that enabled another series of dances in locations as diverse as Machu Picchu, Peru; Bandar Seri Begawan, Brunei; and (in diving gear and filmed underwater) Chuuk, Micronesia (www.youtube.com/watch?v=bNF_P281 Uu4, posted in 2006).[11] A further series followed in 2008, in which (a new turn) Harding's dance was sometimes performed alongside groups of people in, for example, Madagascar, South Korea and Zambia (www.youtube.com/watch?v=zlfKdbWwruY). By 2012 Harding was engaging more deliberately with different groups and the dance forms specific to their cultures. His video shows him teaching others his jig and learning their dances, performing (with varying degrees of fidelity) in a mix of moves that here become glocal: a chorus of disco arms with firemen in League City, Texas; a waltz in Vienna; a formal couples dance in Pyongyang, North Korea. The dance sequences are increasingly choreographed throughout the sequence, with larger groups (in Cairo, Tallinn, Baltimore) performing hand and arm movements in sync with the upbeat signature song, 'Trip the Light' (Gary Schyman, lyrics by Harding and Alicia Lemke; www.youtube.com/watch?v=Pwe-pA6TaZk). 'Me dancing' (solo, amateur, shared) has become 'We dancing' (plural, professionalized, globalized) on a world-wide dance floor that merges local forms with the banal jig of a man having fun.

Harding's case is a good illustration of YouTube's economy of performance. The dance itself is amateurish and easy, a cross between running on the spot and pumping one's arms loosely on the vertical axis. It emerged as a casual piece of silliness, a young man doing a 'stupid dance' as a quirky personal signature. The performance is idiosyncratic but easily adoptable. While not initially conceived for YouTube, the dance took hold in the public sphere through its posting on the video sharing channel. It can easily be presented in short segments – Harding's videos collate often very short clips. It is contextless, in that it can be performed anywhere, as Harding set out to demonstrate. On the other hand, there is something colonial about this series of world tours that puts pins in the map through video capture of Harding's boots on the ground. Initially Harding didn't go to Rwanda or Peru to learn the dances of local people; rather, to place his body *in situ* a little like a summiter's flag. From a North American perspective, the dance is exported to the distant and exotic.

Even so, YouTube facilitated this as a global project that, proliferating specific locations, appeared to efface borders. As the project developed it did acquire more of a flavour of exchange, as Harding adopted the dance forms of other cultures. As he notes in an 'Ignite Talk' given at Gnomedex, Seattle in 2008, the Internet facilitated much of this work, making this a project clearly of the digital era (www.youtube.com/watch?v=ue1GZ4IUFiU). If geographical boundaries were crossed, so were those between mediation for personal and commercial purposes. Sponsorship by the chewing gum manufacturer was followed by a series of TV commercials for Visa that aired in Asia and the Middle East (www.wherethehellismatt.com/about). The naïf appeal of Harding's original performances was subtly defrayed. A different sort of unravelling occurred in the narrative of inauthenticity that spun out when Harding claimed the project to be a hoax. This episode is redolent of the category-shifts facilitated by social media, where perceptions of action, time and location can hover between the actual and the fabricated, sometimes inhabiting one category erroneously, sometimes moving pleasurably across both. It illustrates both the instability of 'truth' that attends presentation through video (which can be manipulated), and the fascination with authenticity that attends digital cultural production.

Harding gave a presentation at The Entertainment Gathering conference in Monterey, California, in 2008 (duly followed by a video released on YouTube) claiming that the entire project was a pretense, and that he had performed all along in front of a blue screen with exotic locations composited behind him. On the face of it, Harding tells a story here about the credulity of an online community: 'They sent me responses by the thousands – people who were expressing profound joy of feeling connected to the whole world by watching the simple act of uncoordinated, unselfconscious silliness shared by everyone' (www.youtube.com/watch?v=ogcqFaNbah4). A month later Harding appeared at the MacWorld Expo in San Francisco, California, to reveal that his previous conference presentation had itself been a hoax (www.youtube.com/watch?v=CVAg6YTgTn4). He recounts the tricks 'revealed' in his first conference presentation, that are instead ever more outlandish features of the hoax that is itself a hoax, such as the claim that those dancing with him were a costumed troupe of animatronic robots. For all that this seems amusingly obvious, when the YouTube video of his first presentation was released two days after the conference, it was almost immediately reposted on digg, a site that gathers and reiterates online news, under the headline 'Confession: Where The Hell is Matt? An Elaborate Hoax' (for digg, see http://digg.com/). If the original hoax had pretended that the online community had been credulous, its effect was to demonstrate precisely this credulity. The digg post, as Harding notes, was 'turned into a more or less legitimate news story' on Associated Content, the online publishing platform, and likewise on the travel website Jaunted (for Jaunted, see www.jaunted.com/).

An online project involving serial reiteration of the real (dances in locations) became, for a short period of time, caught up in the serial reiteration of reports of its un-reality. Cultural memes are memes all the more readily because of the pass-on function of Internet dissemination. In any event, actual dancing was resumed – in a way that indicates the meme-like quality of the jig itself. David Pogue, Harding's interviewer at the MacWorld Expo, informs the audience that 'at the end of the show, Matt has graciously agreed to let you join him on the stage while your friend runs the camcorder, for one more dance.' The ensuing moment deliciously encapsulates features of this project. The image of a host of Mac users taking to an actual stage to perform a short jig sums up the merging of tropes of digital culture, embodiment, presence and pastiche. It demonstrates the attraction of both performance and performance-capture, as doing a dance is something for which one 'runs the camcorder'. The project has a centrifugal energy, spreading dance across a range of individuals. What's also clear is its centripetal force, with Harding (persona, performing body and now personality) at its core.

Harding's website engagingly traces a trajectory of celebrity. The initial YouTube posting made him 'micro-famous'. The second video made him 'quasi-famous'. The third '*not-entirely-un*-famous' (emphasis in the original). This is an affable way of saying that Harding was, on the face of it, an ordinary guy performing a 'stupid dance' that proved to be popular (and then became professionalized). Fame, here, is not a settled state, but the result of serial appearance, distribution and reiteration. Nor, Harding suggests, is it fully achieved. It is a spreading condition, to do with the sort of reach and recognition enabled by online dissemination. The numbers? By the beginning of 2015, Harding's 2008 video had received over 48 million views – it is but a few clicks from a dance on holiday in Hanoi to the 'YouTube sublime'.

## Me singing

Many of the characteristics of 'me dancing' apply just as well to 'me singing'. Two instances here help us briefly to consider some additional features of YouTube performance, not least its way with space, rapport, purpose and all the stuff that appears not to be performance (but really is). The first, uploaded in 2008, is entitled 'Me Singing Should've Said No by Taylor Swift' (www.youtube.com/watch?v=7BVvNE78lyc, at time of writing over 27.5 million views). It features a girl in big close-up, directly in front of the computer screen, we assume. She sings badly, wobbly of voice and tune, in a performance of earnest replication. This is amateurism in the raw. This instance reminds us that performance stages a scene. Here, the scene suggests cultural consumption (a TV plays in the background), celebrity fascination, aspiration, domestic centredness, vulnerability, and a lack of self-awareness that we might term innocence. For all its naivety, the very fact of performing to camera means that there is something calculating to this self-display. In a subsequent posting, Nichole presents a compilation from her video blogs from 2008–12, a series of head shots of Nichole uttering her opening line, 'Hey guys, it's Nichole' (www.youtube.com/watch?v=2fE7YvzTjKQ). As with Noah Kalina's six-year series of stares, Nichole's archive presents a form of growing up, a video album of diverse hairstyles, experiments with clothing and the appearance of teeth braces. A rolling text sign-off at the end says 'Thanks for your continued support.' Nichole's solipsistic, home-alone series is a way of communing. When she looks into the camera Nichole sees a world looking back.

Online denizens of this world are cruel as well as kind, as the comments beneath Nichole's videos demonstrate. They take us back to the Georgian coffee house or the Roman market place, and a very public circulation of discourse of approbation and disapprobation, mockery and celebration. Peters and Seier observe that 'If we wanted to define teenagers' bedrooms as heterotopias as described by Foucault, they might be understood as equally private *and* public, actually existing *and* utopian, performative *and* transgressive spaces' (2009: 199). Nichole's bedroom is accordingly heterotopic. What she shared here, no less, is a life in the living, spatialized in ways particular to teenage experience and then re-spatialized through its circulation online. Place, performance and presence fuse into a single mediation. In the interests of maintaining a thread introduced earlier in this chapter, I should also mention Nichole's rendition of 'Gangnam Style' (www.youtube.com/watch?v=Hi2 LGp-dh08), which is notable for the slight ratcheting up of production values in the form of flashing lighting. Inhabiting a song recorded by someone else is a form of remediation – particularly so in that the *copying* of performance emphasizes performance itself.[12] Hartley suggests that '*purposeless entertainment* has nurtured demand for creative self-expression and communication among the young' (2009: 130, original emphasis). As Hartley's closing clause suggests, what appears to be purposeless is also deeply functional, to do with agency, connectivity and cultural identity.

Finally, consider 'Me Singing "Rolling in the Deep"' – a video uploaded on 25 April 2011, in which Bethan Horton sings a song released by Adele (www.youtube.com/watch?v=EwLvj3mw78I, at time of writing over 1.1 million views). Note here the spoken introduction prior to the performance of the song – throwaway in tone, a conversation with a familiar online audience concerning 'which video you would like next', with an apology by Bethan if she looks down at the lyrics on her laptop, 'because I just learnt it like two seconds ago'. This unedited take, replete with verbal slips and full of casualness, is part of the production of a persona. An extra-performance moment, before we get to the song, it is itself (in-video) part of the performance of self. Lange suggests that:

> videos of affinity have observable characteristics such as a presentist focus that aims to transit feelings of connection and maintain an open, active communication channel. They often contain ephemeral content that the videomakers themselves label as existing in the intercies [*sic*] of their work. Seen not as a cinematic end point, but rather as a mediated moment in an ongoing social relationship, the videos help maintain connections between individuals and groups of people in a social network, large or small. . . . In videos of affinity, people often produce evidence of their live body and provide a spontaneous, present-status update.
>
> (Lange 2009: 83–4)

The viewing hits for some of these videos of affinity, often in excess of 25 million, represent a reach that would have been the envy of the producers of garage bands or makers of fringe theatre in another age. There are some broad principles that lie behind YouTube's phenomenal coverage. The format depends upon the agency of its users, who are themselves responsible for the creation, production and distribution of their artifacts, but also then the ongoing curation of their output. It facilitates sharing and response, thereby sustaining a form of genuine interaction where those involved can make a difference to that with which they interact. Axel Bruns coins the term 'produsage': a mix of producing and usage that accords with the principles of convergence culture. We can now be creator, performer, disseminator, correspondent and consumer through the same communication platform.

Much of this activity displays a form of ultra-localism. Videos are made in intra-domestic spaces (living rooms, bedrooms). Offered out of these interior rooms, they are an act of intimacy – which is to say a form of permission and privilege. They are private and personal, while also being everyday and ubiquitous. This goes for YouTube's facilitation of peer learning, by way of the many instructional videos showing, for example, how to play specific songs on the guitar or piano.

The turn to simultaneous self-presentation and performance; the projection of 'me'; the everyday settings, bodies and clothes: all this in some small way reclaims the self and the body in a highly mediatized, corporatized culture, even while it apes the modes of that culture.[13] Personal identities are laid out, indeed developed over time. The presence of the producer's body as an authentic body – even if also a persona – figures the postdramatic turn to performance, while the mode of presentation slips between pastiching another, performing oneself and being oneself. For all its entanglement with corporatism, YouTube has allowed us to repossess our bodies even while we lend them out to others.

## Notes

1  For an account of shifts in creative practices in media production, see Havens and Lotz 2012: 127–144. The subsequent chapter considers dominant practices in traditional distribution platforms (145–164).
2  For accounts of YouTube's history see Burgess and Green 2009; Suhr 2012: 55–6; and Snickars and Vonderau 2009: 9–21. See Grusin 2009: 62 for a brief discussion of diverse scholarly responses to YouTube.
3  www.youtube.com/yt/press/en-GB/statistics.html.
4  All links in this chapter were live at 2 January 2015 except where indicated.
5  On YouTube as an archival platform, see Snickars and Vondereau 2009: 11–15.
6  www.bbc.co.uk/news/technology-20812870.
7  When I accessed it on this day the tally was 101,355,837.
8  http://en.wikipedia.org/wiki/Gentleman_(Psy_song).
9  For information on 'Gangnam for Freedom', see http://en.wikipedia.org/wiki/Gangnam_for_Freedom and www.independent.co.uk/arts-entertainment/art/news/anish-kapoor-goes-gangnam-style-for-freedom–and-ai-weiwei-8340784.html. For information on 'Gangnam Style', see http://en.wikipedia.org/wiki/Gangnam_Style. See Hartley 2009 for a discussion of the capacity for multiple-platform multitasking of a generation of digital natives.
10  Pullen's article focuses on Beyoncé's video (accompanying her song) 'Single Ladies' (2008), and the thousands of re-creations to which it gave rise, demonstrating 'the ambivalences built into dancing bodies (Pullen 2011: 148). See also Carroll 2008 for a discussion of power, participation and representation in the meeting of (refunctioned) dance practices and digital sharing. See Salvato 2009 for a discussion of discourses and practices concerning amateurism and professionalism in relation to YouTube.
11  For a brief account by Harding of the sponsorship arrangement, see Sachs, Andrea (2006) 'The Guy Who Danced Around the Globe', *The Washington Post*, 22 October 2006, www.washingtonpost.com/wp-dyn/content/article/2006/10/20/AR2006102000373_2.html.
12  For a compilation entitled 'Top 10 Female Youtube Singers', see www.youtube.com/watch?v=l5iNIKQP-yM, whose performers are still broadly in the home movie tradition; and 'Top 12 Best Youtube Singers 2012', www.youtube.com/watch?v=OQXn6NALYqU, which marks the increasing professionalization of this mode of performance. For an instance of further remediation, in which YouTube videos are remade in a live theatre piece under the aegis of Israeli artist Renana Raz, see www.youmakeremake.com/ymr/#/about.
13  See Turner 2006, who argues that micro celebrity remains within the dominant structures and processes of the media industry; and conversely Pullen, who insists that 'the pleasure of the dancing bodies' overrides commercial messages (2011: 151). See Jenkins 2006: 271–296 for a discussion of civic discourse in and through YouTube.

# Chapter 7

# Viewing and acting (and points in between)

## The trouble with spectating after Rancière

Many recent events and performance pieces have challenged the distinction between viewing and acting, from the promenade performance experiences organised by Punchdrunk, to the games-based events of Blast Theory, to immersive installations by, for instance, Anthony Gormley and Olafur Eliasson, to the incorporation of 'experts' of the everyday in the work of Rimini Protokoll. If such work were in search of a manifesto, it might find it in Jacques Rancière's *The Emancipated Spectator* (2009a). Rancière's account – that of a provocateur – explores a philosophical and political framework for spectatorship that bears directly on this gathering artistic trend.

One of the delights of *The Emancipated Spectator* has been the prospect of taking at least parts of it literally. It sometimes appears to exhort us to participate rather than spectate, act rather than watch – we hear a call to the barricades. Its saliency resides in its application to a wider array of spectator transactions, including those where you don't necessarily have to leave your seat in order to enter the playing arena, nor stop watching in order to be in action. Rancière is concerned with the political aspect of spectating by way of spectators having a place, and knowing what that place can be and mean. People can remain spectators in the midst of various degrees of emancipation. *The Emancipated Spectator* also lends itself to forms of heightened viewing, whereby spectators at (for example) multimedia installations, promenade performances and sports matches can experience themselves in the act of watching. Rancière doesn't directly focus on the nature of such experience. I shall suggest below that his analysis can be turned towards this double-edged development in cultural consumption.

To be precise, *The Emancipated Spectator* is the title of both a short essay and a collection of writings that derive from a series of talks and articles presented between 2004–2008. This seems worth mentioning, because it indicates the iterative and accumulative nature of Rancière's intellectual production, and the historical contiguity of these particular pieces with the artistic outputs instanced above. The book takes its place in Rancière's larger project: to identify and reconstitute the political, as it is manifested both in art and in the organization, consumption and context of artworks. It is part of his ongoing series of arguments about the nature of visual images and their effectiveness within culture. And it provides both a parallel commentary and a set of challenges to contemporary theatre's turn towards spectator engagement.[1]

Rancière's focus in *The Emancipated Spectator* tends to be on art that can be looked at. Just looking, Rancière observes, can be dangerous, for 'To be a spectator is to be separated from both the capacity to know and the power to act' (2009a: 2). Spectators cannot 'know' since the *process* of production is not represented. They are by definition separated from the power to act, since spectators watch. Rancière notes the argument (without *quite* doing anything as categorical as propose it himself) that there should be 'a theatre without spectators, where those in attendance . . . become active participants as opposed to passive viewers' (4). The artwork, in this analysis, should rather transform spectators 'into active participants in a shared world . . . [for] [e]mancipation begins when we challenge the opposition between viewing and acting' (11, 13).

If this appears drastic, Rancière acknowledges a balance of considerations. As he wryly notes, 'Being a spectator . . . is our normal situation' (17). And in any case, 'The spectator also acts . . . She observes, compares, interprets. . . . She composes her own poem with the elements of the poem before her' (13). Spectatorship is not effort-free, not as passive as all that, and throughout the piece Rancière troubles 'the established relations between *seeing*, *doing* and *speaking*' (19, original emphasis). The agenda is to identify new configurations of spectatorship that replace a relatively detached looking with more overt forms of engagement.

Rancière often writes glancingly and allusively. It is productive to composite a case from the analysis developed across a number of different lectures and essays rather than derive it from any single output. His work circulates around certain key terms and understandings, albeit that the precise configuration of these shifts across various writings. Characteristically, terms are shaded with nuance, complication and sometimes counter-intuitive readings, and often entail a sort of negative definition. Hence 'emancipation' is not so much liberation as the possibility of disagreement. The 'emancipated spectator' is not a looker-on but someone who is involved. Which raises all sorts of questions for spectatorship, agency and participation.

In order to elaborate spectator engagement and address some of the problems it poses, I will explore Rancière's use of three key terms: 'Equality', 'Dissensus' and 'Sensus communis'.[2] I argue below that these contribute to a nexus of ideas that run through his work more broadly and help to create the underpinning texture of *The Emancipated Spectator*. I then consider how they might apply to a variety of encounters between spectator-participants and artworks or events in Chicago, a city that offers a rich diversity of cultural engagements. For present purposes, I focus on a studio theatre production, a civic sculpture, a museum event and a basketball game.

## Equality

*Equality* stands as an abiding principle across much of Rancière's work. It is understood as the capacity for individuals to take their own perspectives, and be free of what Rancière describes as 'the police' – an ordering function in society that establishes commonalities and conformities, thereby enforcing inequitable power structures.[3] Equality is bound up with the political. As Rancière observes in *Disagreement*: 'Politics . . . is that activity which turns on equality as its principle' (Rancière 1998: ix). To that end, as Steven Corcoran notes, politics is 'an activity in which *all* can partake' (Corcoran 2010: 7). Equality betokens the prospect of individual agency. Something similar might be said of performance, in the light of *The Emancipated Spectator*. One of the threads through Rancière's thinking concerns the ability of (or at least the desirability for) individuals to think and act for themselves.

Rancière presents a case for a radical understanding of equality in *The Ignorant Schoolmaster: Five Lessons in Intellectual Emancipation* (1991), where he addresses the pedagogic principles of Joseph Jacotot. A Frenchman, Jacotot found himself teaching literature in the Flemish city Louvain in 1818. He undertook an experiment whereby he asked students who spoke only Flemish to read a book in French, with a parallel translation; learn the translation by rote; then write about the book – in French. He found that they did so with aplomb. The discovery, as Rancière assesses it, was of the power of intelligent self-development. What, in that case, was a teacher? Perhaps even, what use a teacher? For Jacotot, the teacher who *explains* is in a structural relationship with someone who needs something explaining to them – therefore, someone definitively inferior in the teacher-pupil relationship. As Rancière engagingly suggests, 'It is the explicator who needs the incapable and not the other way around . . . To explain something to someone is first of all to show him he cannot understand it by himself' (1991: 6). Jacotot's premiss, by contrast, was to establish a mode of relation whereby both teacher and pupil would learn together – with learning enabled by a facilitator rather than an elucidator. Rancière suggests:

> The method of equality was above all a method of the will. One could learn by oneself and without a master explicator when one wanted to, propelled by one's own desire or by the constraint of the situation. . . . one can teach what one doesn't know if the student is emancipated, that is to say, if he is obliged to use his own intelligence.[4]
>
> (Rancière 1991: 12, 15)

Rancière's enjoyment of this model is consistent with a sustained anti-authoritarianism in his work, and of course it chimes with developments in learning and teaching practices that favour independent enquiry. Mark Robson observes in Jacotot's scheme 'the community of equals, a community based on the *presumption* of a shared intelligence, a shared capacity' (Robson 2005: 84). The model is inherently levelling. Everyone has the same prospect of access to knowledge and an equality of competence is assumed. The paradox of the ignorant schoolmaster is analogous to that of the spectator who is also an actor – equally engaged in activity, capable of independent action and thought. *The Emancipated Spectator* is built on foundations laid by Joseph Jacotot.

Equality applies communally, in that it entails equivalent prospects and opportunities across groups. This is, nonetheless, not a theory of mass action. Rancière's conception of the communal proposes a free space of individuation. That's to say, communities are not so much defined by their *togetherness* as by their facilitation of *difference*, the fact that they enable individual expression. There is a trace of Rancière's poststructuralist inheritance here. As Peter Hallward puts it, 'When crowds form in Rancière's work, it isn't (as with Sartre) in order to storm the Bastille or its contemporary equivalents; they come together to stage the process of their own disaggregation' (Hallward 2009: 147). Strikingly, the model of equality is in some respects a model for individual libertarianism within a communal (shared) context.

The axes of this thinking are threefold, and readily apply to an understanding of what it is to be one among spectators. Equality is desirable. It is predicated upon a sense of the capacity of each and every individual. The facilitation of difference characterizes a productive relationship to one's community (with which one is able to disagree) – and is a feature of the operation of equality.

## Dissensus

In thesis 8 of 'Ten Theses on Politics', Rancière suggests that 'The essence of politics is *dissensus*. Dissensus is not a confrontation between interests or opinions. It is the demonstration (manifestation) of a gap in the sensible itself' (Rancière 2010: 37).[5] The sensible, in Rancière's usage, indicates that which is perceived and felt. The distribution of the sensible (*partage du sensible*), his celebrated coinage, evokes the manner in which things (artefacts, events, social transactions) are disposed for feeling and perception through cultural production and consumption. Rancière develops the idea that the sensible can entail a break in and of perception in *Aesthetics and its Discontents*:

> Politics consists in reconfiguring the distribution of the sensible which defines the common of a community, to introduce into it new subjects and objects, to render visible what had not been, and to make heard as speakers those who had been perceived as mere noisy animals . . . creating dissensus.
>
> (Rancière 2009b: 25)

As he suggests elsewhere, dissensus means that 'every situation can be . . . reconfigured in a different regime of perception and signification' (2009a: 49).

There is a Brechtian aspect to this, and one can draw a dotted line from Brecht's idea of *verfremdung* (whereby things that we thought we knew only too well are made strange, defamiliarized) to Rancière's argument that a redistribution of the sensible is politically efficacious. The latter case is couched in terms that do not depend, as Brecht's analysis does, upon the need for *meaning* as an overt outcome. Brecht is rearticulated to accord with contemporary modes of production. These are not necessarily rationalist in their operation. They may instead produce affect, sensation and experience – new feeling, or what Rancière describes as 'a sensorium, a new partition of the perceptible' (2010: 122) – rather than (Brechtian) new awareness and right-thinking. Rancière is careful to note that the fact of a redistribution of the sensible isn't in itself a guarantee of 'a new topography of the possible', a formation that might be understood to describe a sort of political and social efficacy. Rather, one seeks 'scenes of dissensus' in the face of the 'beast' of consumerism and commodification (2010: 49). This is a project for artists and arts practitioners, you'd think, who might seek to facilitate such scenes. It is also a project for critics, who might identify scenes of dissensus in and through a disruption of commodification.

Despite its scrupulous basis in difference and dissent, there is something troubling or, at least, volatile about this model. Dissensus depends upon momentary configurations rather than ongoing transactions between groups of consolidated identity. It requires a break, a split or a fissure – it endlessly needs change. The model of equality developed is productive in that it implicitly renounces the sentimentalism of a homogenizing, conformist view of communal identity. Nonetheless it is partial. Peter Hallward asks sceptically:

> To what extent does Rancière's conception of equality remain a merely transgressive one? [. . .] Rancière's emphasis on division and interruption makes it difficult to account for qualities that are just as fundamental to any sustainable political sequence: organization, simplification, mobilization, decision, polarization, taking sides, and so forth.
>
> (Hallward 2009: 153, 155)

If dissensus always requires new configurations, it is difficult to conceive of it in terms of a systematic political project designed to secure measured and lasting benefits. This relates to the play between individual and communal experience discussed briefly above. Rancière is not really interested in dissensus as a programme of collective action or expression – rather, it appears to have more to do with a form of cultural transaction that is available to individuals in a moment of change or new awareness.

According to Rancière, *The Emancipated Spectator* marks 'a change of approach' with regard to a critical project understanding the relation between the individual and society, and the prospect of politically efficacious emancipatory practices (2009a: 48). There is no *explicitly* political project as such, no sense of converting, mobilizing, rescuing or educating a group.

> What there is are simply scenes of dissensus, capable of surfacing in any place and at any time. What 'dissensus' means is an organization of the sensible . . . It means that every situation can be cracked open from the inside, reconfigured in a different regime of perception and signification. To reconfigure the landscape of what can be seen and what can be thought is to alter the field of the possible and the distribution of capacities and incapacities. This is what a process of political subjectivation consists in: in the action of uncounted capacities that crack open the unity of the given and the obviousness of the visible, in order to sketch a new topography of the possible.
>
> (Rancière 2009a: 48–49)

Dissensus occurs through difference and alteration. Its consistency lies in Rancière's insistence that it form part of a texture of aesthetic-political exchange. Spectators, then, engage to greater or lesser extent with and within 'scenes of dissensus'.

### Sensus Communis

Rancière's essay 'Aesthetic Separation, Aesthetic Community' in *The Emancipated Spectator* discusses, in part, a project by the artists' collective Campement Urbaine (Urban Encampment) which created a space of solitude in Sevran-Beaudottes, a down-at-heel suburb of Paris. The essay leads off with Mallarmé's proposition, 'Apart, we are together' (2009a: 51). Rancière is attracted to this conceit, and his essay in effect suggests that together we are also apart: 'To the extent that it is a dissensual community, an aesthetic community is a community structured by disconnection' (2009a: 59).

Such disconnection was realized logistically by Campement Urbain in *Je et Nous* (2003 6), the subject of Rancière's analysis. Among its other outcomes, the project manifested a space that could only be occupied by one person at a time. Oliver Davis notes that the community evoked (indeed facilitated) by this work 'will necessarily be a "dissensual" community, whose members reinterpret the works they encounter in the light of their own experiences and their knowledge of other works' (Davis 2010: 155). You could say that this is the case when any individual takes herself to an event, installation or performance, and that its civic art project *Je et Nous* simply throws the interpretative role of the spectator into starker relief. The space for solo occupation is emblematic, for if each spectator 'composes her own poem', as Rancière puts it (2009a: 13), we must acknowledge the endless variation across individual engagements. Davis nevertheless wonders how Rancière's 'insistence . . . on the dissensual character of the community' can be squared with his otherwise 'broadly Kantian vision', to do with 'the development of a *consensual* community' (Davis 2010: 157). Davis suggests that Rancière has rather too hastily privileged dissensus over consensus.

It is the case that 'consensus' is rather a dirty word in Rancière's work, smacking as it does of bland agreement and the subtle (or not so subtle) operations of that which constitutes the 'police'. 'Consensus' implies a set of assumed norms that are nonetheless held in place by vested interests, and that serve to sustain power structures that do not foster equality. In 'Ten Theses on Politics' Rancière argues that:

> The essence of consensus . . . does not consist in peaceful discussion and reasonable agreement, as opposed to conflict or violence. Its essence lies in the annulment of dissensus as separation of the sensible from itself . . . Consensus is . . . simply a return to the normal state of things – the non-existence of politics.
>
> (Rancière 2010: 42–3)

This non-existence, as we have seen, means the absence of difference, and the sway of convention and conformity.[6]

There is a distinction to be drawn, however, between consensus and community, and the latter term runs as a shadow through Rancière's thinking. We've already seen that a conception of 'the common' – the gathered interests of a group – is important here. This needs teasing out a little. In his 'Afterword' to a collection of essays by others on his work, Rancière observes that 'A common sense does not mean a consensus but, on the contrary, a polemical place' (2009c: 277). In 'Aesthetic Separation, Aesthetic Community' he writes:

> What is common is 'sensation'. Human beings are tied together by a certain sensory fabric, a certain distribution of the sensible, which defines their way of being together; and politics is about the transformation of the sensory fabric of 'being together'. . . . An aesthetic community is not a community of aesthetes. It is a community of sense, or a *sensus communis*. A *sensus communis* involves three forms of community.
>
> (Rancière 2009a: 56–7)

The first form, in Rancière's scheme, is 'a certain combination of sense data' (2009a: 57). The second Rancière terms a 'dissensual figure', entailing conflict or contradiction – he suggests that this is between artistic representation and power structures, form and context. The third level entails 'a community between human beings', which sounds rather vapid and is glossed, more particularly, as the sense of community that arises when the first level (sense data) itself relates to the second ('the intertwining of contradictory relations') (2009a: 58). I take this to mean the realization, in mind, body or both, of divergent possibilities (Rancière's new topographies of the possible) – perhaps, better, the *experience* of that realization.

*Sensus communis*, then, is an important and intriguing coinage. It is not at all the same as 'consensus' in the Rancièrean lexicon. It is not blind or blank agreement for the sake of it. Instead it is the experience of being located meaningfully within a community. It evokes the longstanding leftist view of the centrality of community to effective social interaction. It does so by gesturing towards the tropes of an individualist (indeed a consumerist) era, such as subjective perception, felt experience and personal engagement. Herein lies the congruence with the notion of dissensus: it is as *individuals* that we experience community, and we do so where the aesthetic realm facilitates our dissensual relationship with culture.

The connections between community (or 'the common') and dissensus (or difference) need careful calibration. As Jean-Luc Nancy says, 'One could extrapolate from Rancière that art is a means (and perhaps the most common one, considering all the forms of knowledge and power) of understanding our communal existence and the very modes of being-in-common (what brings us together and separates us)' (2009: 92). That seems right, and yet this isn't quite the same as saying that art *produces* communities as homogeneous groupings, nor that it is even necessarily about the *desirability* of communities. There is a countervailing scepticism in Rancière's work concerning what might be thought the sentimental view of the beneficent aspects of community (or indeed, we might add, a gathered audience). Rancière would much rather emphasize the prospect of difference and separation. Nonetheless, he does so according to the implicit premiss that 'being-in-common', to use Nancy's phrase, is preferable to the segmentations and subjectivations of the police order.

In *The Emancipated Spectator* Rancière discusses the community that pertains to theatre by way of the engagement of spectators. The means by which performances transcend the separation of stage and auditorium entail the figuring of individuals in 'their place of communion. For the refusal of mediation . . . is the affirmation of a communitarian essence of theatre as such' (2009a: 15–16). Mediation is nowhere more emphatically refused than in the moment when the spectator is folded into the event. We are interested, then, in situations where spectators are not passive. These situations will say something about modes of spectatorship and their relation to cultural production, politics and pleasure.

## Spectator engagements in Chicago

In Chicago in 2010 I experienced a number of scenarios where spectating was itself rendered visible; where the ingraining of the spectator into the event (or artefact) was an important feature; and where in various ways I saw myself in the act of spectating. I propose to explore how Rancière's thinking might apply to – or be tested by – these instances, and address their connections with more widespread developments in spectatorship. Taken together they help to illustrate larger questions, possibilities and tendencies in the relationship between a 'spectator' and an 'event'.

## A studio theatre production

*The Twins Would Like to Say* was presented by Dog & Pony Theatre Company at Steppenwolf's Merle Reskin Garage Theatre, a studio space underneath a car park next to Chicago's celebrated Steppenwolf Theatre.[7] The production was programmed as part of Garage Rep, Steppenwolf's Visiting Company Initiative designed to promote 'new, provocative work emerging from Chicago's diverse and vibrant theatre scene'.[8] Established in 2002, Dog & Pony Theatre Company started out by staging contemporary plays – Michael Frayn's *Clouds* (Chicago Cultural Center, 2004), *Osama the Hero* by Dennis Kelly (Athaneum's Studio #3, 2005), Sheila Callaghan's *Crumble (Lay Me Down, Justin Timberlake)* (Athenaeum's Studio #2, 2005) – and was named 'Best Theater Troupe' by Chicago Magazine in 2007. The company turned to devising pieces, working with extant materials and a looser engagement with space and setting. *As Told By the Vivian Girls* (Theater on the Lake, Fullerton & Lake Michigan, 2008), adapted from the circumstances, drawings and writings of the reclusive artist Henry Darger, was presented as a promenade piece in a two-storey former sanitarium. In a manner reminiscent of Punchdrunk's *Masque of the Red Death* (2007), the audience wore masks and wove their own journeys through simultaneous scenes of performance. *The Twins Would Like to Say* was likewise a promenade production, but within the confines of a studio.

Written and directed by Seth Bockley and Devon de Mayo after an initial devising process, *The Twins Would Like to Say* dramatizes the unusual story of the identical twins June and Jennifer Gibbons, Caribbean immigrants to Wales. In the 1970s the twins lived out a pact to speak only to each other, which in part saw them committed to Broadmoor, a secure psychiatric hospital.[9] Dog & Pony's production began with a prologue in the theatre's foyer, involving puppets of parrots and a Master of Ceremonies character called 'Mr Nobody'. The audience was led by this figure into the studio, in which we traversed through a corridor made of black drapes, dividing the studio into sections and creating a destabilizing effect – we didn't know quite where we were going, or the space's proper proportions. A preliminary scene introduced us to the twins, played by Paige Collins and Ashleigh LaThrop. We were then led into the larger spaces of the studio, which was arranged by designer Grant Sabin as a set of stations of performance, each broadly figuring a specific setting. There was a lounge, for instance, a bedroom, and a doctor's office (Figure 7.1).

The audience gravitated towards these various settings, standing and disporting themselves around the foci of action. There was a certain casualness to this, especially as the show went on and we became more familiar with the pace, format and rules of engagement. We sat on rostra on either side of the bedroom set, for instance, to watch a scene played end-on by Collins and LaThrop. In other instances, scenes took place simultaneously, so we choose which to watch, or drifted between different physical settings in order to catch something of everything. The show, then, figured certain sorts of fluidity, decentring, multi-perspectival possibilities and seriality – its form gestured

*Figure 7.1* The doctor's office in *The Twins Would Like to Say* (left to right: Ashleigh LaThrop, Paige Collins and Kasey Foster, seated)

Source: Peter Coombs

towards fracture as opposed to strict linearity, albeit that the play (for this was, decidedly, a play) told its story chronologically and the production was more restrained in its dismantling of space than might have been the case.

The style of the piece was also mixed. The show was part-narrated. It featured broadly naturalistic scenes. It included shadow and rod puppets and a cartoon-like pastiche (the story of a boy addicted to Pepsi). The twins unfolded a picture book to tell of the burning down of a school. There were some choreographed movement figures expressing, for instance, the routine of the girls' mother and father on the sofa watching TV, or the doctor and Mr Nobody in the doctor's office. The twins danced in a sequence dealing with a fantasy-story involving a trip to the disco. Toward the end of the production a curtain was drawn across the studio, dividing the playing area in two. The simultaneous scenes that closed the piece entailed both a denial of spectating (for the first time, given we had previously been free to choose what to watch) and a privileged viewing access (in that one half of the audience saw something denied to the other half).

The production was not particularly groundbreaking, but usefully exemplifies some tendencies in this sort of promenade performance. Actions were presented in different parts of space. The spectators had relative freedom of movement. The staging entailed fairly frequent changes of position, so that there was a continual negotiation of one's viewing space alongside others. The audience was treated as a community of individuals facilitated in making small decisions as to what to watch and how, or from where, to watch it. A not inconsiderable feature of this was that one became very aware of other spectators. They were in your sight line, sometimes in your way, sometimes in a space that you'd like to be standing in, or else you politely adjusted your position in order to facilitate someone else's viewing. We didn't just watch the drama. We observed and accommodated acts of observation.

The configurations enabled some low-level effects of dissensus – the feeling of seeing things differently, of not having drama presented for the gaze, but rather textured into a space that itself became a site of freer flow and negotiation. This returns me to the point that dissensus can achieve its effects as if innocent of meaning or cognition. The production created a *texture of affect* a little different from that of theatre pieces where the spectator sits in a single place and watches. Were we emancipated? Perhaps it suffices to say that we were free to make modest choices relating to positions of viewing. This in itself is a figure for a cultural process that dislodges us from fixed perspectives and moves us towards divergent places of engagement. In its contained way, *The Twins Would Like to Say* performed a nod towards a spectator who is in action rather than inactive.

## A civic sculpture

*Cloud Gate*, nicknamed 'the Bean', is a public sculpture by Anish Kapoor. Located in the AT&T Plaza in Chicago's Millennium Park, it is made of 168 stainless steel plates, highly polished to provide a seamless reflective surface, that displays both the surrounding cityscape and the observer in slightly distorted perspectives (Figure 7.2). It was unveiled in a partially completed form in 2004, as part of the opening of Millennium Park, and formally on 28 August 2005.[10]

Kapoor explored the possibilities of a series of reflective orbs and roundels in the late 1990s, and *Cloud Gate* connects with the pieces in his wider 'void language' and 'mirror language' series.[11] His sculpture *Turning the World Inside Out* (1995) – a steel ball, dimpled on top – displayed a similar fascination with the exuberant gathering of reflection (in this case the ground, ceiling and walls of the gallery, all co-present to the gaze). In *Iris* (1998) a convex stainless steel mirror, placed either on floor or wall, plays back the surrounding space in a way that both condenses it (within the circle) and releases it (through the distortions and abstractions of the convex form). *Iris* makes an eye of itself while staging the act of viewing. This play of perspectives and incorporation of the viewer into the scene of the sculpture occurs in another civic piece, *Sky Mirror* (2006), located in the Rockefeller Centre in New York. This is in effect a huge two-sided mirror formed of a stainless steel disc 10.5 meters in diameter,

*Figure 7.2 Cloud Gate*, Millennium Park, Chicago
Source: Andy Lavender

tilted at an angle of sixty degrees. The convex side of the sculpture points downwards, meaning that viewers can see themselves reflected. The concave side points upwards, embracing skyscrapers and sky, to create an image that looks peculiarly out of place against the sombre backdrop of the Rockefeller Centre's neo-classical façade.

*Cloud Gate* takes the two separate sides of *Sky Mirror* and puts them together in a different shape entirely. It is a machine for spectating. As an art object, its function is to be viewed within its situation. Cool, calm and contextual, it squats in the Plaza as a sophisticated sort of eye candy. The sculpture's organic shape (evoking a coffee bean or a kidney), curved lines and pristine surfaces are sensuous and seductive in themselves. More pertinently, however, *Cloud Gate* restages the city that surrounds it. Chicago is figured in 360 degrees, with the sculpture providing a panoptical survey of plaza, park, skyscrapers and sky. The city is the most densely populated in the world in terms of high-rises. *Cloud Gate* – its name indicating the aerial scope of this crouching piece – pictures the city in both horizontal and vertical axes, embracing its buildings, citizens and visitors, and opening out to the heavens.

While the Bean enables a vernacular replaying of Chicago to itself, its key enticement is the way in which it entails a form of motional spectating. 'I believe in the making of art, the viewer is all important', says Kapoor (quoted in Kent 2011: 32). You walk around *Cloud Gate* to view its (re)perspectives on the city. And you view yourself in the act of viewing. Visitors experiment with stepping closer to and further from the sculpture, testing its hall-of-mirrors effect on their bodies and groupings. People photograph themselves in touristic delight at the sculpture's warping remediations. As Crone and Von Stosch suggest, it produces 'a kind of estrangement for the spectator who must also decode a distorted view of his own shape among the others' (Crone and Von Stosch, 2008: 43). The work is tactile. Kent observes that, 'Invariably, people also touch it as if to verify that the object really is present. . . . There were fingerprints everywhere on the sculpture that evening, going up as high as a person could reach' (Kent 2011: 31, 35). And you walk into and through the Bean, for *Cloud Gate* is a form of gateway. Rather than open onto any particular new territory, it provides a pure passage through a curved arch from one side to the other, an emphatically processual walking through. Not that you simply traverse. At its apex the arch is around 12 feet high, and it gives onto an omphalos whose centre is 27 feet high, its concave ceiling serially distorting the reflections of those beneath (Figure 7.3). You stop in the middle, to admire the sudden vortexical dynamic of the reflection presented above you (Figure 7.4). This peculiar void, reminiscent of the black holes in otherwise diverse pieces by Kapoor such as *Descent into Limbo* (1992), *Marsyas* (2002) and *Marsupial* (2006), sucks its spectators into a sudden rendition as tiny figures seen at a seemingly impossible distance.

*Cloud Gate*'s dissensual character lies in its reimaging of Chicago, the refiguring of its spectators, and the incessant movement of individuals taking up subject-viewing positions that simultaneously place them as objects within – and inter-actants with – the sculpture's larger *mise en scène*. It is egalitarian, a civic artwork that is available to all, but in the terms in which Rancière describes the substance of equality. It facilitates dynamic individuation as the watchers (who are also in

*Figure 7.3 Cloud Gate*: the arch
Source: Andy Lavender

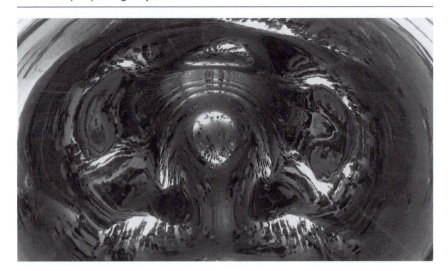

*Figure 7.4 Cloud Gate*: the omphalos
Source: Andy Lavender

motion, in action) determine their own journey, pace and relation to the object. As David Anfam suggests, 'The fact that Kapoor's sculptures make us participants (by enticing us to peer in, walk around, guess their full extent and so forth), rather than just thinking observers, renders their hypnotism profoundly embodied' (Anfam 2009b: 105). Does this also produce a *sensus communis*? Tourists and passers-by gather at *Cloud Gate* as participatory witnesses, and as individuals among a group of many, implicated in the dynamic and self-regulating act of spectating. In that sense *Cloud Gate* is an emblem for a pleasure-economy that commodifies presence, looking and self-recognition, and does so *en masse*.

## A museum event

As part of a trend in a number of museums and galleries, the Museum of Contemporary Art (MCA) in Chicago stages a monthly free-form rendezvous called 'First Friday'. As the museum's website explains:

> Happy hour takes on a new meaning with First Fridays at the MCA. Relax after a long workweek with a cash bar featuring specialty drinks and free Wolfgang Puck appetizers. Enjoy live music from local DJs, the world's only iMac G5 digital dating bar, creation stations, and more.[12]

First Friday extends the commercial activities of the organization. According to MCA's sponsorship prospectus, the event has 24,000 opt-in email subscribers, a potent database:

### Attendance and Demographic

The event attracts city influencers between the ages of 25–45. The crowd is ethnically diverse urbanites working in and around downtown Chicago, whose household income ranges from $75,000–250,000 annually. On average, we welcome between 1,400–2,200 attendees to each event.[13]

Such events refunction the spaces of the museum or gallery and put the viewer at the centre. They are perambulatory and participatory. When I visited the MCA's First Friday, the first thing I did was get a drink from the bar at one end of a gallery space, then some food from a large buffet branded with the name of an Austrian-American celebrity chef. A number of other people were milling around, eating, drinking and chatting. In a separate gallery was a table of *petits fours*, which one could consume standing on the terrace outside, looking out over nearby basketball courts towards Lake Michigan. The food facilitated a sense of purposive drift, as individuals, couples and groups percolated through the spaces, stopping to graze on the dips and chips. There wasn't necessarily anywhere to go, but the event created a texture of flow and impermanent settling as people moved around the building for the sake of taking a promenade or paused in order to rest, eat, watch or chat. It was possible to be a little more directional. I watched a group of people sitting around a set of tables making paper flowers (a 'creation station', Figure 7.5); browsed around one of the exhibitions; then went upstairs, where a suite of iMacs featured an interactive task that indicated the types of people I might be attracted or attractive to. It was perhaps happenstance that the computers featured this particular software, although there is something exemplary about the focus on the inspection of others, and their inspection of you, in an event that is so readily to do with viewing, consuming and being available as a participant. The party aspect of First Friday underscored one of its signal features. The museum was curating us, making an exhibition out of its spectators, who were inherently both observers and observed. The gallery environment enhanced the watchability of those present. The trope of looking, intrinsic to the museum's function, was revitalized in a set of transactions that offered different sorts of sensory stimuli. The museum's usual *mise en scène* was refunctioned as a *mise en événement*, an arrangement of spaces and engagements that created a participatory encounter, the purpose of which was entirely to be experiential.

It was here among strangers, perhaps more so than among different strangers at the Steppenwolf Garage or the AT&T Plaza, that I felt the *sensus communis* of which Rancière writes. The 'sensory fabric' of the museum was refigured by certain small and arguably dissensual rearrangements of its spatial organization. I was folded into the galleries as a participant rather than an observer, yet I was free to be a gawper, guzzler or chatterer entirely as I chose, in each case refuting the museum's main identity as a repository of cultural artefacts and a place of contemplation. Such possibilities are fairly trivial in the grander scheme of cultural process, but they nonetheless figure such a process where it offers

*Figure 7.5* First Friday 'creation station'
Source: Andy Lavender

a form of demotic agency, multiple options for pace and focus, and consumption according to personal preferences. It might be argued that this wasn't exactly the *communis* Rancière had in mind when he wrote of Campement Urbain and the opportunity to contemplate difference – not least given the MCA's account of the wealthy demographic of its visitors. I shall return to this reservation after my last instance of spectator engagement in Chicago.

### A basketball match

On 3 April 2010 the Chicago Bulls played the Charlotte Bobcats at the United Centre in Chicago's West End. Figure 7.6 shows the basketball arena. The central dais above the playing area gives spectators the chance to see the action in close-up, follow timings and statistics relating to the game, and view other messages, adverts and fillers. Electronic data bands around the arena convey messages either in still or moving form. The club lays on additional entertainment by way of the Luvvabulls (female cheerleaders), the Matadors (male dancers) and the IncrediBulls (comedy artists), who perform at diverse opportunities, including external events by arrangement. Mascot Benny the Bull, likewise, 'is available for personal appearances [and . . .] frequently attends

*Figure 7.6* The basketball arena, United Centre, Chicago
Source: Andy Lavender

birthday parties, community parades, festivals, walk-a-thons, school classroom appearances, college, high school and grade school sporting events, golf outings and more!'.[14]

If this extends the reach of the club into its communities, spectator engagement during the course of the game takes a number of forms. In Figure 7.7, the spectators at one end of the court, waving red and white balloons, are barracking a member of the Charlotte Bobcats who is taking a free shot. Signs are displayed that say 'BOO'. This might seem unsporting, but such involvement is packaged here as part of the fun of the event.

Figure 7.8 shows The Dunkin' Donuts race. Three animated characters race around a small track. The spectators have a number on their ticket – 1, 2 or 3. The spectators with the number of the winner can claim a free donut from the foodstalls in the foyer areas behind the seating blocks. A third are winners! There is more noise generated by this three-lap race than during the game itself.

There is a continuum between the engagement of the crowd during and outside gametime. Figure 7.9 shows an animated bull who drums and dances, and leads the crowd in a chant of 'Let's Go Bulls!'. Instructions to the spectator are relayed on the advertising strips around the arena and on the screens, with reactive graphics indicating how much noise is made and thereby encouraging the crowd to redouble its efforts.

During the breaks there are various sequences on the screens that feature the spectators at the event, who become briefly the focus of attention. Figure 7.10 shows a close-up of a spectator eating. Some of this material is clearly pre-recorded, given that the footage is sometimes sped up to make for some comic chomping. In another sequence, a cut-out head of hair appears on the screen. This frames the head of a spectator caught in a live close-up. Some of the spectators are watching the screen, others not, and the latter are nudged or called as the hairpiece settles on them. There are looks of recognition and recognizable utterances ('It's me!'), waves to the camera (Figure 7.11) and warm

*Figure 7.7* Barracking the opposition

Source: Andy Lavender

*Figure 7.8* The Dunkin' Donuts race

Source: Andy Lavender

*Figure 7.9* 'Let's Go Bulls!'
Source: Andy Lavender

*Figure 7.10* Burger at the basketball
Source: Andy Lavender

ripples of laughter from around the auditorium. In a sequence entitled 'Dance Fever', a live camera settles on individuals as 'Shake Your Boogie' plays. Individuals dance (or not) when on camera. Every now and then a recording of one or other of the Bulls players, dancing, is superimposed, further imbricating the spectators with the objects of their fandom.

*Figure 7.11* Waving to the camera

Source: Andy Lavender

*Figure 7.12* Hot dogs on parachutes

Source: Andy Lavender

The audience gets its reward. Hot dogs attached to parachutes are shot from a cannon, to cheers from the crowd (Figure 7.12). The cannon operator waves at a section of the crowd. They respond, wave, stand. He shoots. People whoop. The screen shows the crowd. There is much self-presentation for the camera.

## The implicated spectator: consumer of the watchable

Rancière suggests that 'The modern aesthetic break is often described as the transition from the regime of representation to a regime of presence or presentation' (2009a: 121). We might add that the latter regime entails a further development, towards the presence and presentation of the spectator herself – the implication of the spectator in the event, where we do not just witness new modes of presence, but experience them as a key feature of our engagement. In the instances above, such encounters are structured dramaturgically (or quasi-dramaturgically) to theatricalize experience in the face of the event. The body's implication helps to valorize the event's (or object's) presence, disposition and – ultimately – its pleasurable watchability. Indeed, we become consumers of the watchable, where we are part of that which is consumed by others.

In an uncharacteristically direct statement, Rancière observes that 'Emancipation begins when we challenge the opposition between viewing and acting' (2009a: 13). Yet the mere fact of such a challenge is not necessarily a guarantee of the dissensual expression of life within a culture that is celebrated in much of his work. What is the action undertaken by the non-passive spectator in the examples above? It is a sort of parallel engagement, a desired involvement of self (presence, body, action) in the fabric of the event, where the main mode remains one of watching – relatively risk-free. Here, however, one watches both the event (the play, civic sculpture, museum gathering, basketball game) and sees oneself in person, mirrored or on a screen, or in the echoing bodies of other spectator-participants. This may well produce the *sensus communis* of which Rancière speaks, but it is questionable whether it also routinely produces dissensus beyond a superficial refiguring of customary spaces and relations. The turn is rather towards the curated production of watchers as a guarantee of their engagement – facilitating a heightened sense of involvement in the now-moment, which is part of the commodification of time, presence and experience in late-capitalist culture. There is a would-be innocent pleasure in self-recognition, the striking moment where one says 'that's me!' and both experiences and observes oneself in the moment of participation, as simultaneously sensory subject (enjoying *sensus*) and meaningful object of a gaze that is both personal and shared with others (experiencing *communis*).

The appearance is of a redistribution of the sensible aspects of events and presentations. It suggests that we have moved from a society of the spectacle (objects out there to be seen) to a society of implicated spectaction (to adapt Boal's term 'spectactor'), where the spectator completes the event through her active presence. And yet this is a neutral (or perhaps issue-lite) spectation. It folds the participant modally into its procedures, promising that we are part of the thing rather than merely witnesses to it.

Rancière's problematizing of the relationship between viewing and acting is timely. It is the outcome of a grainy celebration, running through much of his writing, of work ethic, dignified artisanry, free agency and critical difference. Yet we cannot say that non-passivity liberates us, nor even that it will be dissensual. For while the spectator is implicated, the work itself – at least, in the instances above – remains peculiarly unenterable. You don't change the event, here; you merely complete it. Nor do you change yourself. Rather, you consume culture and enjoy the visual affirmation of yourself as participating consumer. In this matrix of engaged experience, the offer is of a safe, secure arrangement for redistributed spectating. The spectator is implicated, even incorporated, rather than emancipated.

I am reminded of Peter Hallward's suggestion, quoted above, that in Rancière's account crowds 'come together to stage the process of their own disaggregation'. They do, theoretically. But these particular crowds in Chicago acted as semi-free agents, expressing individual response and engagement, within a process of agglomeration. We are equally able to respond independently, but within the overarching arrangement of our place as consumers. Hewlett suggests that 'At times it is not clear if Rancière is in fact developing a praxis-informed, progress-oriented, emancipatory theory or if he is thinking more in aesthetic terms of the Utopian and an impractical ideal, which might ultimately inspire the practical but is itself quite removed from it' (2007: 107). This neatly articulates the dilemma of *The Emancipated Spectator*. We are free to view differently, indeed to act, but to what end?

Then again, perhaps in the face of these objects and events we are released into a *sensus communis* that is the antidote to consumerism even while it depends upon consumption. Rancière himself suggested as much. As he observes in relation to the trend towards reality art: 'In one respect, at issue is to restore a certain sense of community to counter the bond-dissolving effects of consumerism' (2010: 146). That in itself is a form of dissensus not to be taken lightly.

## Notes

1 Rancière addresses the split between viewing and acting from a different perspective in Ranciére 2011: 175–232. He explores a 'displacement' through the second part of the nineteenth century from forms of popular performance that involved their audiences also as inhabitors of artworks (hence, 'the workshop poet in his relationship with his brothers') to those that constructed a more disconnected kind of spectatorship (featuring 'the artiste in his or her responsibilities towards their popular audience') (2011: 213). *The Emancipated Spectator* addresses a different trajectory, from detachment to enhanced engagement, but from a similar view of the pertinency of relations between artistic production and consumption.

2 For a useful glossary of Rancièrean terms, including 'Equality' and 'Dissensus' (but not '*sensus communis*'), see Rockhill 2004: 80–93.

3 Žižek describes 'the police' as 'the structured social body where each part has its place' (Žižek 2004: 70). See also May 2010: 9, 108; and, taking issue with May's 'anarchist project', Chambers 2011: 20.

4 For an account of the principles of Jacotot's pedagogy, see Hewlett 2007: 93.

5  The article was first published in English in 2001, trans. by Rachel Bowlby and Davide Panagia, in *Theory and Event*, 5:3. See www.after1968.org/app/webroot/uploads/RanciereTHESESONPOLITICS.pdf.

6  Rockhill traces a development in Rancière's thinking whereby the distinction between consensus and dissensus becomes less strictly marked. It nonetheless remains decisive. See Rockhill 2009: 200–15.

7  The production ran from 18 February – 25 April 2010. I saw it on 1 April 2010.

8  Press release for *The Twins Would Like to Say*. Dog & Pony Theatre Company's website is at www.dogandponychicago.org/index.php.

9  The play draws on *The Silent Twins*, Marjorie Wallace's biographical account (London: Vintage, 1998 [1986]). Wallace's book followed her screenplay for a docudrama, *The Silent Twins* (BBC2 1986). It informed an opera, also entitled *The Silent Twins*, by April de Angelis and Errollyn Wallen (Almeida Theatre, London, 2007) and Shared Experience's production *Speechless*, presented at the Edinburgh Festival in August 2010. The story of June and Jennifer Gibbons has inspired other artworks, including the Manic Street Preachers' song *Tsunami* (1999).

10  See Kent 2011: 31–49, for an account of *Cloud Gate*'s conception, construction and completion, in which the contributions of structural engineer Christopher Hornzee-Jones and the project's fabricator, Ethan Silva, are writ large.

11  For images, see Anfam 2009: 217–55 and 337–9; and Crone and Von Stosch 2008: 41–2, 90, 99.

12  https://boxoffice.mcachicago.org/public/default.asp, accessed 22 November 2011. I visited First Friday on 2 April 2010.

13  http://mcachicago.org/assets/downloads/ff_sponsor.pdf.

14  The Bulls' website is at www.nba.com/bulls/. Game entertainment was detailed at www.nba.com/bulls/tickets/game_time.html, accessed 22 November 2011.

# Chapter 8

# Audiences and affects

## Theatres of engagement in the experience economy

How do you know that you are having an experience? In this chapter I connect the notion of experience with that of affect, in order to explore how performance events make us feel – and what that feeling might mean, what it might permit or efface. I focus below on four instances of audience engagement: an end-on theatre production, a sporting event, a promenade performance and an interactive game-based piece. Each displays various strategies by which *experience* is facilitated, with perhaps unpredictable affective consequences for their audiences.

### The production of experience

In their paradigm-setting book *The Experience Economy*, Joseph Pine and James Gilmore connect the production of experience with a model of theatre and theatricality. The volume is intended as something of a bible for entrepreneurs entering the new millennium, and its key proposition concerns wealth creation: '*goods and services are no longer enough* to foster economic growth, create new jobs, and maintain economic prosperity. To realize revenue growth and increased employment, the staging of experiences must be pursued as a distinct form of economic output' (2011 [1999]: ix; original emphasis). By way of example, Pine and Gilmore trace the trajectory of coffee from its status as a crop (harvested), a commodity (traded as coffee beans), a good (packaged for personal consumption), to a service that is variously experiential (depending on whether you order your espresso from a station forecourt, a ubiquitous Starbucks or – in the authors' example – the Florian café in St Mark's Square in Venice). Of course, the greater the attribution of experience the more costly the transaction.

In this analysis, value is created 'by boldly treating services as the stage and goods as the props for staging engaging experiences.' Hence the turn to theatre as 'a *model* for human performance in staging experiences' (xviii, original emphasis) and for what Pine and Gilmore describe as 'experience orchestration' (66).[1] If this also suggests the analogous field of music, it nonetheless emphasizes the quasi-artistic finesse that is required for certain sorts of post-millennial money-making. The providers of experiences are always at some level tuning the theatricality of their enterprise, which is all about the exercise of creative choice (they determine what is revealed and presented); the organization of action (since a dramatic paradigm entails people doing things); and the arrangement of the sequence, duration and rhythm of events (157–9). You'd think you should look to theatre directing programmes in drama schools to find the most effective business people.

This account has been influential in social and economic studies.[2] Informed by Richard Schechner's *Performance Theory* (1988), it resonates with the turn in theatre and performance towards experience-production – which must also be seen in the context of a cultural shift towards experience-seeking. *The Experience Economy* has a supply-side focus, where provider-producers manage the experiences of customer-consumers (see Darmer and Sundbo 2008: 2, 5). Even so, the implication of an experience-driven model is that the producer will focus on how things *seem* and *feel* to those who pay for, receive and consume the experience. This leads us to the range of affects that help to calibrate our experience, to which I turn later in the chapter.

Pine and Gilmore provide a diagram of 'realms of experience', which can be adapted to help us address affective engagements in contemporary performance scenarios. The diagram features a simple pair of axes: the horizontal runs from 'passive' to 'active'. The vertical runs from 'absorb' (at the top) to 'immerse' (at the bottom) (46). There are immediate problems in applying each axis to theatre settings. First, the Brechtian/Rancièrean analysis tells us that the members of an audience should never be thought of as 'passive', even when sitting silently in a darkened auditorium watching action unfolding in front of them. Individuals can make decisions, affiliate with characters or ideological positions, adjudicate the events presented, and perhaps take actions outside (or indeed inside) the theatre as a consequence. Second, while Pine and Gilmore mean to distinguish between a reflective perspective, akin to stroking your chin, and a full-scale plunge, 'absorption' and 'immersion' are now too close in meaning (at least in digital gaming and performance studies) to be useful to my own analysis. What's more, 'immersion' has become routinely used in theatre criticism as a descriptor for the sorts of events produced by companies including Punchdrunk, Coney, Wildworks and dreamthinkspeak (see Machon 2013: 64–5). The virtue of the intersecting axes, however, is that they figure different *modes* of spectator engagement and different *degrees* of independent agency that help us to unpack ways in which audiences enjoy experiences. To this end, I suggest adapting the diagram as indicated in Figure 8.1.

No word is innocent of its baggage, and the terms here must be taken as gestures towards some predominant correlates. 'Consumption' indicates the act of consuming and perhaps enjoying the event. It suggests a reception model of spectatorship. 'Production' denotes the making of materials and the facilitation of experiences. It indicates an individual agency that can effect change – the transformation that production always entails. It is possible to be

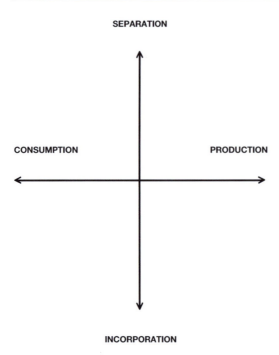

SEPARATION

CONSUMPTION                          PRODUCTION

INCORPORATION

*Figure 8.1* Axes of spectator-participant engagement
Source: Adapted from Pine and Gilmore 2011: 46

a consumer of materials and experiences that one also helps to develop, in which case one would be somewhere towards the middle of this particular axis. In 1980 Alvin Toffler coined the term 'prosumer' to denote the consumer who is proactive and producer-like in diverse ways, adapting goods and devices to suit their own ends, operating like 'professionals' in what had previously been specialist practices, and interacting with companies in ways that drive product development (Toffler 1980). This shift is all the more pronounced in digital culture, and its implications are now regularly seen in contemporary perform-ance. Alston, for example, talks of audience members as 'producing receivers' in his account of immersive theatre (2013: 131; see also Ridout 2008: 129). What was previously a clear distinction between performers and spectators is now a negotiable spectrum.

Likewise the vertical axis proposes a spectrum. 'Separation' indicates a functional detachment of the individual from the entity that is presented. We know that audience members sitting in a darkened auditorium can be no less engaged than games players at a console; the term here designates a structural relationship between spectator and event that points to a geo-physical distance. 'Incorporation' denotes a necessary interdependence, whereby the presence of the individual *affects* the event, and her body (*corpus*) is typically bound up within it. Of course, without the bodies of audiences there would not normally be theatre in any setting. 'Incorporation' here denotes a procedural function to the spectator-participant's presence: an imbrication of the body/action of the individual in the event as it unfolds. In his account of digital gameplay, Gordon Calleja proposes the metaphor of 'incorporation' as a means of avoiding the terms 'presence' and 'immersion', which in gaming assume that the 'external world' can be excluded (2011: 169). 'Incorporation', on the other hand, 'occurs when the game world is present to the player while the player is simultaneously present, via her avatar, to the virtual environment' (169). Both sides of the coin are essential: the player's assimilation of the game (a form of absorption), and her embodiment within it. In the model that I propose here, the twin operations of assimilation (of the game, performance, event) and bodied entry into it can be undertaken *in person* in actual spatial environments such as those produced by 'immersive' theatre companies. Whether your body is virtually or actually in action in the event-world, by way or your avatar or your fleshy self in transit, your involvement requires embodied action that results from autonomous decision.

The two axes divide a field into four quadrants that I will describe in phrases rather than single terms, in order to avoid being too reductive (Figure 8.2):[3]

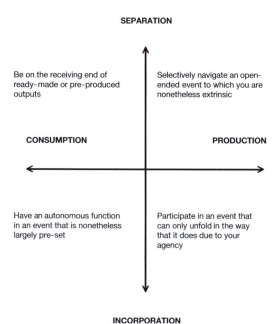

*Figure 8.2* Realms of spectator-participant engagement

Source: Adapted from Pine and Gilmore 2011: 46

Distinctions between the zones are not hard and fast. There is a bleed from one to another, and one's status or situation as a spectator-participant might change within any single event. The very fluidity of the model is critical in a contemporary culture of experience production, where there is a continual negotiation of the relationships between consumption, production, separation and incorporation in determining the extent to which the event is *felt*. This is not a straightforward matter of experience being produced more readily in one realm than in another, as we shall see. Rather, it gives us a way to consider the structuring of experience in diverse performance-related scenarios.

## The experiencing of affect

As soon as we speak of the production of experience, we must consider the sensations and feelings that tell us what experiences we are having. This brings us to affect. The study of affect spreads across a range of disciplines, including neuro-cognitive and psychological bioscience, cultural studies and philosophy, aesthetics, social geography, and anthropology, and (in theatre studies) the fields of spectatorship and theatre for change.[4] This makes the term 'affect' rather slippery, or at least shimmery, like a fish whose colour appears to change depending on the water in which it swims. Affect has come into view in performance studies as part of a wider interest in phenomenology (which deals with matters of perception and response), audience experience, and a new actuality that is concerned with the bodies of spectators as much as those of performers. A phenomenological approach considers how the thing that is affective (the performance, event, piece of acting or design) is offered to and perceived by the spectator. As we saw in Chapter 4, Deleuze and Guattari provide a pithy way of thinking about this: 'What is preserved – the thing or the work of art – is *a bloc of sensations, that is to say, a compound of percepts and affects*' (1991: 164, original emphasis). It is by way of being sensation-oriented that the work moves from concept into consumption and thereby (for the spectator) into conception. Every artwork proposes a felt response. A form of communicability is key, 'something passing from one to the other. This something can be specified only as sensation. It is a zone of indetermination, of indiscernibility . . . this is what is called an *affect*' (Deleuze and Guattari 19 91: 173).

Brian Massumi's key text on the subject, *Parables for the Virtual*, is notably Deleuzean, and develops a case about movement in relation to felt experience. Affect here is part of a set of becomings and intensities relating to motion and action. It can be analysed precisely because it is a category inside sense-experience. In a characteristic flourish, however, Massumi suggests that 'The autonomy of affect is its participation in the virtual' (2002: 35). The latter is not to be understood by way of its normal digital designation but as a term for what Massumi calls 'the "real but abstract" incorporeality of the body' (21) – in other words, its feeling capacity.[5]

Theatre is self-evidently a place where we will find and feel affects, given its arrangement around (re)presentations that are intended to be moving, provoking, exciting and absorbing. Theatre is affective in at least three connected ways. As a medium of communication, it presents us with ideas and figurings. These produce in us responses (that make us feel, for example, fearful, desiring, delighted), relating to the things we see and hear, that are shaped by our past experiences, memories and acculturation. Our responses are also visceral, in relation to our specific experience of space, shape, flow, rhythm, volume and the like – what we might describe as the aesthetic and somatic intensities of presentation. And they can arise from shared, communal involvement with others, to the point where we might find ourselves party to 'affective contagion' (Thrift 2008: 235). Affects usually come upon us outside of our control. We cannot help but *feel* in the moment. They are to that extent immediately corporeal – they belong to the body. But they exist alongside cognition. Affects are sometimes produced because we know the import of a theatrical encounter (the work of memory and acculturation, again). In addition, we can understand what it is that we are feeling and sometimes, afterwards, rationalize it in order to do something with the feeling that we had.

The operation of affect is fundamental to theatrical exchange. It is part of theatre's now-moment and its feeling-machinery. This isn't to relegate it to a simple register of sensation, sentimentality or consumer satisfaction. It has its own politics, to do with notions of invitation, involvement, identity, renuncia-tion, pleasure, community, and agency. In *Theatre & Feeling*, Erin Hurley argues that 'theatre's solicitation, management, and display of feelings – what I will call its "feeling-labour" – is the most important aspect of theatre's cultural work. It is what finally makes theatre matter' (2010: 4).

While affect is usefully understood in relation to cultural practice, it is first and foremost biological in its operation. Hurley describes it as an 'immediate, uncontrollable, skin-level registration of a change to our environment . . . affects are sets of muscular and/or glandular responses' (2010: 13–14). The case is fleshed out, so to speak, in Teresa Brennan's *The Transmission of Affect*, which seeks to establish a broad scientific basis to explain how affect works on both the mind and the body. Brennan has a tilt at neo-Darwinism, which she sees as too narrowly concerned with biological determinism in accounting for animal (and specifically human) affective behaviours. She argues instead for an understanding of affect that allows for 'social and historical context' (2004: 74), tracing pre-Hellenic, Christian and psychoanalytic frames of reference. She finds reverberations, for example, across notions of what we now think of as narcissism, inertia, envy and anger. Her insistence on the social and historical is useful in relation to performance and spectating, whose affects and pleasures can always be understood culturally.

Brennan nonetheless develops a bioscientific (rather than predominantly cultural) understanding of the transmission of affect, drawing on neurological, psychoanalytic and endocrinological (glandular and hormonal) approaches. She describes the key process of 'entrainment', a term taken from neurology, 'whereby one person's or one group's nervous and hormonal systems are brought into alignment with another's' (9). This happens partly through the 'electrical' work of the nervous system, operating through sight, sound and touch (70); partly through the memory-inducing work of smells, sounds and images; and partly through a form of chemical communication due to the operation of pheromones – substances that are released externally from the body. 'Pheromones are literally in the air', Brennan reminds us, operating as 'human chemosignals' that help to align the affective disposition of individuals in a group or shared situation (69, 77).

Affects, then, come upon us through a variety of means and *position* us in relation to others. We can think of an affect as a kind of immediate sensory access that has a basis in biochemical human interactions. It shapes how we feel, and moreover how we feel about that feeling. That said, scholars of affect differ somewhat in their account of the place of feelings and emotions. For neuroscientist Antonio Damasio:

> The term *affect* is often used as a synonym of 'mood' or 'emotion' although it is more general and can designate the whole subject matter we are discussing here: emotions, moods, feelings. Affect is the thing you display (emote) or experience (feel) toward an object or situation, any day of your life whether you are moody or not.
>
> (Damasio 1999: 342, n.10)

Brennan defines feelings as 'sensations that have found a match in words' (2004: 140). They involve an understanding of that which is felt, which is understood because put into language. Affect, here, is the operation of the senses – let's say, the access of sensings – that allows one to have feelings, for 'the things that one feels are affects. The things that one feels with are feelings' (23). Brennan acknowledges that this is paradoxical (116). It might also be thought confusing etymologically, in that we would normally understand 'feeling' in the pre-linguistic sense – that's to say, the thing felt. As Welton observes, the term 'feel' in English 'describes a sensory-affective continuum whose terms range from the particularity of various emotional states to sensations at the tips of the fingers' (2012: 8). Affect, then, is bound up with stimuli that come upon us unannounced, those neuro-physical responses that cannot be controlled in their moment of access. It can involve anticipated excitation (where, often, the anticipation itself is affective). And it entails perceptions that enable feeling; emotional registers that shape our responses to stimuli and situations; and touch-sensations specific to the moment.

Affects can be calibrated, although due to our different biological, cultural and emotional histories they are also roundly subjective, and what one individual finds affective another might not.[6] The problem, of course, is that affect is located in the individual, and as such can too easily be self-referential, self-authorized and immediately unavailable to shared standards of proof or agreement. On the other hand, we know that activities, events and encounters produce feelings not only in us but also in others. Adjudicating the nature of such feelings, and the relationship between the person, the event, the felt engagement and its cultural context is the task of performance criticism.

In the Experience Economy, entrepreneurs and organizations seek to provide experiences (usually for some kind of cost). In the sophisticated consumerism of late-capitalism, experiences offer something that goods cannot: visceral sense-engagement in and across time. In an era that privileges presence and immediacy, they locate us in the affective now-moment. In an era of individual agency, they provide the authentic guarantee of personal involvement. 'You had to be there' used to be a mantra to describe the special buzz of an event. In digital culture there are different ways of being 'there'. More to the point, you have to *feel* it. Theatre and performance organize this feelingness. As Hurley suggests: 'the theatre offers "super-stimuli": that is, it concentrates and amplifies the world's natural sensory effects' (23). We are not interested solely in the sensualities of performance and the quasi-erotic charge of felt sensation. The production of feeling is an effect and guarantee of presence and, more, of something *mattering* to you. For those involved in theatre and performance, it enables an embodied experience of representation and (or) cultural process. It takes us beyond cognition, although often in ways that we can remember and think about. Cognitive acts always come later than the feeling for, in Massumi's celebrated formulation, 'the skin is faster than the word' (2002: 25). Yet feelingness, the having of experience, can also shape an engagement with processes and sites of representation – with the cultural and ideological work of a performance or event. It belongs to the tactics of a late-capitalist experience economy, but also helps to reveal its places of pleasure and spaces for resistance.

Given the *topos* of individual experience, I concentrate below on events that I attended. My own modes of engagement necessarily inform the critical procedure. This is not intended autobiographically. As Brennan suggests, 'Subjectivity means studying what one has experienced oneself and valuing it, or valuing the subjective side of one's interactions with the object studied' (19). I have chosen the instances not so much because I enjoyed them (or otherwise), but for their resonance within current discussions of performance, presence and engagement. Each stands for something larger than itself, whether in a lineage of theatre production; as an emblem of a certain sort of encounter; or an example of developing relationships between audiences (consumers, participants) and their objects of engagement. Each can be located in one of the four realms of the Engagement diagram in Figure 10.2. They help us consider affect as a correlate of experience in the event-zones of contemporary theatre, performance and spectatorship.

## Consumption – Separation | *Audience*

In the top-left of the Engagement diagram, the spectator is a consumer rather than a producer, and the event entails a separation between performers and audience. *Audience*, by the Flemish company Ontroerend Goed, stages this separation as its subject matter, and challenges the divisions that it sets up by focusing on the audience as the topic of the show.

Founded in 1994 and based in Ghent, the company creates performances and events that gnaw at the authenticity of experience.[7] This is so, for example, in its trilogy of pieces addressing how it is to be a teenager, which foregrounds the inner life and emotional turmoil of adolescent years, revealed through personal testimony. *Once and For All We're Gonna Tell You Who We Are so Shut Up and Listen* (2008) features 13 young people (aged 14–18), sitting on a line of chairs, behaving with varying degrees of unruliness and sharing their thoughts whether grave or juvenile. *Teenage Riot* (2010) slims down the cast to eight teenagers contained in a large cube onstage, a space not unlike the always-closed bedroom to which the teenager retreats. The show performed an inversion, however, by mediating the various games, musings and doodlings that went on inside the room by way of a video projection, on the wall facing the audience, of the capture from a hand-held camera inside the cube. When I saw it in Edinburgh, I was struck by how raw, immediate and uncensored the material seemed, utterly distinct from other sorts of cultural engagement with teenagers (through schools, youth clubs, or the work of applied theatre companies) that arrange a patina of comportment. In this instance the achievement of director Alexander Devriendt and his collaborators was a kind of visceral unmuzzling, as the teenagers spoke graphically of their fantasies, angers, anxieties and transgressions. The trilogy concluded with *All That is Wrong* (2012), and a further paring down to a single performer, the 18-year-old Koba Ryckewaert, who wrote the piece. Ryckewaert is also its writer in a different sense, as during the piece she scribes a personal text in chalk, across a series of black surfaces, of her desires and fears as she moves definitively into adulthood.

Another trilogy entails a different kind of personal attention – this time, with the spectator as the centre of attention.[8] *The Smile Off Your Face* (2003) involves the audience member being led on a journey in a wheelchair, blindfolded with hands bound, and subjected to a range of touch and sensation encounters. In *Internal* (2007), the spectator reveals secrets in a one-to-one encounter with a performer, only to find these divulged in a denouement with all participants present. *A Game of You* (2009) is structured around watching and being watched, facilitated by a set of curtained spaces and mirrors. As Groot Nibbelink observes, 'Ontroerend Goed is fascinated by the potential of the direct encounter of performers and spectators in the theatre' (2012: 417). *Audience* is different from the company's 'immersive trilogy', as a studio theatre piece for an audience watching end-on, but it shares the trilogy's fascination with scenarios of intimacy, attention, trust and betrayal. You don't find yourself stroked as you sit in a wheelchair, or chatted up in private by a solo performer, as you do in other pieces, but the encounter of the audience with *Audience* is no less full of feeling than in the immersive productions. I will describe the piece in some detail in order to reflect upon the affective work of its staging and performance.[9]

As the audience enters, we are offered the opportunity to leave our bags and coats, which are placed on racks on the edge of the stage, left and right. This, we are told, is in order not to block the aisles. We sit in an end-on arrangement, facing the stage. The performance begins with a woman speaking to the audience in a pre-show discourse about what to do and what not to do as an audience member at the theatre.

We are familiar with the pre-show instruction, issued over the sound system or sometimes by front of house managers. We are familiar with performers who speak directly to us, often through a microphone (as in shows by The Wooster Group or Forced Entertainment). Complicite's *A Disappearing Number* (2007) begins ostensibly with a stage manager informing us about a necessary delay to the beginning of the show due to technical difficulties. The Builders Association's *Super Vision* (2005) starts with one of the performers speaking directly to us, recounting apparent details of our demographic, as revealed by the statistical rendering of data collected during telephone and online booking of tickets. This trope is the one-way conversation. It interpellates us as an audience, people who are expected to behave in certain ways at an event that itself is expected to behave in certain ways.[10] The performer in *Audience* who talks uninterrupted is meta-theatrical. She observes that there is no drinking permitted in this particular theatre. Someone is drinking, from a plastic glass issued by the bar staff before the show – so already this is a game, a joke. Likewise there is no eating allowed. No coughing (this gets a laugh). She speaks of applause, and the moment when you decide to stop clapping, depending on how favourable you find the performance. The opening sequence is a riff on conventions of spectatorship. The spotlight, so to say, is already facing outwards.

This becomes more uncomfortably apparent when a man positions a camera upstage centre. Here, Handke's requirement that the audience considers itself is manifested in a new-media environment. Very slowly the lights come up on the audience, and the camera's view is projected on the white cyclorama across the back of the stage. As Freshwater observes, 'The confrontational stare, where performers, out of character, stand and silently watch an audience, has now become a recognizable theatrical trope' (Fielding 2009: 50). The camera intensifies this silent stare. *Audience* stages the camera as the device *par excellence* for contemporary scrutiny (Figure 8.3). Here, it is large, overt, and usually onstage looking outwards. An image on the screen is present almost throughout, usually showing one or more members of the audience. The camera is initially set to a medium close-up, so that it catches details of people's clothing, hands, faces and hair. It pans across the audience. There is some laughter, and not much movement among audience members. This brings to mind Nicholas Ridout's discussion of embarrassment, which takes its cue (so to speak) from the moment that Samuel West as Richard II addressed some of his lines directly to him. I too can say with Ridout, 'When I was young and Brechtian I was all for eye contact' (2006: 70). This doesn't change the feeling of embarrassment when the eye of the performer fixes one to the spot and – worse – draws the eyes of others. At *Audience*, the direct address is to the gathered throng (we're in it together), and produces (in this spectator, at least) a feeling of considerable discomfort based on uncertainty. Will I be asked to respond to a question? Or to do something? Worse, to do something against my will, that makes me look stupid or feel out of control?

In his seat at the Swan Theatre in Stratford (or perhaps the Barbican, London), Ridout had it easy. There was no onstage camera scrutinizing him, as there is at *Audience*. The camera dwells on individual faces, accompanied by a speculative voiceover from four performers, dotted around the auditorium, who speak into microphones. They articulate presumed doubts, attitudes and observations of those under scrutiny: 'I've never seen my face so large before'; 'I'm looking more and more like my father'. One of the performers conveys statistics about the audience. 'Eleven people came in alone. There is one group of five. Five of you have free tickets. There are three fat people – you know who you are. Predominant colours are blue and black. The brightest dresser is. . .' The camera pans to a man wearing a yellow jacket. This crossing of a line – making us the reference point of scrutiny, jokes, insults – induces a form of bodily closure. Audience members press back in their seats. There is little movement, for movement attracts attention.

The racks of coats deposited by members of the audience on entering the auditorium are revealed in silhouette behind the cyclorama. The actors hold up individual jackets. They then come onto the stage, 'modelling' the coats to an ironic commentary that decides whether or not the item is fashionable. Three performers each bring a bag on stage and empty its contents. One contains a spare pair of underwear. Another has cigarettes and condoms. Two have moleskines (a fashionable notebook). One has two pots of lip-gloss. The performers accompany this sifting with an ironic commentary. 'Ah, a moleskine, how original. . . . And another moleskine.' This is on the face of it a violation of privacy and property. We have moved from interpellation to a form of disinterment, the presentation of personal effects standing in for an extended kind of calling to account. There is laughter along with some initial gasps.

Matthieu Sys, one of the performers, 'trains' the audience in applause. He starts with one finger clapping, then two, and so on up to a standing ovation. We must cut the applause when he says. This is filmed from onstage. The camera, with its implacable gaze, maintains a continual scrutiny, which sustains an atmosphere of fear. If don't obey instructions, presumably you will be easily spotted and possibly confronted. This makes for an uneasy complicity by spectators with the instructions that are issued. *Audience* does not so much

*Figure 8.3* Reflexive spectating: the audience under scrutiny in *Audience*
Source: Robert Day

stage the audience, as the authority that comes with surveillance, along with the uneasy relations between command, control, choice and compliance. Remember Massumi's dictum, 'The skin is faster than the word'. We *feel* surveillance and its blithe presumption.

The show has an epicentric moment of confrontation. Sys picks on a young woman in the front row. 'You're not intelligent', he says. 'You're not even good looking. You're ugly. You want to know what you look like? Look.' The video projection shows her in big-close-up. 'You know why I'm saying these things to you? Not because of the seat you're sitting in. No, it's because of who you are.' The woman smiles, nervously. 'You think that's funny?' says Sys. Her smile wavers, but sustains, as if there is nothing else for it but to play along at playing along.[11]

Sys says to the young woman that he will only leave her alone if she parts her legs and the camera gets a shot. 'Just one shot, we'll get the shot and then we can move on.' He suggests that in order to help her, the audience get a chant going, 'Part your legs'. The video projection shows her legs, in close–up, crossed. He starts by asking people in the front row to chant. One man complies and starts chanting quietly. Sys offers another man a ten–pound note to join in, but he declines. The audience does not adopt the chant. Sys gives the money to the man who started chanting. He gives the girl a countdown of five. She doesn't move her legs. Someone from the audience says 'I think you should move on.'

The moving on takes the form of the four performers (with Sys now in the audience) raising questions and issues to do with the sequence just presented. The show ends with a wide shot of us, the audience, figured as a crowd, mixed with a shot of us applauding (recorded in the earlier part of the show when applause was practiced). The image then dissolves into a montage showing crowds of different sorts – at a football match, a Nazi rally, the crowd before Martin Luther King at the Lincoln Memorial in Washington. The sequence takes crowds – audiences – out of context and history. It suggests that the crowd is a single phenomenon of homogenized mass compliance. A title comes up: 'Applaud'. Most audience members do. The titles change, to tell the audience to imagine that the performers are on stage and then leaving the stage, and to decide when to stop clapping. The applause is mixed and some audience members do not applaud at all. To a muted atmosphere the performers return coats and bags from the racks, now positioned on the front of the stage again, to audience members as they leave.

In *Audience*, the audience is not properly interactive – the actions of individuals do not change anything in the event – and barely participatory. We are in the top-left zone of our diagram of audience engagement, for this configuration entails separation rather than incorporation, and consumption rather than production. That said, the event has a high experiential function, as we feel the sort of embarrassment and discomfort, magnified, that Ridout describes. Interpellated as 'audience', we are the subject of a set of exchanges that thematize the tension between instruction and compliance, embodied here in the relationship between the stage (as authority) and the auditorium (as place of passive obedience). To that end, the show stages power structures and the place of the consumer/citizen within them. This dramatizes themes common in avant garde theatre from Büchner to Brecht to Handke. The performers chide, harangue and insult the audience, but do so from within a *mise en scène* that retains the geo-physical and spatial separation between stage and auditorium. *Audience* effaces this separation thematically through the staging of personal property (coats, handbags) and the almost perpetual scrutiny of the camera, replaying the spectator to herself but also making her a spectacle for others.

*Audience* comes over as a partially achieved experiment, negotiating the lines between stage and auditorium, the individual and the group, care and command, in a way that depends upon older theatrical strategies: stage-centredness, direct address and a fixed positioning of the audience in the auditorium. The images towards the end, showing other sorts of crowd, fit less well within the hyper-real mediation of the camera replaying the spectator to herself. However, if crowd behaviour eventually appears to be the *topos*, the show really hinges on the production of feeling. It is less interested in dramatizing compliance and behaviour (as in Pirandello) or playing out an associated discourse (as in Handke), and more in the creation of affective moments. *Audience* depends upon the uncomfortable feeling of being looked at when unprepared. It induces a long collective squirm. This is a theatre of affect, and while it takes the end-on format characteristic of much modern theatre, its affective aspects are intensified by its work across the fourth wall and its interpellation of its spectators. It operates within – and in response to – a performance culture that trades in agency and certain sorts of involvement. This production is made to be *felt*.

## Separation – Production | England v. India

The second zone of the Engagement diagram, reading across, entails physical separation from the performers and yet productive agency on the part of the spectator. By way of example, I consider a sporting event that I accessed online on 25 July 2011. I am working in the British Library in London. Yet I wish I were at the cricket. This particular game is the 2,000th international test match. It takes place at Lords cricket ground, the so-called 'home of cricket' in St John's Wood, London, between England and India. It features Sachin Tendulkar, widely acknowledged as one of the best batsman ever to have played the game, and expected to retire from the Indian team before it will play again in England. He has scored a total of 99 centuries (a score of one hundred runs or more) – but has never scored a century at Lords. Batsmen who achieve such a feat have their name inscribed on an honours board in the pavilion. India have been set a score of 458 in their second innings, and at the start of the day's play require another 378 runs to win. Such scores are never normally achieved in the fourth innings of a game. And yet India has a batting line-up much feared and respected, which partly explains why (at the point when this match was played) they are ranked as the leading nation in test cricket. As Kennedy observes, sporting events 'are overt contests and are teleological or outcome-oriented' (2001: 278). The outcome often relates to more than simply the match result. If England beat India in this four-match series by two matches or more, they will take India's place at the top of the test rankings.

I am sitting at a desk in the British Library, wishing I'd taken my son to the cricket as I read about it online on my laptop. I feel rather more sanguine about this when I discover that people have been queuing since 2am and turned away at 9.30. I do not want to plug in headphones to listen to the commentary by the Test Match Special (TMS) team on the radio – for if I did, I would do no work. But I can follow the BBC Sport live video scorecard ('India 2nd Innings In Play') and news updates, by way of blog postings by the BBC's correspondent Tom Fordyce, along with quotes from TMS commentators and pundits; emails, texts and tweets from members of the public and in one case a former England test cricketer; and tweets from BBC journalists and correspondents.

For my part, a desiring mechanism is in play, to do with the affiliation that sports fans feel for their team, and the anticipation that attends sporting events where something appears to be at stake. The desire (at least in my case) is not exactly for victory in and of itself, but for a close engagement with its processes – a combination of high technical achievement on the part of the players, sophisticated teamwork, peak performance in the pressure-zone of elite sport, and the enjoyment of narrative tension and delivery. I confess too an interest in seeing India do well, sustaining their recent ascendancy over the former colonial ruler. The desiring mechanism is geared around witness and uncertainty. It envisages a present-tense encounter with an event whose outcome could go either way. The principles of theatre and performance are evident here. The match itself takes place in an arena with the players surrounded by spectators. It is time-based, albeit that the timeframe is that of test match cricket, which can last (bizarrely, gloriously) for up to five days. The match has its narrative arc. As suggested above, the stakes are high for the participants and indeed historical in terms of the game of cricket. Performance, meanwhile, revolves around the application of focused skills in the sense of delivering a task to best effect, and of course around the players as entertainers, given the place of sport in the leisure economy. Meanwhile, the stage on which I can play, if I choose, is that provided by social media and remediated in the BBC's online coverage.

As discussed elsewhere in this volume, the advent of digital technology and its collapse of time and place have enabled widespread user-engagement with cultural activity. Amid the quiet rustle of scholars working in the Rare Books and Music reading room of the British Library, a couple of miles from Lords, I enjoy a silent and virtual connection with the game. In *Watching Sport*, the philosopher Stephen Mumford suggests that 'Watching should be understood broadly to mean observation through any sense faculty' (2012: 2) – and, we might add, through any medium. I am closer to being a 'purist' than a 'partisan' in terms of Mumford's two fundamental types of sports fan: interested in how the game is played, and the 'key moments of drama' (10).[12] I feel a great sense of atmosphere and theatre: the spectacle and import of the event are clear, even though I am in a library and not at the game. Mumford's account of the relationship of sport to drama is largely to do with what the actors/characters/participants do, and the mode in which they do it, where they are playing a role of a certain kind. We can add the consideration of narrative and what appears to be at stake. From my seat in the Library I have an acute awareness of what I can indeed only call 'drama'. The game has action, consequence, momentness. My connection is affective.

The BBC's online text commentary, cohering around Fordyce's blog, with new entries added every couple of minutes, goes as follows:

### 1025

The queues outside Lord's this morning? Extraordinary. The 20,000 tickets went on sale at 0830 this morning, and by 1000 they were turning them away at St John's Wood Tube station. The queue is four deep and stretches from the North Gate all the way up the Wellington Road, past the hospital, along the side of the garage, past the newsagents . . .

**TEXT via SMS**

**From James, Chalfont St Peter:** 'Got to Lord's at 9.30 and they were already turning people back. Hopefully I'll get home for start of match!'

**1032**

Wonderful scenes inside the ground, and we're still half an hour from the start – as the England team jogged slowly around the perimeter of the outfield, they were given a standing, shouting ovation by the giddy fans lucky enough to have made it in. I was excited before. I'm now a little shaky.

[via twitter]

**From samnics:** 'Measured the queue from when I joined at 8:50. Took 1hr, 15 mins and was 0.82 miles long. So happy to get in.'

**From Tony in Jakarta, TMS inbox:** 'Waiting in hospital for my wife to deliver our second child. I need advice on how best to break it to her that the baby is only the second-most important happening in the world at this time – slowly or quickly. Please help.'

**BBC Test Match Special's Michael Vaughan** [a former cricketer turned pundit]

'The players must cherish days like this. They arrived at 9am and they saw the queues, they had an amazing ovation when they warmed up and if they can bowl at a decent pace on a good length they will be able to take wickets throughout the day. I think Swann [an England bowler] will tie an end down, but the pacemen are going to be key.'

**From Karina in Hampshire, TMS inbox:** 'Mother in law and myself are in and settled in the grand stand. Sun cream on, first cuppa down the hatch and ready for a great day's play, come on England.'

**1055**

A reminder, amid all the giddiness, of the match situation going into this final day. India need another 378 runs to win; England nine wickets. Sachin Tendulkar cannot bat before 1240 or the fall of the fifth wicket (off the field for most of Sunday, has to make that time up); no word yet on where or how Gautam Gambhir will bat after he injured his elbow while fielding. All set?

**From David Rees, TMS inbox:** 'RE: Tony in Jakarta. If your wife is delivering your second child as well as birthing it, frankly I would keep schtum.'

**1104**

### THE SUN IS OUT

### India 80–1 (target 458)

Here we go – [England bowler] Chris Tremlett pawing the ground in front of the rammed pavilion, snorting, three slips, a gully, backward point, deep square leg, fine leg. . . [Indian batsman] Laxman blinking calmly into the bright sunshine, tapping the toe of his bat into the crease, edging down into the ground and through to second slip to pantomine ooohs all around. Short, jabbed off the chest to midwicket for the first single of the day. 582 balls left in the day. Can someone keep a tally?

Thus the day's play commences. This discourse not only reports and thereby remediates the event; it reflects metatheatrically on its eventness. A wicket falls ('GOT HIM! . . . Huge moment for England'). BBC TMS pundit Phil Tuffnell blogs:

> 'That is just what England wanted. The shot was very unlike Rahul Dravid – he fished at one outside off stump and was gone. This is an unbelievable atmosphere: I have never heard a forward defensive being met with oohs and aaahs before. Cracking stuff.'

> **From Marcus, TMS inbox:** 'Apologies to all in carriage C going south from Inverness on the Highland Cheiftan [*sic*] for the whooping at the fall of the Wall [Dravid's nickname on account of his obdurateness].'

**1143**

India 98–1 (target 458)

Febrile atmosphere around the famous old ground, the sun bright, the scene as close to sporting perfection as you could wish for. The three slips wait with hands on knees, Skipper Strauss in a stiff-brimmed sunhat, Swann and Anderson in blue caps. [. . .] If there were some giant control room somewhere where you adjust every tiny nuance of the scenario in front of us here – the sort of giant mixing-desk you'd expect to see George Martin leaning over during a 'recording of Sergeant Pepper' retrospective – you wouldn't touch a single button.

I am enjoying a form of participatory engagement. This is not exactly spectatorship (I do not watch the match), nor is it precisely witness (I was not corporeally there), although it is a form of both. Kennedy comments on 'how powerful witnessing has become in an age of electronic simulations. We are all mediatized spectators now; surrounded daily by televisual enactments and luminant fantasies, we have achieved a new relationship to the live event' (2001: 282). This relationship is further enabled by the Internet.

Temporality is a critical feature, and my experience of the game involves distributed time. The event takes place in real time although I follow it with interruptions, and with a time-lag given that the blog updates always come after the moment they describe. I am, nonetheless, in continual engagement with a quasi-present, knowing that the event is afoot and not knowing what happens next. Mumford discusses the enhanced enjoyment of watching live as opposed to watching a recording: 'We want to watch in shared time because this means we are experiencing the emotional highs and lows of the game simultaneously with many others' (2012: 118). This kind of collectivism enhances the affective nature of the event. In the case of online engagement, shared time is enjoyed entirely through a form of remediation, reiteration and reverberation. The events undergo reflection and commentary through the blogs, texts and tweets. My encounter is amplified by personal interventions by others for whom the game matters. These include Andrew Flintoff, a former England test cricketer, whose tweet is retweeted: 'Would love Sachin to get 100 today and England win – Obviously.' Flintoff's personal incursion into this sphere of public discourse is affirming: he is on the same level – in the same mode of textual production and circulation – as his public, and his participation underscores the wide communal reach of the match. There are extra-game discussions about, for instance, taking sick leave in order to be at the ground, making the match a priority over a birth, enjoying the drama from the seat of a train. This evocation of other places and perspectives amplifies the focus on the event itself. It also democratizes the game. If I wanted to, I could tweet or text my own intervention.

Writing in 2001 – before the advent of live blogging from sports events – Kennedy observes (after Raymond Williams) that sports contests often escape full control by governments or media organizations, given their rootedness in social settings and fanbases. As he suggests:

> It may be that the chief distinction of sports is the freedom fans assume to create, in a public forum and communally, a new text out of their spectation, separate from the text of the game or the meanings assigned to it by the media or official agencies.
>
> (Kennedy 2001: 283)

Internet blogging manifests that text in a literal way, as scripted demotic discourse. Further, it indicates the ongoing *textuality* of digital culture that I remarked upon in Chapter 2. Embodied practices are accompanied by their texts in cyberspace – which are realized through the corporeal exercise of writing.

It goes without saying that such engagements make no difference whatsoever to the game itself, which plays out blithely in 'the middle' irrespective of the anxieties or excitements of this remote community. The spectators present at the ground might be thought to have some bearing on the match, as their concentration and audible response may incrementally affect the nature of the play. For the virtual spectators no such influence can obtain. This doesn't change the intensity of the engagement, however. We would say the same of sports matches that have taken place in other times and places, mediated through the radio or television. Fans are invested, and take enjoyment in respective moments of discovery and revelation, howsoever they are conveyed.

In his discussion of football spectatorship in pubs, Mike Weed suggests that 'the two key features of sport spectating experience are, first, a desire to experience physical proximity to the live event, and second, a desire to have an experience that can be re-told to others after the event' (2008: 192). The pub, in this analysis, is a 'third place' for viewing (being neither the stadium nor the home) that offers a 'shared communal experience' (Weed 2008: 193). Online participation provides neither the physical proximity nor the 'transforming' of a material location that Weed discusses, but it does enable a community of proximate affiliation. And because it remediates, it has an inherent 'retelling' function. This means that we have both a vicarious engagement with the match as seen through the eyes of others (Fordyce in particular), and an actual *in situ* engagement, enjoying its process experienced as a form of drama. Amid the studious ambience of the British Library I am enjoying co-presence with a group of cricket fans.[13]

The rhetoric of the blog underscores the collective affective nature of our virtual engagement. There is indeed much that is pub-like to this discourse. I am aware of its blokishness and the fact that this is a notably male constituency.[14] However, I'm not convinced that – as Weed goes on to argue – the need is for proximity to other blokes (with metaphorical pints in hand) sharing in the experience, as opposed to proximity to the event. Rather, the co-enjoyment of others emphasizes the *access* of the event in the phenomenal sense. Its presence is affirmed. Remote engagement with this particular sort of theatre *re-performs* the event in its moment, and does so in ways that both facilitate and stage its affectiveness. In my online engagement, I do not change the cricket match, but I can gain a form of access and contribute if I so choose to the 'stage' that is the online blog. I *feel* like a participant: connected, engaged, immersed, and able to get involved.

## Consumption – Incorporation | *The Drowned Man*

As an instance of an encounter where you have an autonomous function in an event that is largely pre-set, I return to Punchdrunk and one of its immersive productions. 'Immersive' theatre is now a feature of the contemporary performance landscape, although for some the adjective is sufficiently slippery to warrant hazard-light quote marks. 'Immersion' is used in discussions of digital games-playing to describe the feeling that you are inside the game-world that you engage with through your device monitor (Calleja 2011: 2). On the other hand, as Josephine Machon notes, it also refers to the sort of theatrical event that 'owes more to landscape as location, architectural inspiration, installation art (in visual, sculptural and sonic fields) and festival environments than it does to digital practice' (Machon 2013: 65).[15] There is a connection between both modes of immersion, to do with what Calleja describes as 'the shortening of the subjective distance between player and game environment' (2). Immersive events and productions by (for example) Punchdrunk, Wildwork, dreamthinkspeak, Collective Unconscious (all UK), Fiction Pimps and Signa (Denmark), Dream Theatre Company and (under the aegis of Stageworks Media) Speakeasy Dollhouse (USA), Interactive Theatre International and The Rabble (Australia) are often modular in their arrangement of different spaces, non-linear in the journeys they facilitate, and require navigation by visitors, like the games and virtual worlds of online entertainment. In all these instances, immersion is also to do with innovation, and the promise to the spectator-participant that she will find herself in a new and unique encounter.

It is not untypical to view immersive theatre as an extension of site-specific theatre practice, cohering around particular spaces that are adapted, refunctioned and scenically dressed (Carlson 2012; Worthen 2012; White 2012). This labour with and within space is designed for witness and felt experience – not only in relation to sites, but also to self, as you experience yourself in the act of being a spectator-participant in the midst of performance. In this sense immersive theatre participates in larger trends towards the theatricalizing of cultural production (the world becomes theatre) and the commodification of experience. Another common view is that it offers free rein to the spectator, who can choose her own journey through a piece. This is not always straightforward, however, in that some journeys are more constrained than others, and the event often permits far less agency than appears to be the case. This tension between what is open to you and what is constructed for you is key to the feeling-mechanism of this form of theatre.

I will explore this further by discussing a visit to *The Drowned Man: A Hollywood Fable*, an immersive piece by the British-based company Punchdrunk, arch-exponents of the form. Two signal productions established the company as a force in British theatre: *Faust* (2006–7), staged in a disused tobacco warehouse in east London; and *Masque of the Red Death* (2007–8), an adaptation of short stories by Edgar Allan Poe, presented across many of the various spaces of south London's Battersea Arts Centre (formerly a municipal town hall). Its international reputation was cemented with the hit show *Sleep No More*, based on Shakespeare's *Macbeth*, initially produced in London in 2003, remade for an outing in Boston in 2009, and again in 2011 for an extended run in New York across three disused warehouses made up as 'the McKittrick Hotel'. Other turns to canonical works and dilapidated buildings have included an opera-inflected treatment of *The Duchess of Malfi* in a former pharmaceutical facility in London's docklands (2010), *Tunnel 228* (2009), drawing on Fritz Lang's *Metropolis* and presented in abandoned tunnels beneath London's Waterloo station, and *The Firebird Ball*, after *Romeo and Juliet* (2005), realized in a former pickle factory in south-east London.[16]

*The Drowned Man: A Hollywood Fable*, presented by Punchdrunk and the National Theatre, directed by Felix Barrett (the company's artistic director) and Maxine Doyle, draws loose association from Buchner's *Woyzeck* (Zaiontz also observes 'Nathanael West's Depression-era novel *The Day of the Locust* (1939), Billy Wilder's noir-film *Sunset Boulevard* (1950), and David Lynch's neo-noir-film *Mulholland Drive* (2001)' (2014: 408). It took place in a former sorting office next to London's Paddington train station – a building proffered (not untypically) as a different sort of faded facility; in this case Temple Studios, the London outpost of a now defunct Hollywood production corporation. Spectators were free (up to a point, as some doors are closed off) to wander through four floors, each of which features different spaces designed to convey various atmospheres and settings consistent with the piece's 1950s and early-1960s timeframe. The film studio setting provided the event with its spatial and thematic rationale. On entering the space, I was handed a slip.[17] On one side was the following:

### William and Mary

William and Mary struggle to make ends meet outside the gates of a film studio. When Mary meets Dwayne, a drugstore cowboy, they strike up an affair and William's fragile world starts to fall apart. William confronts Mary about the infidelity, but she denies everything. As William's paranoia becomes uncontrollable, he goes to a party and in horror witnesses Mary and Dwayne's affair first-hand. William's state of delusion and panic accelerates until he leads Mary into the wilderness and murders her.

On the reverse of the slip is the same text, except that it bears the names Wendy and Marshall, specifies that the couple meet inside rather than outside the studio gates, and that Marshall's affair is with Dolores, 'the studio diva'.

Armed with these mirror texts as one enters the space, you understand that there is a parallel narrative, set in and around the film studio, concerning the two love triangles. This establishes a context – but any spectator would be hard pressed to piece the story together without several visits. In any case, this aspect is significantly downscaled by the company: the narrative is not a first-order concern. The scenic space reveals interior and exterior locations and a wash of mid-twentieth-century Americana. The spectator's discovery of it takes precedence. Just as space is encountered, so too is narrative. It becomes segmented and distributed, composed not of a single linear flow but a texture of interrelated events 'collected' as you go. The work is a challenge to epistemology. Everything matters – or not very much matters, as it is all contingent. The story, then, is a vehicle for a touristic encounter with scenographies and scenarios (Barrett, Livi Vaughan and Beatrice Minns are credited as the production's designers). In a small office space, for instance, part of the floor is divided into squares filled variously with hay, stones, sand and old books – an anti-realist treatment. A scene takes place in which a woman dunks a performer wearing whiteface make-up in a fish tank. This is my first encounter with either. I do not know these characters, nor (yet – if ever) how they fit into the story-world. As W. B. Worthen observes in his discussion of *Sleep No More*, 'The actors are fully absorbed, meticulously *doing* what they *do* ... "what the actor is doing" is what we attend to' (2012: 91, original emphasis). The *mode* of performance – a sort of intense immediacy – is foremost. The whiteface performer leaves. The woman changes into a party dress. I follow her into a large studio with a black and white chequered floor. A formalized dance ensues, featuring a number of characters.

My experience was of fleeting and fragmented actions and representations that took on the affective structure of discovery on the one hand and deflection or deferral on the other. I was inside theatrical worlds that seemed oddly remote because often empty of action or casually inhabited by actions that moved or referred elsewhere. The fact that everything is in play simultaneously and can therefore be missed means that no action can be held to be central, unless the denouement to which we were directed at the end of the piece. This produces an odd anxiety (what am I missing?); a floating sense of serendipity (what am I discovering?); or a necessary disaffection (it doesn't matter to me what I am missing).

On the first floor, I move through faded office spaces given a 1950s patina and a pronounced feel of decrepitude. Indeed the tropes of abandonment and decay are widely prevalent in immersive theatre productions, suggesting a cultural nostalgia for recognized pasts and a certain sort of fashionable necrophilia. In the case of *The Drowned Man* (Figure 8.4) this conflates the period setting of the drama (the 1950s and '60s), the thematic treatment of a story of decaying relationships, and the site-specific nature of this particular building (a former post office pretending to be a film studio from half a century ago). More broadly across the immersive genre, it allows for a palimpsestic production of space, where we encounter the functionalities of sites in their first designation (department store, factory, school) along with a performed redolence, where they are remodeled as something else. There is an affective tenor to such spaces, to do with tinges of loss, redundancy and neglect. In this particular performance economy, the past too is available for evocative experience. This may have something to do with late-capitalism's drive to innovation, which leaves a continual wake of outmoded forms and practices whose passing we have little time to mourn, even if we notice it. Immersive theatre permits us this space (literally) for a communal engagement with the passed. I also see this as an extension of the longer postmodern privileging of presence. Our own appearance, in the midst of spaces that are refunctioned and *replayed* (from another time), means that we can inhabit and possess the past while savouring our own now-moment of possession.

On the next floor I come across a dressing room area, with racks of clothes, and chairs dotted along a wide theatrical make-up mirror. Close to this is a patio in which is embedded two rectangular ornamental pools, leading onto

*Figure 8.4* Amid scenic plenitude: Fernanda Prata and Jesse Kovarsky in Punchdrunk's
     *The Drowned Man: A Hollywood Fable*

Source: Brinkhoff & Mögenburg

the scene of a wood, with tree trunks, a couple of caravans in a clearing, and
a small marquee with a table and stage inside it and some strings of party lights.
I watch a couple perform a routine on stage. Later I watch the whitefaced man
of my previous encounter perform a mime routine on this stage-within-a-stage
as if trying to impress the woman (another character) he is with. Separately on
this floor is a bar, fitted out in keeping with the American (Hollywood) setting
of the piece. This is also the bar for the event, where you can buy a drink, sit
at a cabaret-style table, take in the music played by a small band, and perhaps
rest or reflect on what you have seen or where you will go next. Money
changes hands – your money, if you buy a drink. Your economic participation
is ingrained into the flow of the event-world; encouraged as part of its rhythmic
diversity.

The next floor includes a row of motel rooms, a diner and a saloon bar
with a serving area surrounded by an oval-shaped bartop. This is a scenic space
that houses evental action – you can't buy a drink here. I pass through this
space three times: once when there is a male character drinking at the bar;
once when a woman performs on it; and once when the barman is alone. This
space provided me not so much with three scenes as with a space of scenography
to be encountered *diversely*. I got to know it by seeing it in different phases
of its life in the performance. The effect – the reward – is of familiarity, a sort

of possession (the space as an old friend) and pleasure in the face of animation. It feels good to witness action, which is to say, to be part of a space that (at last!) is operative. Spectatorship is a matter of privileged encounter, hence the frissons of pleasure as you appear to come across something yourself alone – this is a peculiarly atomized entertainment.

On the highest floor there is a desert-like setting (outside Hollywood) with a sandy hill at one end. A church made of corrugated iron stands to one side. I watch a black-veiled woman daub a white substance on the face of a bare-chested man and a black substance on his torso. He performs an anguished dance in a dim downlight, half-writhing onto the sand-hill. When the dance is over he takes a spectator by the hand and leads her to a small tent. He starts to wash in a small tin basin set on the floor. By gesture and touch he gets the woman to use a sponge to clean his body of the daubs that we had previously seen applied. The scene is intimate and might be erotic, performed by actor and spectator with concentration and intensity.

Gareth White reflects on the moment when he found himself in a one-to-one performance at Punchdrunk's *Tunnel 228*, concluding that:

> the inside of a piece of drama . . . is not a place of substance, but the set of surfaces that provokes depths of feeling in us as audience. . . . the inside it brought me to was the inside of the production of the drama rather than the inside of the drama itself.
>
> (White 2012: 231)

This is, I think, partly a function of the splintered and mosaic nature of the pieces. Even when you are constructed as a performer, you are not a persona in a narrative, but instead have a phatic role in playing out the *possibility* of being an actor and playing back the *fact* of co-relation with a (paid, professional) performer. A drive to interiority is at play, over and above a drive to dramatic exchange.

*The Drowned Man* is borne on some prevailing winds in immersive theatre production. It privileges discovery over narration, scene over story, specific encounter over synoptic overview. Typically you see the trees rather than the wood. We can take this literally, given the impressive woodland setting created in *The Drowned Man*. The show is materialist in a non-Marxist sense. Surfaces, objects and materials are fetishized as the self-evident sufficiency, indeed surfeit, of the scenic space. The production makes its substances available. It works by conjunction – you are always *in* and *with* its constituent parts – and privileges experience through adjacency. The encounter is thereby commodified as theatre precisely at the point where witness and experience are felt. This dimensional (time-, space- and material-bound) affect-orientation of the work is key to its aesthetic arrangement, spatial disposition and evental flow. It marks it as a product of late-capitalism designed to provide experience as the central commodity for purchase, as Pine and Gilmore recommended.[18] Keren Zaiontz coins the term 'narcissistic spectatorship' to describe 'a repertoire of experiential strategies that weaves together competition and comparison, intimacy and entitlement, bodily perception and semiotic analysis', and promotes a neoliberal form of self-centredness in *The Drowned Man* and work like it (2014: 410). Part of the pleasure-economy of the piece is its confirmation of your own sensing self.

As we have seen, theorists of affect have written about the moment at which one realizes that one feels something. For Damasio, ' "feeling" feelings extends the reach of emotions by facilitating the planning of novel and customized forms of adaptive response' (1999: 284).[19] In the context of immersive theatre, you make decisions about the duration of your stay in a particular place, whether you follow a specific performer, whether you accept offers that are made to you (eye contact, an outstretched hand). These choices are sometimes felt as you make them. In Machon's account (2013: 80), such moments are recalled with greater clarity because they become a body memory. My own sense of encounter did not so much intensify the *dramaturgical* emotion in its moment of access, but produce the parallel sense of *being responsive in the moment*. In other words, one has an experience of spectatorship and participation, and a heightened awareness of being at least receptive and perhaps even improvisatory. The production of feeling here is an effect of and guarantee of presence; enables an embodied experience of involvement; and takes us beyond cognition. We *feel* ourselves to be in play and perhaps play differently as a consequence.

This matter of feeling playful is closely bound up with the degree of agency that we have, which in turn derives from a paradoxical *separation* from the event. As is characteristic of much of Punchdrunk's work, the audience for *The Drowned Man* is masked, with the comfort that this brings by way of anonymity and the creation of a community (we are one among a band of lookalikes).[20] The presence of so many identical spectators, necessarily remote by virtue of being hidden, creates a peculiar sense of spectatorial flow. Brennan suggests by way of a general principle of social interaction that 'The affect *in the room* is a profoundly social thing' (2004: 68). Throughout *The Drowned Man* you see yourself as one participant among many, amid an ambience that is broadly shared. Yet this masking is literally an act of effacement, de-individualizing the spectator, who is instructed not to remove the mask (other than in the bar area or perhaps in one-to-one encounters), or indeed to make any noise. There is performance by experts; and spectating by paying visitors who, while in motion, follow some established rubrics of spectatorship. The spectator is fenced off behind the mask. She is in action but changes nothing. Her job is to be noticed as spectator, and not get in the way. Even the woman who sponged the chest of the actor in the tent operated within a system that could have done without her. The system predominates (as it does in theme parks, as I discuss in the next chapter), both as an eventscape and a regulated zone for observation.

This qualifies the place of such an event in the Engagement diagram, above. Spectators are not 'separated' geo-spatially. They have the experience of being inside the work's stages and, sometimes, too enmeshed in its actions (as with the one-to-one encounters that Punchdrunk facilitates). In this respect we are incorporated rather than kept apart. On the other hand, the event plays out through the blueprint determined by the company. There is little room for improvisation and even less for intervention on the part of the spectator. I agree with Carlson:

> The closest model is not actual life, as it is for Ranciere and Artaud, but rather virtual video games, in which one's character is free to move and make choices, but only within the parameters set forth by the game. . . . The spectator has changed from an observer to a player, but the game still remains some[one] else's.
>
> (Carlson 2012: np)

In this case, the affective rewards that are conferred are to do with permission and privilege (access, special encounter, selection for participation) as much as play. If this is a game, it's played with someone else's ball.

The metaphor of the game and structures of games-play run across *The Drowned Man* and across much contemporary performance. As we saw in considering *Audience*, above, Ontroerend Goed presents spectator-baiting as a game. In the instance of online sports spectatorship, the game itself is central. In *The Drowned Man* you are a player in someone else's game. My final instance concerns a performance event constructed explicitly as a game.

## Incorporation – Production | *Can You See Me Now?*

In games we are incorporated and have agency, to the point where often the game plays out uniquely for each participant. The rise of gaming in digital culture has contributed to a gathering change in how the audience is conceived in contemporary performance. The shift is from watching action to experiencing and determining action. It can be traced back to the popularity of analogue video games in the 1970s and 1980s, then the growth of computer gaming as digital technologies became more readily available for commercial exploitation, and the extension of digital gaming principles into games that feature settings and activities in the 'real' world. The earlier video games, such as *Pong* (Atari 1972), *Space Invaders* (Taito 1978) and *Pac-Man* (Namco 1980), established some of the key principles that would be more deeply mined in computer games, including the involvement, agency and experiential interaction of the player. In a related development, role-playing games (RPGs) grew in popularity during the 1970s and '80s, in their tabletop form (involving groups of players who would gather together in a single space), as video games that could be played by a single player, and as massively multi-player online role-playing games (MMORPGs). As Williams, Hendricks and Winkler observe, 'Most RPGs consist of a *setting* and a *system*' (2006: 3) – a fundamental pair of relations that applies just as readily to immersive and games-based theatre outputs of the twenty-first century. In RPGs, fictional personae are placed within a world in which narrative lines are developed through the actions of the characters, in typically quest-based or task-based scenarios. The playing of roles can take place in tandem with the participation of other players. RPGs are thereby potential vehicles for social engagement, even if one is alone at one's terminal. They also provide an experiential engagement as your in-game persona undergoes challenges, interactions with others, and achieves successes.

In such games – the *Pokémon* series produced for Nintendo's Game Boy device (1996 onwards) provides an example – a narrative plays out in both linear and non-linear ways. The game is open (and thereby facilitates improvisation), indeterminate, and affective due to its requirement for real-time play. On the other hand it is determined by structures and rules that typically lead, eventually, to closure. The death of the character often provides a form of finality (albeit that one can usually play again). These games offer degrees of choice and agency: the opportunity to take one's own route, replay sections and develop highly personalized attributes of persona or setting. As Haddon suggests, 'creating their own games and special effects meant that for many playing the game was only part of *a package of experience*' (Haddon 2009, 304, my emphasis). And they are shaped according to performance in both key meanings of the term: the effectual completion of specialist tasks; and the assumption of a role. Effective performance here, across both categories, is affective and pleasurable.

Game-world enjoyment is frequently liminal, based particularly on the movement across boundaries between states and categories that the game facilitates. This aspect of play connects the more obvious games-based products (say the *Grand Theft Auto* series, Rockstar Games 1997; or *Heavy Rain*, Sony 2010) with virtual online worlds such as *Second Life* (Linden Research 2003). The player's in-game or in-world identity, for example, can be a reverberation of what she would see as her usual self, or a deliberate reinvention. The persona offers a cloak of anonymity if desired. *Second Life* is precisely not First Life. In this sort of digital interaction, the virtual world is fantastical and clearly not of this world. And yet the fact of choosing to play a persona in a virtual world – of undertaking this activity in real-time and synchronously with others – means that the digital domain is also a part of one's present experience, and can be carried in desire, pleasure and memory through one's engagements in the 'first world' of daily life. Likewise, temporality in games is *experienced*. Game time is typically either slower than or quicker than real-time, such that one has an experience of speed (with the requirement for quick and immediate decisions) or an extruded time whereby one can leave and come back to a game, remake or replay sections, or develop something (a building, a collection) over a lengthy period. Game activity is often improvisational and usually task-based, and provides an experience of unstructured flow within a structured system of dramatic play and possibility.

All the above offers the sense-pleasure of experiential engagement, within a flux of personal commitment, presence and escape from dailyness (even if the game is played routinely). This is characteristic of digital culture: pleasure is experienced not simply in the act of play, but in the displacements that the play entails, transgressing normative time and space, flirting with boundaries of self, enabling behaviour that is untypical, risky or even (in real life) forbidden. Such displacements are performed – and *felt* in the moment of performance, by way of a texture of agencies (chosen personal actions) and effects (game rewards and consequences) that are simultaneously affective.[21] The affective act of performance is a game requirement and as such – because it is part of the play paradigm – always tensely bound up with absorption and excitement. Role-play is both casually put on and committedly undertaken. It can be (deliberately) a misrepresentation and a ruse. It can entail devotion and indeed ethical commitment. It is the means by which participatory pleasure is calibrated for the individual: more or less fantastical, effective and enjoyed.

In her discussion of spectatorship in cyberspace, Nina LeNoir suggests that 'Role-playing games make everyone into an actor and an audience member at the same time' (2003: 125). The British company Blast Theory has exploited many characteristics of games play, not least this typical fusion of actor-spectator. On the other hand, the company's work over the course of the twenty-first century has done away with both actors and spectators altogether. The former become facilitators; the latter become players and participants. The company makes pieces that usually depend on the application of new but increasingly ubiquitous technologies, including Global Satellite Positioning (GPS) devices, mobile phone text messaging and webcams. They typically involve movement through spaces (usually urban, virtual or a mix of the two), task-based interaction with prompts and instructions, and decisions not only about in-game options but particular subject positions and points of principle. To that end, the work – in keeping with an older theatrical paradigm – fuses aesthetic presentation with social, political and ethical contexts. A number of instances demonstrate the overlapping conceptual, technological and design principles in play.[22]

In *Kidnap* (1998), two individuals from a larger pool of volunteers were apprehended, held in an undisclosed location and placed under video surveillance for 48 hours, available for wider public viewing. *Desert Rain* (1999) took place inside theatres or warehouse/studio-type settings that accommodated a suite of installations. Participants moved through a series of rooms and spaces to end in a hotel room setting, where a swipe card provided access to the video screening of a testimony from an individual touched in some way by the Gulf War, a point of reference for the work. In *Uncle Roy all Around You* (2003), you respond to SMS text prompts to move around an urban location, and eventually at the end of the piece decide whether to make a commitment to a stranger for a period of twelve months. *Ulrike and Eamon Compliant* (2009) circulates around larger questions of commitment and belief, drawing on the actual circumstances of Ulrike Meinhof (of the Red Army Faction) and Eamon Collins (a member of the IRA and an informer on the organization). Participants decide whether to be Ulrike or Eamon, receive instructions by mobile phone, moving through the city accordingly; and undergo a form of interrogation that raises questions concerning what they would kill for. Other pieces are personal in somewhat lighter ways. In *Day of the Figurines* (2006), each participant has a figurine within a model town (named and customized akin to an avatar in an online game), and responds to SMS text prompts that keep the figurine in play over a 24-day period. In *Rider Spoke* (2007), participants take their own route through the streets of the city on a bicycle, responding to prompts from a portable computer, and recording personal and perhaps autobiographical messages that form part of an ever-expanding texture of responses that you access during your journey. As this brief set of instances indicates, the work is determinedly participatory. It adopts games-play structures, and requires personal navigation of space, place and perspective. It operates in a hybrid performance landscape, involving the co-presence of players and facilitators in actual locations, and their interaction across the virtual platforms of new media devices.

I participated in Blast Theory's *Can You See Me Now?* at Tate Britain in 2010, as part of a 'Tate Late' event devoted to games and gaming. By then the piece had become established as a signal creation in the company's *oeuvre*. Developed by Blast Theory in collaboration with the Mixed Reality Laboratory at the University of Nottingham, *Can You See Me Now?* premiered in 2001, won Ars Electronica's Golden Nica in 2003, and has been presented in cities including Barcelona, Chicago, Rotterdam and Tokyo. A relatively early GPS-enabled game, it takes its place amid the number of games-based performances and events developed in the Web 2.0 era in relation to mobile and locative technologies, and it illustrates the affordances of gaming in digital culture.[23] As Montola suggests, pervasive games (of which *Can You See Me Now?* is a relatively early example) 'exist in the intersection of phenomena such as city culture, mobile technology, network communication, reality fiction, and performing arts, combining bits and pieces from various contexts to produce new play experiences' (2009: 7). *Can You See Me Now?* is played at a computer terminal, either remotely or at the venue that hosts the piece (Figure 8.5). The event features 'runners' in urban locations – these are the company's performers, although the role that they inhabit is akin to that of a tracker or attack dog, and their performance is task-based rather than character-based. They operate within a skeletal narrative to do with pursuit, capture and identification, within the structure of a game as opposed to that of a drama. The visitors to the event are no longer spectators but participants. Each is stationed at a computer terminal that shows a map of a specific location, and each has an icon, placed somewhere on the map, that is moved by the player at the terminal. You can also see the position of the runners, whose physical presence in the location is tracked by a GPS system. The map brings together the actual runners in an external location and the virtual icons of players participating through the computer. The game's premiss is to avoid capture by the runners, while the runners win if they take a 'photo' of your icon, which they achieve by getting within five metres of the map coordinate of your virtual figure. Of course they can't see you in the flesh, but can create the effect of a view (a view to a kill) by positioning themselves in the same street as your icon. The game, then, is effusively spatial. It involves a mix of virtual and actual movement through a geographical space, and tropes of stalking, flight and capture.

The affect-production of the piece is bound up in its work across digital and material dimensions. The runners provide a commentary that emphasizes their corporeality and acts as a useful aid for those at the monitors. It conveys in-game information, as they communicate with each other about sightings they have made, or individuals they will track. And it endorses their outdoorsness. One runner comments, 'There's hardly anyone about. And it's getting very cold.' We can also hear their breath on our headphones. Space is physically inhabited and mediated through personal encounter and experience. This particular virtual world is a place of embodiment.

*Figure 8.5* Gaming: a player at work in *Can You See Me Now?* at the InterCommunication Centre, Tokyo, 2005

Source: Blast Theory

Klich and Scheer discuss the piece in terms of its 'proxemics' (2012: 172), while Benford and Giannachi note that '[o]nline players had a "prosthetic" relationship to the physical site' (2011: 30). Feelings of closeness and attachment are in play. Intimacies are produced. A character (another icon, whose controller must be sitting only a few feet away but remains nonetheless unknown to me), spotted at a distance in-game on the screen, induces a conversation. As our icons enter the same space on the map: 'HELLO!' we/they say. Then, with the icons very close to each other, my fellow player says: 'Hey, this feels intimate.' The moment is affective, not so much in the terms in which flirting might be thought to be affective, but in the other flirtation enabled by the game: that between everyday and virtual worlds. A frisson of awareness comes at points when this overlap is negotiated. The moment also felt slightly transgressive. For a short while, at least, my fellow player and I were in an extra-game suspense, neither running nor chasing, but simply pausing, like stepping outside for a smoke. We sustained an intimacy that, oddly, was nothing of the kind. It only *felt* like it.

Games Studies scholars argue that gameplay has increasingly moved into everyday experience (Montola 2009: 11). The reverse is also true, with the 'real world' figured precisely as a reality effect. If the edges between the designed in-game world and the 'real' world are deliberately blurred, so is the passage between them. As a consequence one experiences play *liminally*, as a constant accessing of and departure from both the actual/material and the fabricated/fantastical. There is a parallel movement that concerns the intentionality of your mode of play. In their discussion of the relationship between gaming structures and social life, Williams, Hendricks and Winkler suggest that fantasy games work across 'a continuum, from unstructured dramatic play to structured combative play' (2006: 3). Your participation in *Can You See Me Now?* might be placed at diverse points on this continuum, depending on the choices you make in how to engage. You can rest, tune in and out, or engage zealously, whereby you are in combat with the runners. These distinct modes of play resonate with the sorts of experience described by the philosopher John Dewey in *Art as Experience*. Dewey contrasts 'inchoate' experience – to do with isolated or unconnected instances – with '*an* experience when the material experienced runs its course to fulfillment' (1934: 35, original emphasis). The latter produces forms of knowledge and pleasure that derive from completion and closure. Game play offers both sorts of experience. Inchoate experience, here, is fluid, unclosed, and subject to serendipity. There were moments in *Can You See Me Now?* when I felt myself in the midst of a virtual *dérive* as my icon drifted around an unfamiliar set of spaces (while I was sat at my computer terminal). After the game this feeling persisted – a trace and a memory of flow and uncertainty. Meanwhile my text conversation with another player was an in-game event that could be chalked up as *an* experience (a specific encounter with start and end points). And for all its fluidity, the game was finite and contained, offering itself as *an* experience that one would enter and then leave.

I was caught – or rather gave myself up – by seeking an adventurous encounter after 28 minutes. I flirted with danger twice then sought out a runner in order to commit suicide. A photo was duly taken – a photo of the street, showing no fleshy person, but allowing a coordinate and timestamp that marked the actual place where a runner stood and saw, onscreen, my virtual self in the same location. My digital double was duly terminated. At the beginning of the event you are asked to recall a person whom you haven't seen for a while, perhaps for a long time. Your icon bears this person's name, so that when you are spotted, it is your lost friend who is called to mind at the moment of your digital death. This recourse to memory and a specific person is a nice touch, providing an affectively 'uncanny moment' (Benford and Giannachi 2011: 31), and is all of a piece with Blast Theory's consistent attempts to draw the biographical into its encounters with new media and virtual playscapes. As Joseph Roach suggests, 'Synthetic experience must answer the human need, regulated by both curiosity and fear, to experience life vicariously as well as directly. Vicariousness suggests the derivative nature of experience from some prior authenticity' (2007: 28). *In Can You See Me Now?* you are doubly vicarious, living in the game as both icon and remembered other. We have already considered the derivative experience of space that the piece promotes. The affect here also depends on your relationship to the person named, and the reason why you haven't met for a while – so might be to do with a sense of loss, fondness, guilt, or the tang of time having moved on. However slight the trace, the meeting of endgame and personal history produces a feeling-cluster that is not uncommon in digital culture: the sense of being in a lived present, connected with some other space (and possibly some other time), and with some part of your biography touched.

What did I feel as a player? Certainly a present-tense encounter, working out what to do and where to go in-game. A sense of curiosity, negotiating the rules, discovering the system. Slightly peculiar and fleeting memories of a person, chases, wandering the streets. And a sense of a self that was both vulnerable but also oddly mattered less. This is a classic game paradigm. You can die more easily, because it is only a play-death.

## Engagement and affect

I found the first two engagements, above, the most affective, even though I was not 'incorporated' within either. You might think that the bottom-right-hand zone of the Engagement diagram – represented here by a game with high levels of incorporation and personal production – promises the most concentrated forms of experience and affect. Yet I would characterize my own engagement with *Can You See Me Now?* as one of curiosity rather than absorption. Likewise the promise of immersive theatre – to provide a high degree of affective engagement because of its high level of incorporation – is not always deeply *felt*, at least if my visit to *The Drowned Man* is anything to go by. This may be a function of my age, theatrical acculturation, or the chances of these particular encounters. Nonetheless, there is no single, simple vector for the relationships between performance and participation, or experience and affect.

Nigel Thrift argues for a critical perspective on affect that acknowledges posthumanist patterns and formations while allowing for the agency and feelingness of 'singular bodies' (2008: 222). Feeling-production is about modes of spectator-participant engagements at a particular point in the history of theatre, performance, indeed culture more broadly. It is also about the affordances of culture for individuals, and therefore continually has aesthetic, phenomenological and political aspects. What we see and sense is inescapably part of our historical moment. Two considerations are paramount. It is always worth thinking about feeling, for this is where our pleasures and commitments are clinched. And we cannot say for sure that a particular form or mode of performance will inherently provide deeper engagement than another.

The Experience Economy arises as an expression of late capitalism and is enabled by the shapes and flows of digital culture. It trades, precisely, on our experiences. These remain diverse and not necessarily predictable. If they often surprise us and seem beyond our control, they are also often beyond the control of others. A space remains between techniques of production and our experiencing of affects. This is something to celebrate, for in this gap lies our capacity for resistance, and our deliberate disposition to pleasure.

## Notes

1  See 164–79 where this is discussed more fully. Pine and Gilmore particularly address theatrical aspects of the experience economy in Chapter 6, which examines work as theatre, and acting/performance at work (153–79); Chapter 7, which considers different modes of theatre in relation to business types and operational models (181–207); and Chapter 8, on fulfilling a role (209–40).

2  See, for instance, Boswijk, Thijssen and Peelen 2007; Sundbo and Darmer 2008; and Thrift 2008: 71.

3  Pine and Gilmore suggest four realms: Entertainment, Educational, Escapist, Esthetic (2011: 46).

4  Broadly in order of the categories described – although much of this work is deliberately interdisciplinary – see Brennan 2004; Damasio 1999; Massumi 2002; Deleuze and Guattari 1991; Heller-Roazen 2007; Thrift 2008; Stewart 2007; Ridout 2008; Hurley 2010; Welton 2012; Thompson 2009; and Shaughnessy 2012. See Thrift 175–82 and 223–35 for a discussion of different schools of thought about affect. For a discussion of historical understandings of affect, and changes to the meaning of the term, see Brennan 2004: 98–138. See Welton for a useful bibliography.

5  On the virtual in relation to the digital (and non-digital), see Massumi 2002: 133–43. See Heller-Roazen 2007: 79–89 for an account of Aristotelian synaesthesia.

6  See Massumi on the measurement of embodied intensities of affect (2002: 24–5). See Damasio on neural patterns that constitute feeling – including chemical and electrochemical messages (1999: 281–3).

7 The company's website is at www.ontroerendgoed.be/en/; see also www.art happens.be/en-gb/artist/ontroerend-goed.

8 For a discussion of the 'immersion trilogy', with links to other reviews, see Needham 2013. See Groot Nibbelink 2012 for a discussion of *The Smile off Your Face*.

9 I saw the piece on 14 August 2011, St George's West, Edinburgh.

10 On interpellation, see Note 18, Chapter 4, above, and the discussion in Chapter 4.

11 When the show was first staged the company picked on a member of the audience. A plant from the company was used in subsequent performances, following complaints concerning the victimization of the woman (Needham 2013).

12 Mumford describes this as an 'aesthetic mode of sports watching' (2012: 10; see also 20–5). For a discussion of the affective experiences of participants (as opposed to spectators) in sport, drawing on Thrift's account of non-representational theory, see Thorpe and Rinehart 2010.

13 See also Mumford 2012: 110 on collective experience.

14 In his discussion of sports spectatorship in relation to theatre spectating, Kennedy relates the masculinist culture of sports spectatorship to a post-industrial move 'from the need for the masculine to the performance of the masculine' (2001: 280).

15 See Calleja 2011: 17–34 for an account of immersion in relation to digital games. See Alston 2012: 196–9 and 2013: 128–31 for useful overviews of characteristics of immersive theatre. Machon suggests a lineage for immersive theatre that includes installation art and physical and visual theatres of the 1980s and 1990s (2013: 63–4).

16 The company's website is at http://punchdrunk.com/.

17 I visited the piece on 21 December 2013.

18 If we were in any doubt, the pricing structure of *The Drowned Man* offers the option of a premium experience. For an additional sum you could purchase a VIP ticket that gave you access through a special entrance (no queue!) to a backstage area and a glass of vodka. Similarly, the website for Cynthia von Buhler's *Speakeasy Dollhouse*, an immersive theatre production in New York, offers a 'VIP ticket' with various inducements (www.brownpapertickets.com/event/214593). See Alston 2012 for a discussion of commercial imperatives of Punchdrunk's work. See also Alston and Daker 2012; and Zaiontz 2014: 413.

19 See also Heller-Roazen 2007: 200–1; and Massumi 2002: 13–15 on the feeling of feeling.

20 Punchdrunk's director Felix Barrett discusses the company's use of masks for spectators in Machon 2013: 160. See also White 2009; White 2013: 178–9; and Worthen 2012: 94–5.

21 Calleja notes various forms of affective involvement in games (2011: 146).

22 For the company's website, see www.blasttheory.co.uk/. Dates given in the instances that follow are for first performances/productions.

23 See the company's website at www.blasttheory.co.uk/projects/can-you-see-me-now/ for discussion of the piece and archival materials. See also Benford and Giannachi 2011: 27–34 (the bibliography includes a number of computing-oriented articles on the piece); and Kilch and Scheer 2012: 171–7. See also www.youtube.com/watch?v=hX4kZvEllwY. I participated in the piece on 5 March 2010.

## Chapter 9

# Performance engagements across culture

## Re-theatring

One feature of the period under discussion in this book – after postmodernism – is that it turned 'theatre' into a verb. Processes of theatring were all around us, as cultural production staged individuals (actual and fictional) across diverse platforms, presenting them for spectatorship. The society of the spectacle became a multi-theatred communications zone, replete with the paraphernalia of production, presentation, performance, audience and applause (or at least positive and negative feedback mechanisms). Narratives and issues were theatricalized through various sorts of performance intervention in the public domain. Equally, cultural production traded with feeling, experience and involvement, theatring its participants as actors in the midst of (re)presentation. Spectators were invited into the inside of performance, theatred by way of their incorporation into the event. Engagement was therefore often bi-directional – the event reached out, and the participant performed.

The opening chapter of this book began at the Fast Forward Festival in Athens in May 2014. In its closing chapter we can revisit the Festival a year later, to observe a controversy that touches on this business of theatring along with a number of the themes in *Performance in the Twenty-First Century* as a whole. I will conclude in due course with some reflections upon three theme parks, to consider modes of engagement in other spheres of popular culture. First we can gather the threads of this book's argument with brief reference to two civic installations that were separately shut down at points in their history. Let's return (as so often in theatre) to Athens.

The Belgian artist Kris Verdonck (whose work I discussed in Chapter 5) presented *Stills* at the Fast Forward Festival 2015.[1] As part of the installation, a video of two performers, each naked and sporting multiple tattoos across their bodies, was projected in large scale upon the wall of a building in Klafthmonos Square that was itself inscribed with graffiti (Figure 9.1). Other projections were shown at Sina Street and Vissarionos Street. As Verdonck explained, the piece (originally conceived for an installation in Rome in 2006) depicted its subjects as living caryatids, the sculpted figures that support buildings in classical architecture. In Klafthmonos Square, *Stills* integrated the painted bodies with

*Figure 9.1* The tattooed, trapped caryatids: Martine Morréale and Philippe Sandor in
Kris Verdonck's *Stills* in Klafthmonos Square, Athens, 2015

Source: Stavros Petropoulos

the painted wall, the performers appearing as a pair of living graphical inter-
actants trapped in a sort of *mise en bâtiment*. Early in its run, a priest who was
passing saw it and complained to the police, who instructed the Festival to
take down the video. The matter was reported in both Greek and Belgian
media, and resulted in a Tweet from Greece's Minister of Culture in support
of Verdonck, although the installation was not subsequently remounted.[2] As
we saw previously, the Fast Forward Festival's marketing blurb in 2014
proclaimed that 'the theatre of now is . . . a collage of arts, techniques and
media.' Verdonck's collage – video and mural, body art and graffiti, recorded
performance and installation – fitted this particular bill. It produced a collision
of another kind, between the aesthetic, civic and ecclesiastical, that proved
intolerable for members of the still-powerful Greek Orthodox Church.

In Chapter 1 I looked at the events of 1989 that helped shape the contemporary European project. Those of a quarter-century or so later threatened
the new European order, as European Union officials, finance ministers and
members of the Greek government sought to negotiate a rescue package that
would avoid a 'Grexit': the exit of Greece from the Eurozone single currency
on account of its numbing national debt. Verdonck's piece didn't seek to
comment on the crisis. Nonetheless it attains an added piquancy in its witting
intervention within a contested cultural space that was also, at the time, amid
extraordinary geopolitical and (micro- and macro-) economic stresses.

*Stills* joins other events and performances discussed in this book as an example of a wider set of contemporary theatres of engagement that are particularly sensitive to their context. They are structured in some way by digital paradigms; are definitively post-postmodern; engage variously with ideas of authenticity and actuality; display hybrid forms and processes; and typically work through the mode of affective encounter. *Stills* featured digital video, but also participated in digital culture more sinuously by way of its fusion of intimacy and publicness, and by confounding actual and virtual textures. It wore the transparency of display that characterizes Verdonck's practice, while operating knowingly at the boundary between presentation and representation, artifice and actuality. It had the restless ostensiveness of art that seeks a public space in order to provoke private meditation.

In the same month that Kris Verdonck was being censured and censored in Athens, the Dutch artist and performance maker Dries Verhoeven installed himself in a converted transport container in a square in Utrecht, in a different inhabitation of public and private spaces (Figure 9.2). Verhoeven's *Wanna Play? (Love in the Time of Grindr)* was part of the city's SPRING Festival.[3] The container was in effect an apartment, with a bed at one end, a toilet at the other, and a shower, sink, stove and table also in the mix. It looked like a chic and minimalist bachelor pad, white and grey, chrome and glass. Verhoeven was incarcerated for ten days. Not untypically you'd see him sat at a desk, facing the rear wall (as you looked through the windowed façade that ran along the entirety of one side) that showed the feeds from his Grindr account. Grindr is an online site for gay dating. *Wanna Play?* caused controversy when it was first presented in Berlin (2014), when one of the men invited to Verhoeven's very public residence protested at the invasion of his privacy that the piece performed. A social media storm ensued, addressing matters of artistic integrity, personal trust, and individual privacy. The installation was shut down five days into its intended run of fifteen.[4]

For its second iteration in Utrecht there were new rules of engagement. Verhoeven entered into text chat with other men in private, and at a certain point revealed that he was making an art piece. The conversation was only continued in public where the respective punter gave his permission. Verhoeven's stated intention was to explore the prospect of non-sexual intimacy in this digital-cum-actual environment. A dating site that predominantly facilitates sexual encounters was used instead to seek meetings that would entail a different kind of exchange. The men who agreed to visit Verhoeven in his container in Utrecht variously played scrabble, shaved his head and had dinner with him. One simply sat on the bed with Verhoeven, holding hands.

The piece fulfils the broad parameters for theatres of engagement described above. Its location in a busy city square, and the wide-format viewing window, made it ostensively available, an installation expressly for encountering. The large-scale projections of Grindr screens on the long interior wall exaggerated the public aspect of digital exchanges that are normally transacted in private.

*Figure 9.2*  Public intimacies: Dries Verhoeven at work/leisure in *Wanna Play? (Love in the Time of Grindr)*, Utrecht, 2015

Source: Willem Popelier

Profoundly embedded in digital culture – for what else can we say of Grindr, Tinder and other platforms that facilitate virtual social exchange? – *Wanna Play?* also finessed the digital with its emphasis on presence, corporeal participation, the serial nature of dating chat, and the non-linear flurry of possible exchanges. Verhoeven reached out to men through a social media platform, and some of these contacts endorsed the piece's actuality by entering an artwork precisely as themselves. This wasn't so much a reality effect as a reality grab. Yet for all that *Wanna Play?* stages Grindr, it also turns it inside out. The private meetings were transacted in a sort of phantom public space (Verhoeven drew the curtains when his guests arrived, but some of the meetings were still visible at least in outline) and without sexual consummation. It was lived durationally, and reached its moment of release in Utrecht when Verhoeven came through the door at one end of the container and jogged to join the symposium on his work that was at that moment in session (its delegates watching his exit by way of a live camera relay).

The piece sets out to stage some of the tensions of contemporary inter-relation. In that sense it joins with other pieces by Verhoeven as an artwork with an agenda, socially engaged rather than simply aesthetic or affective. If sex, at least, was absent, other features duly compensated. 'Actuality', 'authenticity', 'encounter' and 'engagement': our keywords apply as readily here as elsewhere. Žižek's notion of the Real having 'the status of a(nother) semblance' (2002: 19) comes to mind in this recuperation of the actual as performance, mediated as quotidian.

Entering the everyday, *Wanna Play?* and *Stills* are decidedly postdramatic in presenting what Lehmann described as a 'theatre of states' (2006: 68), and refiguring spatiality and temporality: they are durational, display-based, framed rectilinearly within civic settings. They go beyond the postdramatic, however, in their reengagement with social discourse. The 'open and fragmenting perception' that Lehmann observed within postdramatic theatre (83) is realigned within a discursive aesthetic paradigm. There is a deliberate entry into the public sphere. *Wanna Play?* was part of HAU Hebbel am Ufer's 2014 *Treffpunkte* ('hangouts') series, looking at 'the status of the private in the public sphere . . . under the current political conditions of neoliberal urban development' and in relation to 'digital data transfer'.[5] The following year, Katia Arfara, artistic director of the Fast Forward Festival, wanted to 'shine a light on the multiple, heterogeneous aspects of the city' and explore 'the dialectical relationship between multimedia, hybrid artistic practices and public and private space' (Arfara 2015). This fresh conjunction of private and public, and the challenges for personal encounter that it sets up, expresses the millennium's abiding topic: the production of interaction (or disintegration) amid spaces and technologies for new engagements with social and cultural exchange.

A few days after seeing *Wanna Play?* I received an email advertising performances at the Britannia Theatre, a variety venue within the Dickens World theme park complex in Chatham, Kent. How different, on the face of it, from the disrupted installations in European cities. And yet, perhaps not so different. To conclude, I turn towards more populist scenes of engagement – for they too bear the stamps of theatricality, actuality, personal performance and experiential encounter discussed in the pages above.

## Synthetic encounters: pleasure and performance in the theme park

To visit Hong Kong's Disneyland on Lantau Island, you take the Mickey Mouse train for a single stop from Sunny Bay, which is otherwise a terminus on the Tung Chung line. Built on reclaimed land in Penny Bay, Disneyland is beyond an end-point. As Michael Sorkin suggests in relation to theme park visits, 'The element of arrival is especially crucial, the idea that one is not passing through some indeterminate station but has come to some place where there is a definitive "there" ' (Sorkin 1992: 215). In Hong Kong, in order to reach 'there' you take a journey in a train that is part of the Disneyland scenography. You have arrived, so to speak, even while you are *en route*. In both raising and satisfying anticipation, the train performs a liminal passage, one of escape from the ordinary world and border-crossing into the promised zone of consumable pleasure.

In considering this zone as a theatre of engagement we are concerned with the dynamics of interaction between visitors (the public), performers (usually specialists), mediated images and scenic space. Visits to theme parks provide an array of performance situations and arrangements that put the visitor amid tropes of theatricality. These enhance the sensation of being in the moment and participating in cultural iconography – experiencing familiar stories, biographies, filmworlds and so forth from the inside. Di Benedetto talks of theme parks as 'extensions of memory machines, constructed so that attendants can navigate an arranged representation of a fictional world to experience or remember their experiences or their conceptions of fictional universes' (2012: 57). The consumption of symbolic capital is thereby consistently experiential. Such places, such visits, synthesize performance, engagement and consumption in a blend of the fictive and the felt.

Given the centrality of experience here, I explore this scenario with reference to visits that I undertook to Disneyland in Hong Kong and Dickens World in Chatham, Kent, attractions that opened within four months of each other in 2005; and the production of a theme park like no other, Banksy's Dismaland.[6] Disneyland provides a touchstone and template for park experiences – corporately extensive, commercially successful and part of mainline consumer culture. As a heritage and entertainment attraction, Dickens World is tiny by comparison but shares many theatrical strategies with its larger cousin. Dismaland mobilizes some familiar theme park tropes to notably different effect.

## A drift in Disneyland (after Debord)

The first Disneyland opened in 1955 in Anaheim, California, and was intended to evoke the sense of being in another world entirely. That said, the Disney model was designed to provide a clean, regulated, systematic engagement for its visitors, different from the more open-ended style (and sometimes sleaziness) of the fairground or the dispersed (and sometimes faded) pleasures of the amusement park.[7] Half a century later, Hong Kong's iteration opened on 12 September 2005. Another park is under development in Shanghai for a projected opening in 2016. One of the key propositions of the cloned Disneylands, and other parks of their kind, is a value-zone in which family-oriented leisure – addressed to a mass market and therefore determinedly inoffensive (at least to a mass market) – is meshed with diverse forms of experience-based action and consumption, including fairground rides, theatrical entertainments, exhibitions, immersion in scenic or thematic scapes, and opportunities to buy food, drink and souvenirs. We are in the midst of what Alan Bryman calls 'Disneyization'.

Bryman is careful to differentiate 'Disneyization' from 'Disneyfication'. As he explains, the former term is not expressly 'about the influence of Disney but about the spread of the principles that its theme parks exemplify': it concerns a more pervasive tendency in late-capitalist culture (2004: 11).

If 'McDonaldization' (a term coined by George Ritzer) is to do with Fordist principles of repeatability and standardization, 'Disneyization' is to do with 'a post-Fordist world of variety and consumer choice' (13). Bryman describes 'a systemscape in the sense of a set of underlying principles that are diffused throughout the economy, culture and society, but which allow considerable variation in how they are implemented' (vii). This principle of variation marks the historical shift from one mode of corporate culture (Fordist) to another (diversifying and consumer-centred). We observe the ongoing extension of experiencing and 'eventing' in this matrix of consumer choice.

The parks may be ideologically complicit with aspects of corporate capitalism that include massification, presentationalism and profit at the expense of localism; and they trade in narratives that present versions of normativity that many would question. They also feature advanced technologies, and a continual quest for innovation in production and interrelation with their visitors. This is a part of their trade in a pleasure economy, for they are nothing if not audience-facing. In his discussion of Universal Studios Florida attractions, including 'Men in Black' and 'Harry Potter', Di Benedetto notes that 'Several strategies for shaping mass experience remain constant between exhibits, such as crowd control, setting up fictional parameters, overt theatricality and participatory strategies' (2012: 58). The performance paradigm is yet more deeply embedded. We know about the theatrical lexicon of Disney parks. Employees are 'the cast'. Public areas are 'onstage'. A job interview is an 'audition', a job is a 'role', performed in a uniform that is a 'costume' (Bryman 2004: 11). Cast members are trained to observe patterns of gesture and behaviour specific to their characters, so that Mickey Mouse in Hong Kong is the same as Mickey in Paris, Orlando or Tokyo. Characters in these skin parts go out of their way to interact with members of the public. Annie Wharmby, Hong Kong Disneyland's Director of Show Operations, talks of the careful facilitation of 'magic moments' where a child is engaged, participates, and gets a special photo to mark the moment.[8] As so often in these sorts of cultural encounters, the child as *experiencer* is the centre of the activity, with the photographic record used as a form of QED (the child was taken to the park, the child was evidently there, the child had pleasure).

A magic moment was constructed for me too. We stopped to watch a dancing band on Main Street – that's to say, a band that sometimes performs dance steps along with its music. Annie Wharmby encouraged me to join the band for a photograph that performs a peculiar inversion. Where ordinarily I might applaud the band, endorsing its activity, here the band endorses my interest through the photographic proof of our co-presence. The band, here, is performing my witness. You could say that my appearance – as a consumer, an experiencer – is more important than that of the band (there could easily be other bands, other musicians). This is a key feature of the theme park. While it is a place of destination, Sorkin's 'there', the park nonetheless only exists *for* its visitors, hence it must also become a 'here'. The visitors are central by way of the production of an experience that is both generic and particularized. The 'magic moment' is endlessly produced, but it is magical insofar as it is bespoke, a memory for the individual. I argued above (in Chapter 7) that in certain settings Rancière's spectator is implicated rather than emancipated. Here the spectator is implicated, you might even say incorporated.

The park presents a number of modes of performance. Its array of street entertainment includes jugglers, magicians and character turns. I came upon Bunsen and Beaker, the Muppet characters, restaged here as a mobile street act in audio-animatronic form. Both puppets are on a small buggy that drives along the park's walkways and open spaces. Cameras in the vehicle deliver a live image-feed to a voice artist at a distance, who voices the characters by way of a live relay through a built-in loudspeaker. Dr Bunsen thereby addresses members of the public. At one point the buggy squirts water at an unsuspecting onlooker, to great amusement. The performance involves triangulated show-operation. In addition to the voice artist, the buggy and its characters have an anonymous operator who stands at one remove from the vehicle, driving it from behind, a remote-control device concealed in his pocket. The puppets' apparent autonomy is delightful. What's produced here is in part a performance, but also a situation of absorption and surprise, enhancing the immersive aspect of the park and its encounters. Bunsen and Beaker are part of the *casual affect* of the park's performance infrastructure. You (probably) don't visit Disneyland expressly to see the Muppets. But suddenly there they are, signalling that here is a place where popular performance manifests under your nose. You might not know whom to expect – but you know that, *en dérive* in Disneyland, you can expect *characters* to appear across your horizon.

This is no less the case in the aptly named *Stich Encounter*, in which the spectators have an interactive exchange with the cartoon character Stich, a mischievous dog-like alien. Stich appears to us as a two-dimensional animation on a screen in a small cinema-cum-viewing-gallery. The computer animation software makes the mouth of the character move in sync with the speech of a live voice artist hidden from view, so that Stich appears to talk directly with the spectators. The pre-determined cartoon action is reanimated by way of this live exchange, shifting the paradigm from the usual fixed flow of the cartoon to a semi-improvised encounter in real time – an effect of cartoon presence.

Part of the action involves Stich incorporating members of the audience in an adventure story set in outer space. During my visit Mr Noe, a member of the audience whose image is captured by a concealed camera, is framed in a graphic as the notorious space criminal Karm, to general amusement (this reminds us how close are the tropes of surveillance and multimedia entertainment; see McGrath 2004). Another audience member becomes Stich's love object in a comic exchange that gently embarrasses the young woman in question. This comes over as a gleeful riff on the part of the voice artist, who is required to be an adept improviser creating the scene in the moment, in sync with the computer-programmed animation.

In the show's denouement, the audience yells as Stich escapes from a space station in a manner akin to a protagonist in a computer game. Stich and his pursuer are figured as moving dots on a diagram of the space station, shown on the screen. Spectators shout out instructions as to which route to take to avoid capture. The interaction here is between audience, voice artist, computer operator and animated character, as if all are playing the game on the fly. Throughout the piece, then, the spectators are implicated in an intermedial realization of cartoon presence and live interaction between screen and auditorium. The screen is both a place for digital imagery and a theatrical space, while the event dissolves the rigidities of proscenium presentation, and distinctions between two-dimensional and three-dimensional spaces for performance and spectatorship.

In his lacerating account of Disneyland parks, Michael Sorkin notes the parallel between televisual space, with its zapping-enabled diversities, and 'ageographical' Disneyland space:

> The highly regulated, completely synthetic vision provides a simplified, sanitized experience that stands in for the more undisciplined complexities of the city. . . . Both circus and Disney entertainment are anti-carnival-esque, feats of atomization, celebrations of the existing order of things in the guise of escape from it, Fordist fun.
>
> (1992: 208)

I don't dispute the ideological basis of Sorkin's analysis. In a broader landscape of cultural production, however, the work undertaken by planners and artistic directors in the parks is not entirely removed from that undertaken in other less corporate environments (a spectrum that includes Punchdrunk, Rimini Protokoll and Blast Theory). Clavé suggests that theme parks 'can be considered places of innovation concerning planning matters regarding the use of land, the management of energy flow, transport and communications' (2007: 155). This applies in relation to aspects of performance presentation and spectator engagement. Some of the tendencies of immersive, promenade and multimedia theatre are in play – and perhaps preempted – here. The parks provide non-linear journeys offering choice, fictive engagement and experience as a feature of consumption. Their 'synthetic vision', to return to Sorkin, is synthetic because escapist (non-actual), but more literally because it synthesizes fictive reference points with sensations of presence, participation and involvement (actualized). Theme parks are inherently hybridizing. For Lehmann, in postdramatic theatre 'Synthesis is cancelled. It is explicitly combated' (83). Disneyland (pre)figures a shift beyond the postdramatic and the postmodern. Synthesis returns, as formal pattern for consumption. The encounter is all.

## Eventing in Chatham

On a grey summer's day in 2012 I took my son Tom and his friend Noah to visit Dickens World at Chatham Maritime in Kent. While Disney's parks are self-contained micro-cities, Dickens World is an interior theme park located in a retail and leisure site in a reclaimed part of the Medway, a relatively depressed region of north-east Kent close to the Thames Estuary. The complex was conceived by theme park designer Gerry O'Sullivan-Beare and built by RMA Ltd, a company specializing in themed attractions.[9] As the press release notes, the theming here is around the 'life, books and times of one of Britain's best loved authors.' Pat Yale observes that 'heritage tourism really means little more than tourism centred on what we have inherited, which can mean anything from historical buildings, to art works, to beautiful scenery' (Yale 1998: 32).[10] In this instance Dickens World presents a pastiche of an historical nineteenth-century heritage – the scenic scape includes a waterway, dark brickwork, Victorian shopfronts and interior spaces – that meshes with a literary heritage figured through Charles Dickens' characters, stories and aspects of his biography. Chatham is a resonant location in that Dickens lived here from 1817–22 as a child, and the town features in his stories. Dickens World is a mash-up of the seemingly historical, the fictional and the experiential. It opened to the public on 25 May 2005, offering a lower-key version of the plurality that characterizes a Disney park, with distinct areas, micro-themes and diverse modes of engagement. It features a number of theatrical arrangements and performance situations that make it a useful microcosm for considering the theatring of engagement.

You arrive at what in effect is a car park with an industrial shed attached (Figure 9.3). This underscores the fact that the theme park is characteristic-ally a place of destination: Sorkin's 'there', albeit rather less glamorous than

*Figure 9.3* Dickens World: the car park with a theme park attached

Source: Andy Lavender

*Figure 9.4* The fairground cut-out: Tom (left) and Noah inhabit the event
Source: Andy Lavender

attractions that are more lavishly funded and enticingly located. As you pass Nandos and Subway on the way in, it is clear that the theme park is also a 'hybrid consumption location', to use Bryman's term, 'whereby the forms of consumption associated with different institutional spheres become interlocked with each other and increasingly difficult to distinguish' (2004: 58, 57).

Hybridity can be thought of as a mingling of forms and procedures, as discussed earlier in this book; and in terms of 'synthetic' production in two senses. The first is a blending of *performance* (which involves presentation, spectatorship and effects of presence); *engagement* (which wraps in event, encounter and experience); and *consumption* (which entails an exchange of things, sights, experiences, and symbolic capital). The synthesis of these activities depends on simulation – certain sorts of pretence or make-believe, copying and reiteration. In this latter respect the cultural production of the theme parks is synthetic in another way – in the sense of being inauthentic, not original. However, this matter of inauthenticity is complicated by the authorizing marks of brand identity, as discussed with respect to Disneyland, above; and the unquestionable fact of one's own actual presence. We were really there. Experience is verified by virtue of engagement in the here and now. Performance, which is here one's evental witness and involvement, corroborates this guarantee of experience. To this end, the greater the degree of performance, the greater the feeling that things are real, even where they are also all the more palpably made-up. The authentic and inauthentic are synthesized.

There are a number of opportunities to partake of performance. In an old-fashioned fairground cut-out, Tom and Noah disport themselves not so much as Oliver and his dog Bullseye than as participants in a staging of their own presence at the event (Figure 9.4). They *inhabit* the event by integrating in its opportunities for appellation and personification. To that end, Tom, Noah and I are 'eventers' – people who travel somewhere to engage and be engaged in a sphere of presentations and experiences. Such eventing is confirmed by its very presentationalism, for it is nothing if not available to photography. Di Benedetto suggests that theme parks can be conceived as 4-D memory theatres, offering 'a network of theatrical action-potentials that hold the potential to summon embodied knowledge' (2012: 62). The photograph is a means by which to retrieve such knowledge.

In the manner discussed in Chapter 4, above, the theme park fuses *mise en scène* – the arrangement of space and action for performance – *and mise en événement* – the arrangement of the event. The central courtyard and its surroundings (Figure 9.5) are both scenic space and event location. They contribute to what Bryman describes as the 'systemscape' of the theme park, a blending of space, scenography, performance and encounter (2004: vii).

We visit the Britannia Theatre, modelled on its namesake in Hoxton, the East End of London, between 1841–1900 – one of Dickens' preferred haunts. As Sorkin observes in another context: 'At Disneyland one is constantly poised in a condition of becoming, always someplace that is "like" someplace else. The simulation's referent is ever elsewhere; the "authenticity" of the

*Figure 9.5* The central courtyard: scenic space and systemscape for encounter

Source: Andy Lavender

substitution always depends on the knowledge, however faded, of some absent genuine' (1992: 216).

An audio-animatronic show plays at advertised times throughout the day. The figure of Charles Dickens stands at a lectern (haunting this theatre, too), and at points during the show talks with his characters Mr Pickwick and Samuel Weller, who appear in life-sized statuesque form standing in the boxes. The show begins with a voiceover featuring Fagin and the Artful Dodger, from Dickens' *Oliver Twist*. It features human actors in a series of videoscapes (Dickens' father, Mr Jingo and William Dorritt, for instance, appear in a mélange of fictionalized biography and quasi-biographical fiction). The animatronic Dickens talks later in the show to figures who appear as illustrations in a large book by way of video projection. As the pages turn, drawings of the characters come to life as Fagin, David Copperfield and Miss Moucher, performed by actors on video. The show is a multimedia, multi-modal production, mixing two- and three-dimensional virtual theatre. Performed to a co-present audience, it exists in the present but also in series, exactly repeatable and thereby profoundly un-live. It is like watching the negative of theatre.[11]

We sat in the courtyard for a more orthodox sort of performance – a potted version of *Oliver Twist*, lasting around 20 minutes or so. This was introduced by one of the actors, in an address to the audience, as an instance of the nineteenth-century street theatre of Dickens' day presented by a small troupe. Here such performance is enabled by sound reinforcement, recorded music, sound effects and a vocal track, to which the actors lipsynch. The mix of live and recorded performance, and the effacement of historical registers by contemporary means of production, make for a strikingly synthetic experience. Another trope of performance and presentation: in the Haunted House there is a series of Pepper's Ghost effects, staging a theatrical trick of the Victorian theatre using video projection via a mirror onto glass. The scenes include a meeting between Scrooge and Marley; a duel; and a parade of characters including Bumble, Oliver Twist, Miss Havisham and Pegotty, who appear to an expository voiceover in the character of Dickens.

Choice (within limits) is characteristic of the theme park. We choose to take the boat ride, which (as the press release has it) winds through 'the dark, dank sewers of London and then up to the city rooftops' (Figure 9.6). The ride is themed to 'relive the story of Magwitch's escape from the prison ship in Great Expectations'. Clavé reminds us that 'theatrical authenticity' is a feature of that which is consumed in theme parks, where leisure is incorporated into life (and vice versa) in a context of high levels of comfort and safety (2007: 158–9). I'm not sure that London's waterways ever provided a compelling eyeline view of the city's rooftops, nor that Magwitch found himself among these in his escape from the hulks. The turn to authenticity here, nevertheless, is in the realist *mise en scène* and the offer of a privileged perspective on that which is normally hidden from sight. The effect is like being in a film set that both documents and fictionalizes, and thereby stages one's experience in the synthetic present.

*Figure 9.6* The boat ride: inside a fictional/documentary *mise en scène*
Source: Andy Lavender

*Figure 9.7* The point of maximal smiling
Source: Souvenir photo from Dickens World

*Figure 9.8* The 'poor boy' costume for wearing . . .

Source: Andy Lavender

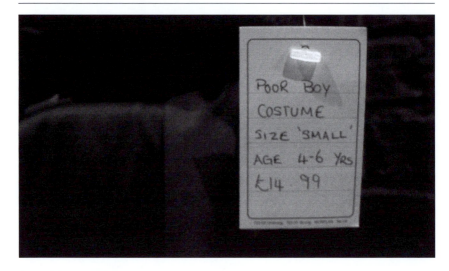

*Figure 9.9* . . . at a price

Source: Andy Lavender

The fairground ride is a familiar pleasure. Here it is retro-packaged by way of the photograph for purchase, taken automatically by a strategically positioned camera at the point at which the boat falls from a height into the water below (Figure 9.7). This souvenir may represent the apogee of our pleasure, and nothing to do with the theme park's synthesis of past, present, history, fiction, site and biography. Perhaps it is simply a kinetic thrill, the point of maximal smiling.

In *Consumer Culture*, Celia Lury argues that relationships between people and things (and I would include here those between people, sites and events) should be understood as reciprocal and iterative rather than linear. That's to say, consumption isn't the end point of production. It is a form of production in itself, what Lury describes as a 'conversion' of transactions into use and use-value (2011: 1–4). Initially at the theme park one consumes situations of encounter. The use value here is a guarantee of presence; the up–close exposure to a particular world, theme or story (*Harry Potter*, *The Lion King*, Outer Space, Victorian London and so on); and the sinking into an engagement that promises various choices, sensations and self-iterations. Typically, the visit here, as with that to the zoo, museum or gallery, entails a journey the final phase of which is through the shop. If the train or car park provides for a liminal phase of entrance, the shop offers a connective link between the visit and its echoes in daily life. First one consumes culture in the park (engaging with symbolic value through situated leisure and pleasure, produced as felt experience); and then has an opportunity to consume goods. The souvenirs sustain the brand's identity and its forms of cultural production (by way of gifts to others who were not present) and also allow for ongoing memorializing of the visit.

Figure 9.8 shows a costume for purchase, part of the general theatricality of the theme park, and the reiteration of the Dickensian as commodity (for acquisition and make-believe). In its price tag (Figure 9.9) we find Dickens World's final cancellation of Dickens. It marks the evisceration of much that we might describe as Dickensian – the social conscience, rage at inequality, fun at the expense of conformity. It's not so much that these things are displaced. They are obliterated through the turn to self-inscription and experience. The poor boy is not for contextualizing, let alone saving. Nor is he even really for sale. He is a costume for inhabiting.

Emerging from the in-world place of event and experience, we become again ourselves in our everydayness. We have arguably no greater understanding of Dickens or things Dickensian. We might even have less understanding. But we have had a degree of fun, placed inside a simulation of history, biography and literature in order to produce our own eventful present.

## Dis(s)engagements in Dismaland

Lastly, an antidote to the theme park: an attraction that advertised its own inadequacy (hence, rather, its specialness) and involved its visitors in various counter-cultural scenarios. The British street artist Banksy, renowned for protecting his anonymity and operating under the radar of civic legislature (while now sustaining a profile as an internationally recognized artist) conceived and produced Dismaland as an installation-cum-experience.[12] Self-styled in its publicity materials as a 'bemusement park' and 'The UK's most disappointing new visitor attraction!', Dismaland was pertinently located at the site of the Tropicana, a derelict lido in the faded North Somerset seaside town Weston-super-Mare. It ran for five weeks (21 August to 27 September 2015) as a dystopian rendering of a Disneyesque park, albeit with artworks by 58 artists, including Damian Hirst, David Shrigley and Jenny Holzer, rather than rides as its central attraction. Tickets could only be bought in person at the event or online, and cost £3. When they first went on sale, the site crashed due to the demand, and all tickets were sold within 90 minutes.[13] The park's helpers wear high-visibility jackets, cheap Mickey Mouse ears on their heads, and determinedly miserable expressions. Attractions include a mordantly dilapidated version of the iconic Disney castle, featuring an installation of a crashed pumpkin coach complete with dead princess; a stall where you throw small balls in an attempt to knock over an anvil; and a pocket money loan booth, where the child has to jump on a trampoline to read the small print outlining the exorbitant interest rate.

Dismaland is a decidedly contemporary theatre of engagement. It is scenographically rich, a meld of carefully designed spaces, buildings, objects and models. Like all theme parks (along with many other civic and virtual spaces) it presents a systemscape for movement and encounter. It is concretely situated, both in its witty makeover of an abandoned pleasure resort, and in its pointed attack on the sorts of management and commodification of pleasure within mainstream leisure culture. It fizzes with intensity and creativity. It is a generation beyond postmodernism's more abstract and ironic disaffectedness, while it sustains postmodernism's systematic procedures of fragmentation and hierarchical revision. In a characteristic fusion of artifice and actuality, it involves the bodies of its visitors in its staged entry protocols (body scans, bag searches) and, through the performance of its sullen helpers, immerses you within scenes of satirical actuality. It implicates its visitors in its counter-cultural energetics, placing you within its scenarios of affective disorder.

Dismaland reminds us that theatres of engagement can also be theatres of disengagement, capable of performing separation, disagreement and resistance – struggling (as Butler has it) 'against disenfranchisement, effacement, and abandonment' (2011) – even while providing fun and *sensus communis*. But this, too, is a form of engagement – the sort of dissensus that we can perform, in some places, in our encounters within culture. The Real is theatricalized as the image of itself within a refigured actuality. Escapism is always embodied (even in its most sedentary or virtual forms), and needn't be mindless. Nor, for that matter, need engagement.

## Notes

1 The piece was scheduled for 21–31 May 2015, with projections at Klafthmonos Square, Sina Street and Vissarionos Street, Athens. Those in the square were withdrawn partway through. The piece was initially presented at the EUR, Rome, on 9 September 2006, with subsequent iterations elsewhere. See www.atwodogs company.org/en/projects/item/162-stills.

2 Conversation with the author, 4 June 2015. See also www.sgt.gr/en/programme/event/1862, which includes a link to Verdonck's director's note. Nikos Xydakis's Tweet is at https://twitter.com/damomac/status/604403716905648128. A video showing the projection is at https://vimeo.com/129102244. See also www.grreporter.info/en/video_installation_athens_has_been_removed_because_priest_does_not_it/12803. Links accessed 28 August 2015.

3 *Wanna Play?* was presented in Heinrichplatz, Kreuzberg, Berlin, 1–5 October 2014, in association with HAU Hebbel am Ufer; and in De Neude, Utrecht, 21–30 May 2015, where I saw it on its final two days.

4 See Rosenberg 2014. The shift in approach for the Utrecht version is made clear in the press release at www.driesverhoeven.com/sites/default/files/uploads/press_release_wanna_play_dries_verhoeven_en_with_photo.pdf.

5 http://english.hebbel-am-ufer.de/programme/archive/treffpunkte/, accessed 28 August 2015.

6 I visited Hong Kong Disneyland on 18 February 2011 and Dickens World (for a second time) on 10 June 2012.

7 See Clavé 2007: 3–18, 21–41 for an account of the development and characteristics of theme parks. See also Swarbrooke 2002, which addresses the development of attractions, management systems and specific case studies. For a well-illustrated synoptic account see A. and P. Wylson 1994. For accounts that focus on Disneyland see Sorkin 1992 and Yale 1998.

8 Interview with the author, 18 February 2011.

9  See Balmond 2005; and, for an account of the project on RMA's website, www.rma-themedattractions.co.uk/dickens-world. For Dickens World's website, see www.dickensworld.co.uk/.

10 See Yale 1998: 32 for a description of the development of 'heritage' as a concept and a term in cultural discourse in the UK from the 1970s onwards.

11 Dickens World remodeled its visitor experience later in 2012, dropping the animated performance and instead offering visitors an interactive guided tour.

12 A website concerning Banksy's work is at www.banksy.co.uk/menu.asp. Wikipedia's entry on Banksy contains useful information, links and references: https://en.wikipedia.org/wiki/Banksy. Dismaland's website is at www.dismaland. co.uk/. For a promotional video, see www.dismaland.co.uk/advert/ or www.you tube.com/watch?v=V2NG-MgHqEk. Jobson's review (2015) includes a number of images. All links accessed 29 August 2015.

13 www.itv.com/news/west/update/2015-08-28/next-ticket-sale-announced-for-banksys-dismaland/, accessed 29 August 2015.

# Bibliography

*All links live at 2 January 2015 unless otherwise indicated by a different date of access.*

Ahmed, Sarah, Jane Kilby, Celia Lury, Maureen McNeil and Beverley Skeggs (2000) 'Introduction: thinking through feminism', in Ahmed, Kilby, Lury, McNeil and Skeggs (eds), *Transformations: Thinking Through Feminism*, London and New York: Routledge.

Allain, Jean-François, Laurence Larroche and Janet Gough (2006) *Collins Robert French Dictionary*, Glasgow, New York, Ontario and Paris: HarperCollins/Diction naires Le Robert-SEJER.

Alston, Adam (2012) 'Funding, product placement and drunkenness in Punchdrunk's *The Black Diamond*', *Studies in Theatre & Performance*, 32:2, 193–208.

Alston, Adam (2013) 'Audience Participation and Neoliberal Value: Risk, agency and responsibility in immersive theatre', *Performance Research: A Journal of the Performing Arts*, 18:2, 128–38.

Alston, Adam and R. Daker (2012) 'Contemporary Theatre "Philanthropy" and the Purchase of Participatory Privilege', *Contemporary Theatre Review*, 22:3, 433–9.

Althusser, Louis (1970) *Essays on Ideology*, London: Verso.

Andrews, David L. and Steven J. Jackson (eds) (2001) *Sports Stars: The cultural politics of sporting celebrity*, London and New York: Routledge.

Anfam, David (ed.) (2009a) *Anish Kapoor*, London and New York: Phaidon.

Anfam, David (2009b) 'To Fathom the Abyss', in David Anfam (ed.), *Anish Kapoor*, London and New York: Phaidon, 88–113.

Ang, Ien (2003) 'Together-in-difference: beyond Diaspora, into Hybridity', *Asian Studies Review*, 27:2, 141–54.

Appel, Hannah Chadeyane (2012) 'The People's Microphone', in Amy Schrager Lang and Daniel Lang/Levistsky (eds), *Dreaming in Public: Building the Occupy Movement*, Oxford: New Internationalist Publications, 260–2.

Arfara, Katia (2015) 'Fast Forward Festival 2: New Media/New Technologies/New Forms', Artistic Director's note, www.sgt.gr/en/circle/77.

Ars Electronica, http://new.aec.at/prix/kategorien/hybrid-art/.

Auslander, Philip (1997) *From Acting to Performance: Essays in Modernism and Postmodernism*, London and New York: Routledge.

Auslander, Philip (2002) 'Live from Cyberspace: or, I was sitting at my computer this guy appeared he thought I was a bot', *PAJ: A Journal of Performance and Art*, 24:1, 16–21.

Auslander, Philip (2008 [1999]) *Liveness* (2nd edition), London and New York: Routledge.

Auslander, Philip (2011) 'Digital Liveness', Keynote lecture at the transmediale *Digital Liveness – Realtime, Desire and Sociability* conference, Berlin, 3 February 2011, www.transmediale.de/content/digital-liveness-philip-auslander-us-about-digital-liveness; http://vimeo.com/20473967.

Austin, J. L. (1975 [1962]) *How to do Things with Words*, Cambridge, MA: Harvard University Press.

Bala, Sruti (2012) 'Vectors of Participation in Contemporary Theatre and Performance', *Theatre Research International*, 37:3, 236–48.

Baerenholdt, Jørgen Ole, Michael Haldrup and Jonas Larsen (2008) 'Performing cultural attractions', in Jon Sundbo and Per Darmer (eds), *Creating Experiences in the Experience Economy*, Cheltenham and Northampton (MA): Edward Elgar, 176–202.

Balme, Christopher (2004) 'Editorial', *Theatre Research International*, 29:1, 1–3.

Balme, Christopher (2006) 'Audio Theatre: The Mediatization of Theatrical Space', in Freda Chapple and Chiel Kattenbelt (eds), *Intermediality in Theatre and Performance*, Amsterdam: Rodopi, 117–24.

Balme, Christopher B. (2008) *The Cambridge Introduction to Theatre Studies*, Cambridge and New York: Cambridge University Press.

Balme, Christopher B. (2014a) *The Theatrical Public Sphere*, Cambridge: Cambridge University Press.

Balme, Christopher (2014b) 'Public Sphere', in Bryan Reynolds (ed.), *Performance Studies: Key Words, Concepts and Theories*, London and New York: Palgrave Macmillan, 16–23.

Balmond, Sarah (2005) 'RMA/O'Sullivan-Beare theme for Dickens World', *Design Week*, 21 April 2005, www.designweek.co.uk/news/rma/osullivan-beare-theme-for-dickens-world/1119186.article.

Barder, Alexander D. and David M. McCourt (2010) 'Rethinking International History, Theory and the Event with Hannah Arendt', *Journal of International Political Theory*, 6:2, 117–41.

Bauman, Zygmunt (1993) *Postmodern Ethics*, Oxford and Cambridge, MA: Blackwell.

Bauman, Zygmunt (1995) *Life in Fragments: Essays in Postmodern Morality*, Oxford and Cambridge, MA: Blackwell.

Bauman, Zygmunt (1997) *Postmodernity and its Discontents*, Cambridge: Polity Press.

Bauman, Zygmunt (2000) *Liquid Modernity*, Cambridge: Polity Press.

Baumgardner, Jennifer and Amy Richards (2010 [2000]) *Manifesta: young women, feminism, and the future*, New York: Farrar, Strauss and Giroux.

Bay-Cheng, Sarah (2012) 'Intermediate Bodies: Media Theory in Theatre', in Megan Alrutz, Julia Listengarten and M. Van Dyn Wood (eds), *Playing with Theory in Theatre Practice*, Basingstoke: Palgrave Macmillan, 63–74.

Bay-Cheng, Sarah (2014) 'Digital Culture', in Bryan Reynolds (ed.), *Performance Studies: Key Words, Concepts and Theories*, London and New York: Palgrave Macmillan, 39–49.

Benkler, Yochai (2006) *The Wealth of Networks: How Social Production Transforms Markets and Freedom*, New Haven and London: Yale University Press.

Bennett, Susan (1990; 2nd edn. 1997) *Theatre Audiences: A theory of production and reception*, London and New York: Routledge.

Bennett, Susan (2013) *Theatre & Museums*, Houndmills: Palgrave Macmillan.

Bertens, Hans (1995) *The Idea of the Postmodern: A History*, London and New York: Routledge.

Bhabha, Homi K. (2004 [1994]), *The Location of Culture*. London and New York: Routledge.

Biehl-Missal, Brigitte (2012) 'Using artistic form for aesthetic organizational inquiry: Rimini Protokoll constructs Daimler's Annual General Meeting as a theatre play', *Culture and Organization*, 18:3, 211–29.

Bignell, Jonathan (2005) *Big Brother: Reality TV in the Twenty-first Century*, Basingstoke and New York: Palgrave Macmillan.

Billig, Michael and Herbert W. Simons (1994) 'Introduction', in Herbert W. Simons and Michael Billig (eds), *After Postmodernism: Reconstructing Ideology Critique*, London, Thousand Oaks and New Delhi: Sage Publications, 1–11.

Bishop, Claire (2004) 'Antagonism and Relational Aesthetics', *October*, 110, 51–79.

Bishop, Claire (2005) *Installation Art: A Critical History*, London: Tate Publishing.

Bishop, Claire (ed.) (2006) *Participation*, London and Cambridge, MA: Whitechapel and the MIT Press.

Blattès, Susan (2007) 'Is the Concept of 'Character' Still Relevant in Contemporary Drama?', in Christoph Henke and Martin Middeke (eds), *Drama and/after Postmodernism*, Trier: WVT Wissenschaftlicher Verlag Trier, 69–81.

Boenisch, Peter M. (2010) 'Towards a Theatre of Encounter and Experience: Reflexive Dramaturgies and Classic Texts', *Contemporary Theatre Review*, 20:2, 162–72.

Boenisch, Peter M. (2012) 'Acts of Spectating: The Dramaturgy of the Audience's Experience in Contemporary Theatre', *Critical Stages*, IATC Webjournal 7 (December 2012), www.criticalstages.org/.

Bohman, James (2004) 'Expanding dialogue: The Internet, the public sphere and prospects for transnational democracy', in Nick Crossley and John Michael Roberts (eds), *After Habermas: New Perspectives on the Public Sphere*, Oxford and Malden, MA: Blackwell, 131–155.

Bonnicksen, Andrea L. (2009) *Chimeras, Hybrids, and Interspecies Research: Politics and Policymaking*, Washington: Georgetown University Press.

Boorstin, Daniel J. (1992 [1961]) *The Image: A Guide to Pseudo-Events in America*, New York: Vintage Books.

Bordwell, David and Kristin Thompson (1990 [1979]) *Film Art: An Introduction*, New York: McGraw-Hill.

Borsò, Vittoria (2006) 'Hybrid perceptions: a phenomenological approach to the relationship between mass media and hybridity', in Frank Heidemann and Alfonso de Toro (eds), *New Hybridities: Societies and Cultures in Transition*, Hildesheim, Zurich and New York: Georg Olms Verlag.

Boswijk, Albert, Thomas Thijssen and Ed Peelen (2007) *The Experience Economy: A New Perspective*, Amsterdam: Pearson Education Beneluz.

Botham, Paola (2008) 'From Deconstruction to Reconstruction: A Habermasian Framework for Contemporary Political Theatre', *Contemporary Theatre Review*, 18:3, 307–17.

Boullemier, Leo B. (compiler) (1985) *The Checklist of Species, Hybrids and Cultivars of the Genus Fuchsia*, Poole: Blandford Press.

Bourriaud, Nicolas (2002) *Relational Aesthetics*, trans. Simon Pleasance and Fronza Woods with Mathieu Copeland, Dijon: Les presses du réel (first published in French as *Esthetique rélationelle*, 1998).

Brecht, Bertolt (1964), 'Short description of a new technique of acting which produces an alienation effect', in John Willett (ed. and trans.), *Brecht on Theatre: The Development of an Aesthetic*, New York: Hill and Wang, pp. 136–47.

Brennan, Teresa (2004) *The Transmission of Affect*, Ithaca and London: Cornell University Press.

Brown, Adrienne Maree (2012) 'From liberty plaza: let it breathe', in Amy Schrager Lang and Daniel Lang/Levistsky (eds), *Dreaming in Public: Building the Occupy Movement*, Oxford: New Internationalist Publications, 79–84.

Brown, Derren (2006) *Tricks of the Mind*, London: Channel 4 Books/Transworld.

Brown, Derren (2010) *Confessions of a Conjuror*, London: Channel 4 Books/Transworld.

Brown, Richard Harvey (1994) 'Reconstructing Social Theory after the Postmodern Critique', in Herbert W. Simons and Michael Billig (eds), *After Postmodernism: Reconstructing Ideology Critique*, London, Thousand Oaks and New Delhi: Sage Publications, 12–37.

Bruns, Axel (2008) *Blogs, Wikipedia, Second Life and Beyond*, New York: Peter Lang.

Bryman, Alan (2004) *The Disneyization of Society*, Los Angeles, London, New Delhi, Singapore: Sage Publications.

Buckley, William F., Jr. (2004) *The Fall of the Berlin Wall*, Hoboken, New Jersey: Wiley.

Bunz, Mercedes (2014) *The Silent Revolution: How Digitization Transforms Knowledge, Work, Journalism and Politics Without Making Too Much Noise*, Houndmills and New York: Palgrave Macmillan.

Burgess, Jean and Joshua Green (2009) *YouTube: Online Video and Participatory Culture*, Cambridge (UK) and Malden, MA: Polity Press.

Burke, Peter (2009) *Cultural Hybridity*, Cambridge: Polity Press.

Butler, Judith (2011) 'Bodies in Alliance and the Politics of the Street', European Institute for Progressive Cultural Policies, www.eipcp.net/transversal/1011/butler/en (accessed 30 August 2015).

Calhoun, Craig (ed.) (1992a) *Habermas and the Public Sphere*, Cambridge, MA and London: MIT Press.

Calhoun, Craig (1992b) 'Introduction' in Craig Calhoun (ed.), *Habermas and the Public Sphere*, Cambridge, MA and London: MIT Press, 1–48.

Calleja, Gordon (2011) *In-Game: From Immersion to Incorporation*, Cambridge, MA and London: Massachusetts Institute of Technology.

Carlson, Marvin (1996) *Performance: a critical introduction*, London and New York: Routledge.

Carlson, Marvin (2006) '*Postdramatic Theatre*' (review), *Theatre Research International*, 31:3, 315–6.

Carlson, Marvin (2012) 'Immersive Theatre and the Receptive Process', unpublished conference paper presented at the International Federation of Theatre Research conference, Santiago, 2012.

Carné, Marcel (director) and Jacques Prévert (writer) (1945) *Les Enfants du Paradis*, France: Pathé Cinema.

Carroll, Samantha (2008) 'The Practical Politics of Step-Stealing and Textual Poaching: YouTube, Audio-Visual Media and Contemporary Swing Dancers Online', *Convergence*, 14:2, 183–204.

Casati, Roberto and Achille C. Varzi (eds) (1996) *Events* (*The International Research Library of Philosophy* 15), Aldershot (UK) and Brookfield (USA): Dartmouth.

Castells, Manuel (2001) *The Internet Galaxy: Reflections on the Internet, Business, and Society*, Oxford and New York: Oxford University Press.

Castells, Manuel (2012) *Networks of outrage and hope: social movements in the Internet age*, Cambridge: Polity.

Causey, Matthew (2006) *Theatre and Performance in Digital Culture: From Simulation to Embeddedness*, London and New York: Routledge.

Chambers, Samuel A. (2011) 'The Politics of the Police: From Neoliberalism to Anarchism and Back to Democracy', in Paul Bowman and Richard Stamp (eds), *Reading Rancière: Critical Dissensus*, London and New York: Continuum, 18–43.

Chapple, Freda, and Chiel Kattenbelt (2006) 'Key Issues in Intermediality in theatre and performance', in Freda Chapple and Chiel Kattenbelt (eds), *Intermediality in Theatre and Performance*, Amsterdam and New York: Rodopi, 11–25.

Chvasta, Marcyrose (2006) 'Anger, Irony, and Protest: Confronting the Issue of Efficacy, Again', *Text and Performance Quarterly*, 26:1, 5–16.

Clavé, Salvador Anton (2007) *The Global Theme Park Industry*, Wallingford (UK) and Cambridge, MA: CABI.

Claycomb, Ryan (2012) 'Voices of the Other: Documentary and Oral History Performance in Post-9/11 British Theatre', in Jenny Spencer (ed.), *Political and Protest Theatre after 9/11: Patriotic Dissent*, New York and Abingdon: Routledge, 93–107.

Cohen Cruz, Jan (2010) *Engaging performance: theatre as call and response*, London: Routledge.

Coleman, Gabriella (2014) *Hacker, Hoaxer, Whistleblower, Spy: The Many Faces of Anonymous*, London and New York: Verso.

Corcoran, Steven (2010) 'Editor's Introduction', in Jacques Rancière, *Dissensus: On Politics and Aesthetics*, ed. and trans. Steven Corcoran, London and New York: Continuum, 2010, 1–24.

Corner, John (2004) 'Afterword: Framing the New', in Su Holmes and Deborah Jermyn (eds), *Understanding Reality Television*, London and New York: Routledge (290–9).

Couldry, Nick (2010) *Why Voice Matters: Culture and Politics after Neoliberalism*, London: Sage.

Cremona, Vicky Ann, Peter Eversmann, Hans van Maanen, Willmar Sauter and John Tulloch (eds) (2004), *Theatrical Events: Borders Dynamics Frames*, London and New York: Rodopi.

Crone, Rainer and Alexandra Von Stosch (2008) *Anish Kapoor*, Munich, London and New York: Prestel.

Czirak, Adam (2011) 'The Piece Comes to Life through a Dialogue with the Spectators, not with the Performers: An interview on participation with Dries Verhoeven', *Performance Research: A Journal of the Performing Arts*, 16:3, 78–83.

Damasio, Antonio (1999) *The Feeling of What Happens: Body, Emotion, and the Making of Consciousness*, London: William Heinemann.

Darmer, Per and Jon Sundbo (2008) 'Introduction to experience creation', in Jon Sundbo and Per Darmer (eds), *Creating Experiences in the Experience Economy*, Cheltenham and Northampton, MA: Edward Elgar, 1–12.

Davis, Oliver (2010) *Jacques Rancière*, Cambridge and Malden, MA: Polity Press.

Davis, Tracy C. and Thomas Postlewait (2003) 'Theatricality: an introduction', in Tracy C. Davis and Thomas Postlewait (eds), *Theatricality*, Cambridge: Cambridge University Press, 1–39.

de Certeau, Michel (1984) *The Practice of Everyday Life*, trans. Steven Rendall, Berkeley, Los Angeles, London: University of California Press.

Deleuze, Gilles and Félix Guattari (1991) *What is Philosophy?*, trans. Hugh Tomlinson and Graham Burchell, New York: Columbia University Press.

Deleuze, Gilles and Félix Guattari (2004 [1998]) *A Thousand Plateaus: Capitalism and Schizophrenia*, trans. Brian Massumi, London and New York: Continuum.

DeLuca, Kevin M., Sean Lawson and Ye Sun (2012) 'Occupy Wall Street on the Public Screens of Social Media: The Many Framings of the Birth of a Protest Movement', *Communication, Culture & Critique*, 5, 483–509.

Dewey, John (1934) *Art As Experience*, New York: Capricorn Books.

Di Benedetto, Stephen (2012) 'Camillo's 4-D Theme Park Attractions', *Performance Research*, 17:3, June 2012, 57–62.

Dixon, Steve, with contributions by Barry Smith (2007) *Digital Performance: A History of New Media in Theater, Dance, Performance Art, and Installation*, Cambridge, MA and London: The MIT Press.

Docherty, Thomas (ed.) (1993) *Postmodernism*, Cambridge: Cambridge University Press.

Dovey, Jon (2000) *Freakshow: First Person Media and Factual Television*, London and Sterling: Pluto Press.

dreamthinkspeak (2010) *Before I Sleep* (production programme), Brighton: dream-thinkspeak.

dreamthinkspeak (a) www.dreamthinkspeak.com/about2.htm.

dreamthinkspeak (b) www.dreamthinkspeak.com/dont-look-back.htm.

Eckersall, Peter (2012) 'Locations of Dramaturgy – Kris Verdonck', *Performance Research*, 17:3, 68–75.

Emden, Christian J. and David Midgley (eds) (2013) *Beyond Habermas: Democracy, Knowledge, and the Public Sphere*, New York and Oxford: Berghahn Books.

Engel, Jeffrey A. (2009) '1989: An Introduction to an International History', in Jeffrey A. Engel (ed.), *The Fall of the Berlin Wall: The Revolutionary Legacy of 1989*, Oxford and New York: Oxford University Press, 1–35.

Engle, Karen (2009) *Seeing Ghosts: 9/11 and the Visual Imagination*, Montreal & Kingston, London and Ithaca: McGill-Queen's University Press.

Fischer-Lichte, Erika (2008) *The Transformative Power of Performance: A New Aesthetics*, trans. Saskya Iris Jain, London and New York: Routledge.

Fischer-Lichte, Erika (2009) 'Interweaving Cultures in Performance: Different States of Being In-Between', *New Theatre Quarterly*, 25, 391–401.

Fischer-Lichte, Erika (2010) 'Modernisation as Interweaving of Cultures in Perform-ance', keynote lecture, International Federation of Theatre Research conference, Ludwig Maximilian University of Munich, 28 July 2010.

Fischer-Lichte, Erika, and Rustom Bharucha (2011) 'Dialogue: Erika Fischer-Lichte and Rustom Bharucha', *Textures: Online Platform for Interweaving Performance Cultures*, www.textures-platform.com/?p=1667.

Forsyth, Alison, and Chris Megson (2009) 'Introduction', in Alison Forsyth and Chris Megson (eds), *Get Real: Documentary Theatre Past and Present*, Houndsmill and New York: Palgrave Macmillan, 1–5.

Foster, Hal (1985) 'Postmodernism: A Preface', in Hal Foster (ed.), *Postmodern Culture*, London and Leichhardt: Pluto Press.

Foucault, Michel (1981) 'The Order of Discourse' [Inaugural Lecture at the Collège de France, 2 December 1970], trans. Ian McLeod, in Robert Young (ed.), *Untying the Text: A Post-Structuralist Reader*, Boston, London and Henley: Routledge & Kegan Paul, 48–78.

Foucault, Michel (2002 [1972]) *Archeology of Knowledge*, trans. A. M. Sheridan Smith, London and New York: Routledge.

Franko, Mark (2007a) 'Introduction: eventful knowledge and the post-ritual turn', in Mark Franko (ed.), *Ritual and Event: Interdisciplinary perspectives*, London and New York: Routledge, 1–9.

Franko, Mark (2007b) 'Given movement: Dance and the event', in Mark Franko (ed.), *Ritual and Event: Interdisciplinary Perspectives*, London and New York: Routledge, 2007, 125–37.

Freshwater, Helen (2009) *Theatre & Audience*, London and New York: Palgrave Macmillan.

Fried, Michael (1998 [1967]) 'Art and Objecthood', in Michael Fried, *Art and Objecthood: Essays and Reviews*, Chicago and London: University of Chicago Press, 148–72.

Fuchs, Elinor (1996) *The Death of Character: Perspectives on Theater after Modernism*, Bloomington: Indiana University Press.

Fuchs, Elinor (2008) '*Postdramatic Theatre* (review)', *The Drama Review*, 52:2, 178–83.

Gamson, William A. and Micah L. Sifry (2013) 'The #Occupy Movement: An Introduction', in William A. Gamson and Micah L. Sifry (eds), 'Special Section: The #Occupy Movement', *The Sociological Quarterly*, 54:2, 159–163 (Special Section 159–228).

Gardner, Lyn (2008) 'One Step Forward, One Step Back', *The Guardian*, www. guardian.co.uk/stage/2008/apr/12/theatre.europeancapitalofculture2008, posted 12 April 2008.

Garner, Stanton B. Jr. (1994) *Bodied Spaces: Phenomenology and Performance in Contemporary Drama*, Ithaca and London: Cornell University Press.

Gauntlett, David (2013) 'Creativity and digital innovation', in Gillian Youngs (ed.), *Digital World: Connectivity, Creativity and Rights*, London and New York: Routledge, 78–90.

Gebauer, Gunter and Christoph Wulf (1995 [1992]) *Mimesis: Culture, Art, Society*, trans. Don Reneau, Berkeley, Los Angeles, London: University of California Press.

Gendlin, Eugene (1999) 'Authenticity after Postmodernism', *Changes: An International Journal of Psychology and Psychotherapy*, 17:3, 203–12.

Giannachi, Gabriella (2004) *Virtual Theatres: An Introduction*, London and New York: Routledge.

Goring, Paul (2005) *The Rhetoric of Sensibility in Eighteenth-Century England*, Cambridge: Cambridge University Press.

Grehan, Helena (2009) *Performance, Ethics and Spectatorship in a Global Age*, Houndmills, Basingstoke and New York: Palgrave Macmillan.

Groot Nibbelink, Liesbeth (2012) 'Radical Intimacy: Ontroerend Goed Meets *The Emancipated Spectator*', *Contemporary Theatre Review*, 22:3, 412–20.

Grusin, Richard (2009) 'YouTube at the End of New Media', in Relle Snickars and Patrick Vonderau (eds), *The YouTube Reader*, Stockholm: National Library of Sweden, 60–7.

Habermas, Jürgen (1991) *The Structural Transformation of the Public Sphere: An Inquiry into a Category of Bourgeois Society*, trans. Thomas Burger with the assistance of Frederick Lawrence, Cambridge, MA: The MIT Press (originally published in German in 1962).

Haddon, Leslie (2009) 'The Development of Interactive Games', in Leah A. Leevrouw and Sonia Livingstone (eds), *New Media: Volume II (Technology: Artefacts, Systems, Designs)*, London and Los Angeles: Sage.

Hallwall, Peter (2009) 'Staging Equality: Rancière's Theatrocracy and the Limits of Anarchic Equality', in Gabriel Rockhill and Philip Watts (eds), *Jacques Rancière: Politics, History, Aesthetics*, Durham & London: Duke University Press, 140–57.

Hammond, Will and Dan Steward (2008) *verbatim verbatim: Contemporary Documentary Theatre*, London: Oberon Books.

Hannerz, Ulf (1992) *Cultural Complexity: Studies in the Social Organization of Meaning*, New York: Columbia University Press.

Hannerz, Ulf (1996) *Transnational Connections: Culture, People, Places*. London: Routledge.

Hardt, Michael and Antonio Negri (2004) *Multitude: War and Democracy in the Age of Empire*, New York: Penguin.

Hartley, John (2009) 'Uses of YouTube: Digital Literacy and the Growth of Knowledge' in Jean Burgess and Joshua Green (2009) *YouTube: Online Video and Participatory Culture*, Cambridge (UK) and Malden, MA: Polity Press, 126–43.

Harvie, Jen (2013) *Fair Play – Art, Performance and Neoliberalism*, Basingstoke and New York: Palgrave Macmillan.

Havens, Timothy and Amanda D. Lotz (2012) *Understanding Media Industries*, New York and Oxford: Oxford University Press.

Heddon, Deirdre and Jane Milling (2006) *Devising Performance: A Critical History*, Houndmills: Palgrave Macmillan.

Heidemann, Frank and Alfonso de Toro (2006) 'Introduction: Rethinking Post-colonialism and Hybridity', in Frank Heidemann and Alfonso de Toro (eds), *New Hybridities: Societies and Cultures in Transition*, Hildesheim, Zurich and New York: Georg Olms Verlag, 9–17.

Heiser, Jörg (2010) 'What is "super-hybridity"?', *Frieze*, www.frieze.com/issue/article/pick-mix/.

Heller-Roazen, Daniel (2007) *The Inner Touch: Archaeology of a Sensation*, New York: Zone Books.

Henke, Christoph and Martin Middeke (2007) 'Introduction: Drama and/after Postmodernism', in Christoph Henke and Martin Middeke (eds), *Drama and/after Postmodernism*, Trier: WVT Wissenschaftlicher Verlag Trier, 1–33.

Herring, Laraine (2007) *Writing Begins with the Breath: Embodying Your Authentic Voice*, Boston: Shambhala Publications.

Hewlett, Nick (2007) *Badiou, Balibar, Rancière: Re-thinking Emancipation*, London and New York: Continuum.

Hill, Annette (2005) *Reality TV: Audiences and popular factual television*, Abingdon and New York: Routledge.

Hill, Annette (2007) *Restyling Factual TV: Audiences and new, documentary and reality genres*, Abingdon and New York: Routledge.

Hill, Annette (2011) *Paranormal Media: Audiences, spirits, and magic in popular culture*, London and New York: Routledge.

Hobsbawm, Eric (1994) *Age of Extremes: The Short Twentieth Century: 1914–91*, London: Michael Joseph.

hooks, bell (2000) *Feminism is for Everybody: Passionate Politics*, Cambridge, MA: South End Press.

Hurley, Erin (2010) *Theatre & Feeling*, Houndmills: Palgrave Macmillan.

Hybrid Arts, http://hybridarts.co.uk/?page_id=1304.

Hybrid.[Theatre].Ensemble, www.facebook.com/pages/HybridTheatreEnsemble/3126 30205359.

Hybrid Theatre Works, www.hybridtheatreworks.org/.

ITU (International Telecommunication Union) (2014) *Measuring the Information Society Report 2014: Executive Summary*, Geneva: ITU.

Jackson, Shannon (2011) *Social Works: Performing Arts, Supporting Publics*, Abingdon and New York: Routledge.

Jameson, Fredric (1991) *Postmodernism, or, The Cultural Logic of Late Capitalism*, London and New York: Verso.

Jenkins, Henry (2006) *Convergence Culture*, New York and London: New York University Press.

Jobson, Christopher (2015) 'Welcome to Dismaland: A First Look at Banksy's New Art Exhibition Housed Inside a Dystopian Theme Park', Colossal, www.this iscolossal.com/2015/08/dismaland/, posted 20 August 2015, accessed 29 August 2015.

Jung, C. G. (1966 [1953]) *Two Essays on Analytical Psychology*, trans. by R. F. C. Hull, in Herbert Read, Michael Fordham and Gerhard Adler (eds), *The Collected Works of C. G. Jung*, Volume 7, London and Henley: Routledge & Kegan Paul.

Jürs-Munby, Karen, Jerome Carroll and Steve Giles (eds) (2013) *Postdramatic Theatre and the Political: International Perspectives on Contemporary Performance*, London and New York: Bloomsbury.

Kattwinkel, Susan (2003) 'Manipulation of the Mind: Fiction in the performances of Penn and Teller', in Susan Kattwinkel (ed.), *Audience Participation: Essays on Inclusion in Performance*, Westport, Connecticut and London: Praeger, 2003, 89–100.

Kattwinkel, Susan (ed.) (2003) *Audience Participation: Essays on Inclusion in Performance*, Westport, Connecticut and London: Praeger.

Kavka, Misha (2012) *Reality TV*, Edinburgh: Edinburgh University Press.

Kaye, Nick (2000) *Site-Specific Art: Performance, Place, and Documentation*, London and New York: Routledge.

Kennedy, Dennis (2001) 'Sports and Shows: Spectators in Contemporary Culture', *Theatre Research International*, 26:3, 277–84.

Kent, Cheryl (2011) *Millennium Park Chicago*, Evanston, Illinois: Northwestern University Press.

Kirby, Michael (1984) 'On Acting and Non-Acting', in Gregory Battcock and Robert Nickas (eds), *The Art of Performance: A Critical Anthology*, New York: E. P. Dutton, 97–117.

Klich, Rosemary and Edward Scheer (2012) *Multimedia Performance*, Houndmills: Palgrave Macmillan.

Korbonits, Márta, David Blaine, Marinos Elia, Jeremy Powell-Tuck (2005) 'Refeeding David Blaine – Studies after a 44-Day Fast', *New England Journal of Medicine*, 353: 21, 2306–7.

Kubiak, Anthony (2002) *Agitated States: Performance in the American Theater of Cruelty*, Ann Arbor: University of Michigan Press.

Kwok-bun, Chan (ed.) (2012) *Cultural Hybridity: Contradictions and Dilemmas*, London and New York: Routledge.

Lange, Patricia G. (2009) 'Videos of Affinity on YouTube', in Relle Snickars and Patrick Vonderau (eds) (2009), *The YouTube Reader*, Stockholm: National Library of Sweden, 70–88.

Lavender, Andy (2003) 'Pleasure, performance and the *Big Brother* experience', *Contemporary Theatre Review*, 13.2, 15–23.

Lavender, Andy (2010) 'Digital Culture', in Sarah Bay-Cheng, Chiel Kattenbelt, Andy Lavender and Robin Nelson (eds), *Mapping Intermediality in Performance*, Amsterdam: Amsterdam University Press, 125–34.

Lavender, Andy (2013) 'The living statue: Performer, poseur, posthuman', *Studies in Theatre and Performance*, 33:2, 119–31.

Lavender, Andy (2014) 'Modal Transpositions towards Theatres of Encounter, or, in Praise of "Media Intermultimodality"', *Theatre Journal*, 66:4, 499–518.

Lee, Newton (2013) *Facebook Nation: Total Information Awareness*, New York: Springer.

Lehmann, Hans-Thies (2006) *Postdramatic Theatre*, trans. Karen Jürs-Munby, Oxford and New York: Routledge (first published in German as *Postdramatisches Theater*, 1999).

Lehmann, Hans-Thies (2007) 'Word and Stage in Postdramatic Theatre', in Christoph Henke and Martin Middeke (eds), *Drama and/after Postmodernism*, Trier: WVT Wissenschaftlicher Verlag Trier, 37–54.

Lehmann, Hans-Thies (2013) 'A Future for Tragedy? Remarks on the Political and the Postdramatic', in Karen Jürs-Munby, Jerome Carroll and Steve Giles (eds), *Postdramatic Theatre and the Political: International Perspectives on Contemporary Performance*, London and New York: Bloomsbury, 87–109.

LeNoir, Nina (2003) 'The Audience in Cyberspace: Audience-performer interactivity in online performances', in Susan Kattwinkel (ed.), *Audience Participation: Essays on Inclusion in Performance*, Westport, Connecticut and London: Praeger, 115–31.

Levin, Laura, and Marlis Schweitzer (2011) 'Editorial: Performing Publics', *Performance Research*, 16:2, 1–6.

Limb, Peter (2008) *Nelson Mandela: A Biography*, Westport, CT: Greenwood Press.

Loviglio, Jason (2005) *Radio's Intimate Public: Network Broadcasting and Mass-Mediated Democracy*, Minneapolis and London: University of Minnesota Press.

Lury, Celia (2011) *Consumer Culture*, Piscataway, N. J., Rutgers University Press.

Lyotard, Jean-François (1984) *The Postmodern Condition: A Report on Knowledge*, trans. Geoff Bennington and Brian Massumi, Minneapolis: University of Minnesota Press (originally published in French as *La Condition postmoderne: rapport sur le savoir*, Paris: Les Editions de Minuit, 1979).

Machon, Josephine (2013) *Immersive Theatres: Intimacy and Immediacy in Contemporary Performance*, Houndmills: Palgrave Macmillan.

Malzacher, Florian (2010) 'The Scripted Realities of Rimini Protokoll', in Carol Martin (ed.), *Dramaturgy of the Real on the World Stage*, Basingstoke and New York: Palgrave Macmillan, 80–7.

Manovich, Lev (2013) *Software Takes Command*, New York and London: Bloomsbury.

Marshall, P. David (2006) 'New Media – New Self: The changing power of celebrity', in P. David Marshall (ed.), *The Celebrity Culture Reader*, New York and London: Routledge, 634–44.

Martin, Carol (2006) 'Bodies of Evidence', *TDR: The Drama Review*, 50:3, 8–15.

Martin, Carol (2010) 'Introduction: Dramaturgy of the Real', in Carol Martin (ed.), *Dramaturgy of the Real on the World Stage*, Basingstoke and New York: Palgrave Macmillan, 1–14.

Martin, Carol (ed.) (2010) *Dramaturgy of the Real on the World Stage*, Basingstoke and New York: Palgrave Macmillan.

Massumi, Brian (2002) *Parables for the Virtual: Movement, Affect, Sensation*, Durham and London: Duke University Press.

May, Todd (2010) *Contemporary Political Movements and the Thought of Jacques Rancière: Equality in Action*, Edinburgh: Edinburgh University Press.

McConachie, Bruce (2008) *Engaging Audiences: A Cognitive Approach to Spectating in the Theatre*, New York and Basingstoke: Palgrave Macmillan.

McGann, Jerome (1996) *The Poetics of Sensibility: A revolution in literary style*, Oxford: Clarendon Press.

McGrath, John E. (2004) *Loving Big Brother: Performance, Privacy and Surveillance Space*, London and New York: Routledge.

McKenzie, Jon (2001) *Perform or Else: From Discipline to Performance*, London and New York: Routledge.

Meakin, Nione (2012) 'Tristram Sharps, dreamthinkspeak', *IdeasTap*, 4 May 2012, www.ideastap.com/ideasmag/the-knowledge/tristan-sharp-dreamthinkspeak.

Melnick, Jeffrey (2009) *9/11 Culture: America Under Construction*, Malden, MA, Oxford and Chichester: Wiley-Blackwell.

Mirzoeff, Nicholas (2012) 'Event? Performance? Or Theatre?', www.nicholasmirzoeff.com/O2012/2012/01/30/event-performance-or-theatre/, posted 30 January 2012.

Moffat, Steven (writer), Hettie MacDonald (director) (2007) 'Blink', *Doctor Who*, BBC1, 9 June 2007. Available on DVD: *Doctor Who: The Complete Series 3*, BBC, 2007.

Montola, Markus (2009) 'Games and Pervasive Games', in Markus Montola, Jaakko Stenros and Annika Waern (eds) (2009), *Pervasive Games: Theory and Design*, Burlington: Morgan Kaufmann, 7–23.

Morgan, Matthew J. (ed.) (2009a) *The Impact of 9/11 on the Media, Arts, and Entertainment: The Day That Changed Everything?* New York: Palgrave Macmillan.

Morgan, Matthew J. (2009b) *The Impact of 9/11 on Religion and Philosophy: The Day That Changed Everything?*, New York: Palgrave Macmillan.

Morris, Tee (2010) *All a Twitter: A Personal and Professional Guide to Social Networking with Twitter*, Indianapolis: Que.

Mumford, Stephen (2012) *Watching Sport: Aesthetics, ethics and emotion*, Abingdon and New York: Routledge.

Nally, Claire, and Angela Smith (eds) (2015) *Twenty-First Century Feminism: Forming and Performing Femininity*, Houndmills and New York: Palgrave Macmillan.

Nancy, Jean-Luc (2009) 'Jacques Rancière and Metaphysics', trans. John Hulsey, in Gabriel Rockhill and Philip Watts (eds), *Jacques Rancière: Politics, History, Aesthetics*, Durham & London: Duke University Press, 82–92.

Nardin, Terry and Daniel J. Sherman (2006) 'Introduction', in Daniel J. Sherman and Terry Nardin (eds), *Terror, Culture, Politics: Rethinking 9/11*, Bloomington, IN: Indiana University Press, 1–11.

Needham, Alex (2013) 'Ontroerend Goed: touch-sensitive theatre', *The Guardian*, www.theguardian.com/stage/2013/mar/11/ontroerend-goed-adelaide-festival, posted 11 March 2013.

NEF (New Economics Foundation) (2010) *Capturing the Audience Experience: A Handbook for the Theatre*, London: New Economics Foundation.

Nelson, Robin (2010) 'Prospective Mapping', in Sarah Bay-Cheng, Chiel Kattenbelt, Andy Lavender and Robin Nelson (eds), *Mapping Intermediality in Performance*, Amsterdam: Amsterdam University Press, 13–23.

Nguyen, Cindy (2004) 'interpellation', *Theories of Media: Keywords Glossary*, University of Chicago, http://csmt.uchicago.edu/glossary2004/interpellation.htm (accessed 3 January 2014).

Norton-Taylor, Richard (2003) 'Courtroom Drama', *The Guardian*, www.theguardian.com/stage/2003/nov/04/theatre.politicsandthearts, posted 4 November 2003.

O'Neill, Kate (2004) 'Transnational Protest: States, Circuses, and Conflict at the Frontline of Global Politics', *International Studies Review*, 6:2, 233–51.

Paget, Derek (1987) ' "Verbatim Theatre": Oral History and Documentary Techniques', *New Theatre Quarterly*, 3:12, 317–36.

Paget, Derek (2009) 'The "Broken Tradition" of Documentary Theatre and Its Continued Powers of Endurance', in Alison Forsyth and Chris Megson (eds.), *Get Real: Documentary Theatre Past and Present*, Houndmills and New York: Palgrave Macmillan, 224–38.

Palfrey, John and Urs Gasser (2008) *Born Digital: Understanding the First Generation of Digital Natives*, New York: Basic Books.

Palfrey, John, G. and Urs Gasser (2012) *Interop: the promise and perils of highly interconnected systems*, New York: Basic Books.

Parker-Starbuck, Jennifer (2011) *Cyborg Theatre: Corporeal/Technological Intersections in Multimedia Performance*, Houndmills and New York: Palgrave Macmillan.

Pavis, Patrice (1982) 'Towards a Semiology of the Mise en Scène?', trans. Susan Melrose, in Patrice Pavis, *Languages of the Stage: Essays in the Semiology of the Theatre*, New York: Performing Arts Journal Publications, 131–61.

Pavis, Patrice (1992) *Theatre at the Crossroads of Culture*, trans. Loren Kruger, London and New York: Routledge. (Pavis, 'From Page to Stage: A Difficult Birth', trans. Jilly Daugherty, 24–47.)

Pavis, Patrice (1998) *Dictionary of the Theatre: Terms, Concepts and Analysis*, trans. Christine Shantz, Toronto and Buffalo: University of Toronto Press.

Pavis, Patrice (2003) *Analyzing Performance: Theater, Dance and Film*, trans. David Williams, University of Michigan Press; originally published in French as *L'Analyse des spectacles*, Editions Nathan, 1996.

Pavis, Patrice (2010) 'The Director's New Tasks', trans. Joel Anderson, in Maria M. Delgado and Dan Rebellato (eds), *Contemporary European Theatre Directors*, London and New York: Routledge, 395–411.

Pavis, Patrice (Section ed.) (2012) 'Special Topics: The Spectator', *Critical Stages: IATC Webjournal*, 7, http://archive.criticalstages.org/criticalstages7/#sthash.n0qWypCs.dpbs.

Pavis, Patrice (2013) *Contemporary Mise en Scène: Staging theatre today*, trans. Joel Anderson, London and New York: Routledge (first published in French as *La mise en scène contemporaine: Origines, tendances, perspectives*, Paris: Armand Collin, 2007).

Pavis, Patrice (2014) 'Postdramatic Theatre', in Bryan Reynolds (ed.), *Performance Studies: Key Words, Concepts and Theories*, London and New York: Palgrave Macmillan, 39–49.

Peters, Kathrin, and Andrea Seier (2009) 'Home Dance: Mediacy and Aesthetics of the Self on YouTube', in Relle Snickars and Patrick Vonderau (eds) (2009), *The YouTube Reader*, Stockholm: National Library of Sweden, 187–203.

Pine II, B. Joseph and James H. Gilmore (2011 [1999]) *The Experience Economy*, Boston: Harvard Business Review Press.

Pluta, Izabella (2010) 'Instance: Robert Lepage and Ex Machina, *The Andersen Project* (2005)', in Sarah Bay-Cheng, Chiel Kattenbelt, Andy Lavender and Robin Nelson (eds), *Mapping Intermediality in Performance*, Amsterdam: Amsterdam University Press, 191–7.

Prior, Dorothy Max (2011) 'Autumn Days', *Total Theatre*, 1 November 2011, http://totaltheatrereview.com/blog/autumn-days, accessed 24 March 2013.

Pullen, Kirsten (2011) 'If Ya Liked It, Then You Shoulda Made a Video: Beyoncé Knowles, YouTube and the public sphere of images', *Performance Research*, 16:2, 145–53.

Radbourne, Jennifer, Hilary Glow and Katya Johanson (2013) 'Knowing and Measuring the Audience Experience', in Jennifer Radbourne, Hilary Glow and Katya Johanson (eds), *The Audience Experience: A critical analysis of audiences in the performing arts*, Bristol and Chicago: Intellect, 1–13.

Rancière, Jacques (1991) *The Ignorant Schoolmaster: Five Lessons in Intellectual Emancipation*, trans. Kristin Ross, Stanford: Stanford University Press.

Rancière, Jacques (1998) *Disagreement: Politics and Philosophy*, trans. Julie Rose, Minneapolis: University of Minnesota Press.

Rancière, Jacques (2009a) *The Emancipated Spectator*, trans. Gregory Elliott, London and New York: Verso (first published in French as *Le spectateur émancipé*, Paris: Editions La Fabrique, 2008).

Rancière, Jacques (2009b) *Aesthetics and its Discontents*, trans. Steven Corcoran, Cambridge and Malden, MA: Polity Press (first published in French as *Malaise dans l'esthétique*, Editions Galilee, 2004).

Rancière, Jacques (2009c) 'Afterword: The Method of Equality: An Answer to Some Questions', in Gabriel Rockhill and Philip Watts (eds), *Jacques Rancière: Politics, History, Aesthetics*, Durham & London: Duke University Press, 273–88.

Rancière, Jacques (2010) *Dissensus: On Politics and Aesthetics*, ed. and trans. Steven Corcoran, London and New York: Continuum.

Rancière, Jacques (2011) 'Good Times, Or, Pleasure at the Barrière', in Jacques Rancière, *Staging the People: The Proletarian and His Double*, trans. David Fernbach, London and New York: Verso, 175–232.

Read, Alan (2008) *Theatre, Intimacy & Engagement: The Last Human Venue*, Basingstoke and New York: Palgrave Macmillan.

Read, Alan (2013) *Theatre in the Expanded Field: Seven Approaches to Performance*, London and New York: Bloomsbury.

Reinelt, Janelle (2010) 'Towards a Poetics of Theatre and Public Events: In the Case of Stephen Lawrence', in Carol Martin (ed.), *Dramaturgy of the Real on the World Stage*, Basingstoke and New York: Palgrave Macmillan, 27–44.

Reinelt, Janelle (2011) 'Rethinking the Public Sphere for a Global Age', *Performance Research*, 16:2, 16–27.

Ricardo, Francisco J. (2013) *The Engagement Aesthetic: Experiencing New Media Art Through Critique*, London and New York: Bloomsbury.

Ridout, Nicholas (2006) *Stage Fright, Animals, and Other Theatrical Problems*, Cambridge and New York: Cambridge University Press.

Ridout, Nicholas (2008) 'Welcome to the Vibratorium', *Senses and Society*, 3:2, 221–31.

Rimini Protokoll (2009) *HAUPTVERSAMMLUNG 8. APRIL 2009/ICC BERLIN*, Berlin: Hebbel am Ufer.

Ringertz, Nils R. and Robert E. Savage (1976) *Cell Hybrids*. New York, San Francisco, London: Academic Press.

Roach, Joseph (2007) *it*, Ann Arbor: The University of Michigan Press.

Roberts, John Michael and Nick Crossley (2004) 'Introduction', in Nick Crossley and John Michael Roberts (eds), *After Habermas: New Perspectives on the Public Sphere*, Oxford and Malden, MA: Blackwell, 1–27.

Robson, Mark (2005) 'Jacques Rancière's Aesthetic Communities', in Mark Robson (ed.), *Jacques Rancière: Aesthetics, Politics, Philosophy*; *Paragraph*, 28.1, 77–95.

Rockhill, Gabriel (2004) 'Glossary of technical terms', in Jacques Rancière, *The Politics of Aesthetics*, ed. and trans. Gabriel Rockhill, London and New York: Continuum, 80–93.

Rockhill, Gabriel (2009) 'The Politics of Aesthetics: Political History and the Hermeneutics of Art', in Gabriel Rockhill and Philip Watts (eds), *Jacques Rancière: Politics, History, Aesthetics*, Durham & London: Duke University Press, 195–215.

Rodenburg, Patsy (1997) *The Actor Speaks: Voice and the Performer*, London: Methuen.

Rojek, Chris (2001) *Celebrity*, London: Reaktion Books.

Rosenberg, Jacob Bard (2014) 'Wanna Play? Game Over', Mute, www.metamute.org/ editorial/articles/wanna-play-game-over, posted 7 October 2014, accessed 28 August 2015.

Salvato, Nick (2009) 'Out of Hand: YouTube Amateurs and Professionals', *The Drama Review*, 53:3, 67–83.

Sauter, Willmar (2000) *The Theatrical Event: Dynamics of Performance and Perception*, Iowa City: University of Iowa Press.

Sauter, Willmar (2004) 'Introducing the Theatrical Event', in Vicky Ann Cremona, Peter Eversmann, Hans van Maanen, Willmar Sauter and John Tulloch (eds), *Theatrical Events: Borders Dynamics Frames*, London and New York: Rodopi, 3–14.

Schneider, Rebecca (1997) '*The Death of Character*: Perspectives on Theater After Modernism', *Theatre Journal*, 49:4, 541–3.

Schneider, Susan (2005) 'Events', *Internet Encyclopedia of Philosophy*, ISSN 2161–0002, www.iep.utm.edu/events/.

Schrager Lang, Amy and Daniel Lang/Levistsky (eds) (2012) *Dreaming in Public: Building the Occupy Movement*, Oxford: New Internationalist Publications.

Shaughnessy, Nicola (2012) *Applying Performance: Live Art, Socially Engaged Theatre and Affective Practice*, Houndmills: Palgrave Macmillan.

Shepherd, Simon and Mick Wallis (2004) *Drama/Theatre/Performance*, London and New York: Routledge.

Sherman, Daniel J. and Terry Nardin (eds) (2006) *Terror, Culture, Politics: Rethinking 9/11*, Bloomington, IN: Indiana University Press.

Shiu-Hing Lo, Sonny (2008) *Political Change in Macao*, London and New York: Routledge.

Snickars, Relle and Patrick Vonderau (2009) 'Introduction', in *The YouTube Reader*, Stockholm: National Library of Sweden, 9–21.

Sorkin, Michael (1992) 'See You in Disneyland', in Michael Sorkin (ed.), *Variations on a Theme Park: The New American City and the End of Public Space*, New York: Hill and Wang, 205–32.

Spencer, Jenny (2012) 'Editor's Introduction', in Jenny Spencer (ed.), *Political and Protest Theatre after 9/11: Patriotic Dissent*, New York and Abingdon: Routledge, 1–15.

Stenros, Jaakko, Markus Montola and Frans Mäyrä (2009) 'Pervasive Games in Media Culture', in Markus Montola, Jaako Stenros and Annika Waern (eds), *Pervasive Games: Theory and Design*, Burlington: Morgan Kaufmann, 257–78.

Stevens, Anthony (1999 [1990]) *On Jung*, London: Penguin Books.

Stewart, Kathleen (2007) *Ordinary Affects*, Durham and London: Duke University Press.

Street, Seán (2009) *The A to Z of British Radio*, Lanham and Plymouth: Scarecrow Press.

Suhr, H. Cecilia (2012) *Social Media and Music: The Digital Field of Cultural Production*, New York: Peter Lang.

Sundbo, Jon and Per Darmer (eds) (2008) *Creating Experiences in the Experience Economy*, Cheltenham and Northampton, MA: Edward Elgar.

Swarbrooke, John (2002 [1995]) *The Development and Management of Visitor Attractions*, Oxford, Auckland, Boston, Johannesburg, Melbourne, New Delhi: Butterworth Heinemann.

Taddeo, Julie Anne and Ken Dvorak (eds) (2010) *The Tube Has Spoken: Reality TV & History*, Lexington: The University Press of Kentucky.

Taylor, Lib (2013) 'Voice, Body, and the Transmission of the Real in Documentary Theatre', *Contemporary Theatre Review*, 23, 3, 368–79.

Teigland, Robin and Dominic Power (eds) (2013) *The Immersive Internet: Reflections on the Entangling of the Virtual with Society, Politics, and the Economy*, Houndmills and New York: Palgrave Macmillan.

Thompson, James (2009) *Performance Affects*, Houndmills: Palgrave Macmillan.

Thorpe, Holly and Robert Rinehart (2010) 'Alternative sport and affect: non-representational theory examined', *Sport in Society*, 13:7/8, 1268–91.

Thrift, Nigel (2008) *Non-Representational Theory: Space | politics | affect*, London and New York: Routledge.

Todd, Janet (1986) *Sensibility: An introduction*, London and New York: Methuen.

Toffler, Alvin (1980) *The Third Wave: The Classic Study of Tomorrow*, New York: Bantam.

Tomlin, Liz (2013) *Acts and apparitions: Discourses on the real in performance practice and theory, 1990–2010*, Manchester and New York: Manchester University Press.

Trend, David (ed.) (2001) *Reading Digital Culture*, Malden, MA and Oxford: Blackwell.

Trottier, Daniel (2012) *Social Media as Surveillance: Rethinking Visibility in a Converging World*, Farnham and Burlington, VT: Ashgate.

Tully, James (2013) 'On the Global Multiplicity of Public Spheres: The Democratic Transformation of the Public Sphere?', in Christian J. Emden and David Midgley (eds), *Beyond Habermas: Democracy, Knowledge, and the Public Sphere*, New York and Oxford: Berghahn Books, 169–204.

Turner, Graeme (2004) *Understanding Celebrity*, London: Sage.

Turner, Graeme (2006) 'The Mass Production of Celebrity: "Celetoids", Reality TV and the "Demotic Turn"', *International Journal of Cultural Studies*, 2:9, 153–66.

Uricchio, William (2009) 'The Future of a Medium Once Known as Television', in Relle Snickars and Patrick Vonderau (eds), *The YouTube Reader*, Stockholm: National Library of Sweden, 24–39.

van Alphen, Ernst and Mieke Bal (2009) 'Introduction', in Ernst van Alphen, Mieke Bal, and Carel Smith (eds), *The Rhetoric of Sincerity*, Stanford: Stanford University Press, 1–16.

Vanderbeeken, Robrecht (2010) 'Relive the Virtual: an Analysis of Unplugged Performance Installations', *New Theatre Quarterly*, 26:4, 362–9.

Van Gelder, Sarah and the staff of YES! Magazine (eds) (2011) *This Changes Everything: Occupy Wall Street and the 99% Movement*, San Francisco: Berrett-Koehler Publishers.

Van Kerkhoven, Marianne (nd) 'Dancer #1', www.atwodogscompany.org/en/projects/item/158-dancer-1?bckp=1 (accessed 2 January 2015).

Vázquez, Rolando (2006) 'Thinking the Event with Hannah Arendt', *European Journal of Social Theory*, 9:1, 43–57.

Verhoeven, Dries (2014 [2008]) *No Man's Land*, printout of performance text, Utrecht version, unpublished.

Wake, Caroline (2013) 'Headphone Verbatim Theatre: Methods, Histories, Genres, Theories', *New Theatre Quarterly*, 29:4, 321–35.

Wake, Caroline (2014) 'The Politics and Poetics of Listening: Attending Headphone Verbatim Theatre in Post-Cronulla Australia', *Theatre Research International*, 39:2, 82–100.

Watt, Stephen (1998) *Postmodern/Drama: Reading the Contemporary Stage*, Ann Arbor: The University of Michigan Press.

Weed, Mike (2008) 'Exploring the sport spectator experience: virtual football spectatorship in the pub', *Soccer & Society*, 9:2, 189–97.

Welton, Martin (2012) *Feeling Theatre*, Houndmills: Palgrave Macmillan.

White, Gareth (2009) 'Odd Anonymized Needs: Punchdrunk's Masked Spectator', in Alison Oddey and Christine White (eds), *Modes of Spectating*, London: Intellect, 219–30.

White, Gareth (2012) 'On immersive theatre', *Theatre Research International*, 37:3, 221–35.

White, Gareth (2013) *Audience Participation in Theatre: Aesthetics of the Invitation*, Houndmills: Palgrave Macmillan.

White, Hayden (1996) 'The modernist event', in Vivian Sobchack (ed.), *The persistence of history: cinema, television and the modern event*, New York and London: Routledge, 17–38.

Williams, J. Patrick, Sean Q. Hendricks and W. Keith Winkler (2006) 'Introduction: Fantasy Games, Gaming cultures, and Social Life', in J. Patrick Williams, Sean Q. Hendricks and W. Keith Winkler (eds), *Gaming as Culture: Essays on Reality, Identity and Experience in Fantasy Games*, Jefferson, North Carolina and London: McFarland.

Wilson, Clare (2005) 'The Great Pretender', *New Scientist*, 187:2510 (July 30 2005), 36.

Worthen, W. B. (2012) '"The Written Troubles of the Brain": *Sleep No More* and the Space of Character', *Theatre Journal*, 64:1, 79–97.

Wylson, Anthony and Patricia Wylson (1994) *Theme Parks, Leisure Centres, Zoos and Aquaria*, Harlow, UK: Longman.

Yale, Pat (1998 [1990]) *From Tourist Attractions to Heritage Tourism*, Huntingdon: ELM Publishers.

Zaiontz, Keren (2014) 'Narcissistic Spectatorship in Immersive and One-on-One Performance', *Theatre Journal*, 66:3, 405–25.

Žižek, Slavoj (2002) *Welcome to the Desert of the Real! Five Essays on September 11 and Related Dates*, London and New York: Verso.

Žižek, Slavoj (2004) 'The Lesson of Rancière', in Jacques Rancière, *The Politics of Aesthetics*, ed. and trans. Gabriel Rockhill, London and New York: Continuum, 69–79.

# Index